CAMBRIDGE SURVEYS OF ECONOMIC LITERATURE

OLIGOPOLY THEORY

CAMBRIDGE SURVEYS OF ECONOMIC LITERATURE

Editors:
Professor Phyllis Deane, University of Cambridge, and
Professor Mark Perlman, University of Pittsburgh

Editorial Advisory Board:
Professor A. B. Atkinson, London School of Economics and Political Science
Professor M. Bronfenbrenner, Duke University
Professor K. D. George, University College, Cardiff
Professor C. P. Kindleberger, Massachusetts Institute of Technology
Professor T. Mayer, University of California, Davis
Professor A. R. Prest, London School of Economics and Political Science

The literature of economics is expanding rapidly, and many subjects have
changed out of recognition within the space of a few years. Perceiving the state of
knowledge in fast-developing subjects is difficult for students and time consuming
for professional economists. This series of books is intended to help with this
problem. Each book will be quite brief, giving a clear structure to and balanced
overview of the topic and written at a level intelligible to the senior undergraduate.
They will therefore be useful for teaching, but will also provide a mature yet
compact presentation of the subject for economists wishing to update their
knowledge outside their own specialism.

Other books in the series
E. Roy Weintraub: Microfoundations: The compatibility of microeconomics and
macroeconomics
Dennis C. Mueller: Public choice
Robert Clark and Joseph Spengler: The economics of individual and population
aging
Edwin Burmeister: Capital theory and dynamics
Mark Blaug: The methodology of economics or how economists explain
Robert Ferber and Werner Z. Hirsch: Social experimentation and economic policy
Anthony C. Fisher: Resource and environmental economics
Morton I. Kamien and Nancy L. Schwartz: Market structure and innovation
Richard E. Caves: Multinational enterprise and economic analysis
Anne O. Krueger: Exchange-rate determination
Steven M. Sheffrin: Rational expectations
Mark R. Killingsworth: Labor supply

Oligopoly theory

JAMES W. FRIEDMAN

The Virginia Polytechnic Institute

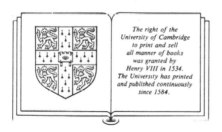

The right of the
University of Cambridge
to print and sell
all manner of books
was granted by
Henry VIII in 1534.
The University has printed
and published continuously
since 1584.

CAMBRIDGE UNIVERSITY PRESS

CAMBRIDGE

LONDON   NEW YORK   NEW ROCHELLE

MELBOURNE   SYDNEY

Published by the Press Syndicate of the University of Cambridge
The Pitt Building, Trumpington Street, Cambridge CB2 1RP
32 East 57th Street, New York, NY 10022, USA
296 Beaconsfield Parade, Middle Park, Melbourne 3206, Australia

First published 1983
Reprinted 1984

Printed in the United States of America

Library of Congress Cataloging in Publication Data
Friedman, James W.
Oligopoly theory.
(Cambridge surveys of economic literature)
Includes bibliographical references and index.
1. Oligopolies. I. Title. II. Series.
HD2757.3.F75   1983   338.8'2   82–22170
ISBN 0521 23827 7 hard covers
ISBN 0521 28244 6 paperback

To Nan and Rob

CONTENTS

PREFACE

Oligopoly theory began with Cournot, more than 140 years ago. Judging from many intermediate textbooks on price theory, one might think it ended with him too. A purpose of this book is to demonstrate fully and clearly that much interesting and useful progress has been made, particularly in the last quarter century, in developing a deeper and fuller understanding of oligopoly theory. The recent advances stem from two main sources. One is game theory. Cournot's oligopoly theory anticipates fundamental developments in game theory, particularly the noncooperative branch, and the fuller flowering of this new discipline has brought fresh insight back to oligopoly, as it has to other fields of economics. The second source is the recent work in dynamic economics. Many processes in economics would be better understood if they were modeled as many-period, or dynamic, phenomena. Capital theory led the way in dynamic economics, along with dynamic programming in operations research, and as the reader can see from Chapters 5 through 8, oligopoly theory has benefited from the development of dynamic models also.

I can offer the reader two reasons why oligopoly theory might be interesting. First, the subject is fascinating on its own, and the markets it depicts represent a considerable portion, perhaps a large majority, of markets in modern industrial nations. A person combining an interest in economic phenomena and an interest in the first principles of how things work will naturally be interested in theoretical economics, including oligopoly. Second, oligopoly theory is that portion of economic theory underlying the field of industrial organization. Although this book is not intended as a text on industrial organization, much research on oligopoly has stemmed from a desire to construct a firm theoretical foundation for that field. Inevitably, such efforts have been only partially successful, because if one insists on great rigor, much generality, and clear theoretical results, it is almost inevitable that one's efforts tend away from the more practical concerns of applications in the field. This tension between theoretical and empirical efforts typifies economics in all areas, of course. I hope that this book will help those persons interested in practical applications to think more clearly about the problems of concern to them, that it will bring useful insights that might otherwise escape notice, and that knowledge of oligopoly theory will enable them to articulate more clearly the directions in which theory might further develop in order to better cope with questions concerning applications.

In selecting the material to be covered, I have made choices aimed at presenting to the reader what I believe to be the important and lasting elements of the field, along with some material that I regard as promising, but whose importance is not yet clear. In following this policy I have unhesitatingly omitted certain developments that have long been staple fare but that I find to be without merit, as well as certain material that may be currently fashionable but whose importance I seriously doubt. An example of the former is the celebrated kinky oligopoly demand curve due to Sweezy. An important topic that is omitted is the group of general equilibrium approaches to oligopoly. The reason is that I think it is much more of interest to include those approaches with a treatment of general equilibrium rather than with oligopoly; I believe the audience for this book is much more interested in the partial equilibrium aspects of the subject. I cannot comment on my inclusions and exclusions without mentioning the matter of fallibility. These choices, of course, reflect my personal tastes and judgment, but inevitably they are also affected by accidental considerations. Despite efforts to be well-read throughout this field, one becomes better acquainted with certain work through refereeing, through the research of one's students, and so forth. Undoubtedly there would have been some different emphases and inclusions had I been more perfectly informed.

The coverage of this book is intended to be thorough without being encyclopedic. It begins with the birth of the theory and carries through to major recent developments. As befits a survey intended to be useful to advanced undergraduates, graduate students, and professional economists specializing in other fields, proofs of theorems are omitted, and much verbal explanation accompanies the formal models and numerical examples. It is assumed that the reader has a solid working knowledge of price theory at the intermediate level, a solid grasp of basic calculus, and the rudiments of linear algebra. Although undergraduates with this training may find the book difficult in places, it should be largely within their grasp. The first three chapters lay a foundation for the rest of the book and cover static oligopoly theory through Hotelling and Chamberlin. After Chapter 3, the reader can jump to any one of the next four chapters. Chapter 8 builds directly on Section 7.3 of Chapter 7. Chapter 9 makes connections between oligopoly and game theory, and much of it can be read following Chapter 3.

In writing this book I have had aid from many sources. Marjorie Adams, Elizabeth Castle, and Janet Wood have carefully and accurately typed the manuscript, including numerous lengthy revisions. Nicholas Economides, Charles Miller, and Paul Segerstrom have offered helpful comments, and the insights of John McMillan and David Salant have improved the focus and clarity of the final product. I am especially grateful for the numerous comments, touching on style, presentation, and economic content, that have come from the painstaking reading of Morton Kamien, Shmuel Nitzan, Robert Porter, Andrew Schotter, and Michael Toman. I am extremely grateful to all of these people and acutely aware that their aid has greatly improved the book. They will see that occasionally I refrained from taking their advice, but usually I followed it. I also want to thank Colin Day of Cambridge University Press, whose candor, kindness, and encouragement have done much to ease the task of writing. Needless to say, I retain responsibility for any remaining errors or shortcomings.

J. W. F.

1

Introduction and overview

A useful way to characterize different market types is by the number of firms on the supply side of the market and the number of buyers on the demand side. An *oligopoly* is a market having few firms (but more than one firm) on the supply side and a very large number of buyers on the demand side, each of whom makes a negligible contribution to the market demand function. A buyer will take market conditions as given, for he cannot affect them, but a seller will inevitably be preoccupied with guessing the behavior to be expected from rival sellers. Furthermore, in a market that will continue in operation for a long time, an oligopolistic firm will naturally be concerned with how its present actions may influence the behavior of its rivals in the future.

The key distinguishing feature that sets oligopoly apart from competition and from (textbook) monopoly is that oligopolists are strategically linked to one another. The best policy for one firm is dependent on the policies being followed by each rival firm in the market. Imagine, for example, a town with four home mortgage lenders in a nation with no national mortgage market. Each lender must select a mortgage interest rate and will, let us say, lend to all qualified applicants. Applicants will not all automatically go to the lender offering the lowest rate, because other details of the contract may differ, not all applicants will undertake the cost of fully informing themselves on alternative lenders, and some will have

1

lenders with which they prefer to deal (provided the cost of doing so is not too high). However, any change in the terms offered by one lender will affect the rate of flow of applicants to each other lender. An interest rate change for one may be profitable or unprofitable, depending on the subsequent rate adjustments the others make as a result of the initial lender's change.

A central feature of the study of oligopoly theory consists of understanding the nature of these *strategic interactions* and in seeing the character of equilibrium choices for firms that face them. Purely competitive markets lack this strategic interaction, because the choices of a single firm have no effect on the market price of the homogeneous good the firms produce. Likewise, the monopolist is not interconnected with any large firms whose policies individually affect it. The monopolist must be sensitive to market conditions, but these are embodied in the demand function for its product and the supply functions for the inputs it uses. No strategic considerations appear. Both competitor and monopolist have straightforward maximization problems to solve when seeking maximum profits – in contrast to an oligopolist, whose profit maximization problem is intertwined with those of several rivals.

Another continuing source of interest in oligopoly stems from the relationship of market form to economic efficiency. Adam Smith (1776) conjectured that competitive economies are economically efficient, and recent research in general equilibrium theory has provided conditions under which Smith's conjecture has been proved true. See the work of Arrow and Hahn (1971) or Hildenbrand and Kirman (1976). These results yield the familiar rule that efficiency requires the price of each good to equal its marginal cost of production. The marginal cost pricing rule is generally violated in oligopolistic and monopolistic markets, because price and marginal revenue in such markets diverge. An economy having a noncompetitive market (i.e., one monopoly or oligopoly) would not be Pareto efficient. That is, it would be possible to make changes in prices and resource uses that would cause all firms to obtain larger profits and all consumers to attain higher levels of satisfaction.

Intuition would suggest that an oligopolistic market would approach ever closer to the marginal cost pricing norm as the number of firms in the market increased. Were this true, then an oligopolistic economy could be close to efficient if the number of firms in each market were sufficiently large. Whether or not prices in a market become close to marginal costs as the number of firms in the market increases is examined in Chapters 2, 3, and 5. It turns out that convergence of price to marginal cost will occur in some situations, but not all.

The first model of oligopoly, along with the first equilibrium concept, is due to Cournot (1838). His analysis is mainly, and most importantly, concerned with static markets. Roughly speaking, his equilibrium is characterized by policies for the firms that cannot be individually improved on. That is, at equilibrium, no firm can alter its policy unilaterally and increase its own profit. Thus, firms take their strategic interactions into account by adopting policies that are individually best in the face of their rivals' policies.

It is shown in Chapters 5 through 8 that Cournot's insight leads to a large variety of possible equilibria when applied to dynamic (i.e., many-period) situations. The nature of Cournot's equilibrium in its original static setting is illustrated with an example in Section 1.1. Then the example is modified to show how Cournot's insight becomes enriched and changed in a dynamic model.

1.1. An example of an oligopoly

As an illustration, imagine a small town that has only three restaurants and is located fifty miles from the nearest town. At a time when business is slow, one restaurant owner might think he* could greatly increase his business and improve his profits by offering half-price dinners on the slower nights of the week. Then it might occur to him that if such a policy would help him, given that neither of the other restaurants did the same, then his two rivals would be in essentially the same position. Any one of them could

---

* In order to avoid complex terminology, the masculine pronoun will be used in the generic sense to mean "he or she."

benefit by being the only one to offer half-price dinners on Tuesday, Wednesday, and Thursday. If all did this, there might not be enough extra business for any of them to make it worthwhile; however, if only one did it, the other two would lose so many customers that they would be better off following suit.

What will the firms do? Two plausible avenues can be imagined. To begin with, none is likely to offer half-price dinners for three nights per week, because in thinking through the effect this would have on the two rivals, the owner would see that such a policy probably would hurt the firm, as compared with the status quo. Imagine that one of the restaurants offered half-price dinners on the three midweek days. For a week it might prosper, but the other two restaurants would see their midweek clientele much diminished and would know the cause. They might perceive that they, too, would do better by offering half-price dinners on the three midweek days. With all three offering them, each could be making less profit than before anyone offered them; yet, any single restaurant might more profitably offer them than not, given the policies of the other two.

This situation is illustrated in Table 1.1, where the three restaurants are called *A*, *B*, and *C*. If none offers half-price dinners, each has a profit of 7, but if all offer them on all three midweek nights, each has a profit of only 2. From the standpoint of one restaurant, say *A*, offering half-price dinners dominates offering no half-price

Table 1.1. *Profits to three restaurants under various policies*

	Half-price nights										
	B and *C* have none			*B* has 3, *C* has none			*B* has none, *C* has 3			*B* and *C* have 3	
A has no half-price nights	7	7	7	0	20	0	0	0	20	−4	9	9
A has 3 half-price nights	20	0	0	9	9	−4	9	−4	9	2	2	2

dinners when the policies of the rivals are fixed. If B and C offer none, A can increase its profit from 7 to 20 by offering them. If one of the pair B and C offers them, A can increase profits from 0 to 9 by following suit, and if both B and C offer them, A can increase profits from -4 to $+2$ by doing the same.

However, a second possibility is that the three restaurant owners discuss the situation and decide that the half-price idea is a good one as long as they do not all do it at the same time. So, one might take Tuesdays, one Wednesdays, and the third Thursdays. Such a policy might make all of them better off, and it might be in no one's interest to pursue a different policy. In terms of the example of Table 1.1, say that each restaurant has a profit of 15 if each has one half-price night of its own. Alternatively, a firm might, on its own, pick only one of the three nights as a half-price night. Its purpose in taking only one night would be to allow its rivals a means of following suit in a manner that would leave them all better off after all of them had reacted to one another's actions.

The two outcomes for the restaurants anticipate an interesting aspect of oligopoly behavior that is highlighted in subsequent chapters. Imagine that the restaurant owners must decide early Sunday morning on policy for the whole week, that they cannot collude, and that they are so short-sighted that each Sunday each one cares about the profits of only the coming week. In this situation the first outcome must prevail, because irrespective of the policy of the other two, each restaurant will be more profitable offering half-price dinners on all three midweek days. This is an example of a single-period *Cournot equilibrium,* and it is studied in various forms in Chapters 2 and 3.

If the restaurant owners each look to maximizing a discounted profit stream and look well beyond the current week, either the second or first outcome could prevail. A policy of myopic Cournot behavior by all firms produces an equilibrium in the many-period market, but the second outcome could prevail if there were a means to curb the temptation each would have to offer half-price dinners on all three days. That means could be an understanding that each restaurant will continue with the one-night-for-each-restaurant arrangement as long as everyone continues to honor it. Should one fail to honor it and offer half-price meals on two or three nights, it is understood that the others will, in all succeeding weeks, each offer half-price meals on three nights. In other words, if the one-night-per-restaurant arrangement is violated, the restaurants will shift to the first outcome. From the viewpoint of one restaurant, if it violates the one-night-each arrangement it can get a profit of 20 for one week, but that will be reduced to 2 in all succeeding weeks. Compared with the one-night-each arrangement, which will yield 15 per week indefinitely, with a suitably low rate of discount, the extra one-week profit of 5 will not repay the loss of 13 per week in all succeeding weeks.

This second equilibrium is in the spirit of Cournot in the sense that it is a *noncooperative equilibrium*. Each firm is maximizing profit with respect to its own strategy (i.e., its long-range policy or plan), given the strategies of the others. Yet, the move to a multiperiod model has opened up possible outcomes that are not attainable in a one-period model without collusion. Such a model is examined in Chapter 5, and it illustrates the importance of studying oligopoly in a multiperiod setting.

A striking welfare difference between these two equilibria emerges in later chapters. As the example suggests, the myopic Cournot outcome is nearer to marginal cost pricing than is the second outcome, in which the firms have profits higher than Cournot profits. But, additionally, if the market were enlarged by increasing the number of active firms, the Cournot equilibrium price would move closer to marginal cost; however, the quasi-cooperative outcome (with the restaurants coordinating on the half-price dinner offer) need not become any nearer to a competitive equilibrium.

1.2. **Oligopoly in comparison with other market forms**

To set oligopolistic markets into proper perspective, recall the nature of competitive and monopolistic markets. A *competitive market* has multitudes of both buyers and sellers, none of whom looms large enough to have a noticeable effect on the market demand and supply functions. For example, take a typical wheat farmer or an average New York City restaurant. For all practical purposes the wheat farmer can sell any quantity of wheat at a well-established market price whose level will be unaffected by his own transactions. Therefore, his actions will not impinge on other wheat farmers, and he need not be concerned that his policy today will affect the future policies of other wheat farmers and, consequently, influence through them the environment in which he operates in the future.

New York City restaurants do not really provide an appropriate example of a competitive industry unless some unrealistic simplifying assumptions are made. They differ in terms of location, type of menu, decor, and quality of both food and service. They provide a good example of *monopolistic competition,* a market form characterized by many small producers, each of whom makes a distinctly different variant of the product of their industry. But assume the differences aside and imagine a restaurant meal to be a standard product. Then, as with wheat, there will be a going price for dinner at which any restaurant can sell as many as it wishes. The *strategic interdependence* of the small-town restaurants will be absent.

At the opposite end of the spectrum sits the *monopolist,* who is the sole supplier of a good whose demand function is, at most, affected negligibly by the actions of any other single firm. The point of this last proviso is to remove from the monopolist any strategic concerns coming from other parts of the economy. The monopolist, like the competitor, has a straightforward maximization problem to solve when making decisions. Neither needs to worry that his effects on others will influence his later environment in ways that are difficult to predict. Indeed, the only difference in terms of economists' usual modeling is that the competitor faces a horizontal demand curve, whereas that of the monopolist is downward-sloping. It is quite possible that no market exists for which the textbook model of monopoly is a good approximation. The usual examples of monopoly that occur to people are the various public utilities. Although it is correct that one generally cannot buy telephone services, natural gas, or electricity from more than one supplier, the prices of these commodities are likely to affect the policies of firms in related industries, and the behavior of these firms, in turn, will affect the utilities. For example, the price of natural gas will affect the design of gas-using products (e.g., appliances and furnaces), and the design of these products will affect the demand for gas. Were these related products produced in either monopolistic or oligopolistic industries, there would be oligopoly-like strategic linkages between these firms and the monopolist utility.

In the sense of numbers, oligopoly lies between monopoly and competition, but analytically and conceptually it is quite different from both because of the strategic interdependence of the firms in an oligopoly. There is no counterpart to this in the other two market forms. This difference accounts for the peculiar difficulties and fascinations of the subject. In terms of quantitative importance, oligopolies loom large in the United States and in all industrialized economies. Virtually every large firm one can think of, be it in steel, chemicals, petroleum, automobiles, food retailing, department stores, or computers, is in a position of strategic interdependence with several other firms in the same industry. Furthermore, many much smaller firms are parts of oligopolies, for many markets are geographically local in nature, with particular market areas being served by a handful of firms. Banking in a small town is an obvious example. A town of 50,000 inhabitants may have only two or three banks. For most banking services, particularly loans, a person or firm in the town may be unable to take his business to any but the local banks.

Where is the line to be drawn between oligopoly and competition? At what number do we draw the line between few and many? In principle, competition applies when the number of competing firms is infinite; at the same time, the textbooks usually say that a market is competitive if the cross effects between firms are negligible. Up to perhaps six firms one has oligopoly, and with fifty or more firms of roughly similar size one has competition; however, for sizes in between it may be difficult to say. The answer is not a matter of principle, but rather an empirical matter. If the several firms of an industry choose to ignore their cross effects (i.e., their strategic interdependence) and if demand is very elastic for each of them, with each taking its own market price as virtually given, then the industry is best analyzed as if it is competitive. Conversely, when nonzero cross effects exist, and the firms take account of them, though they may be small, then the industry is best viewed as an oligopoly even if the number of firms is two hundred. In Chapters 2 and 5 the transition from a clearly oligopolistic market to a competitive market, as the number of active firms grows, is examined.

It can be argued that strategic interdependence between a firm and some few other firms is nearly universal. In industries having many small firms, it is typical that they are not competitors in the textbook sense. Take, for example, retail food stores prior to the rise of the supermarket chains. Each store would primarily cater to a neighborhood clientele, and the location of the store would partly define its product. In other words, because of location alone, one could not claim that various stores sold identical items. Surely a bag of flour available at one location was not the same commodity as an otherwise identical bag of flour located in a store two miles distant. A person near one store would incur significant additional costs in going to the second store to purchase food. With food stores located every few blocks along major streets, a single store's products were more akin to the products of nearer stores, and the closer two stores were to one another, the larger the strategic interconnection between them. Stores separated by a distance of five miles may have had no effect on one another.

The food stores described provide an example of *monopolistic competition.* I believe that the vast majority of firms in modern economies are either oligopolistic firms or monopolistic competitors. Either way, strategic considerations become paramount, in contrast to the situation with competition and monopoly. The remaining chapters are concerned with the study of markets in which strategic considerations are of central concern.

1.3. **Outline of the remaining chapters**

The topics covered include a mixture of the standard literature that has been taught for many years and recently developed material. Chapters 2 through 4 deal with single-period models, whereas Chapters 5 through 8 are concerned with multiperiod, mostly infinite horizon models. Chapter 9 makes connections between the material of the earlier chapters and the theory of noncooperative games.

Chapter 2 is mainly an exposition of Cournot's model (1838) of oligopoly. It is a single-period model in which a fixed number of firms produce a perfectly homogeneous good, with each firm choosing its output level as its only decision variable. As far as we know, this model was the first treatment of oligopoly, and although it was originally published more than 140 years ago, it is still presented in modern textbooks in much the same form as it first appeared. Cournot's equilibrium concept, under which the output choices of the several firms form an equilibrium if no single firm can increase its profit by using a different output level, is noteworthy in two respects: First, it is very close to the definition of equilibrium behavior usually used in competitive models. In the latter, equilibrium obtains when no single economic agent can change its behavior and increase its utility (if a consumer) or profit (if a firm) and when the choices of all the economic agents cause markets to clear. In a competitive model, the choices of one agent have no discernible effect on the utility or profit of any other agent, and in Cournot's model the firms undertake to clear the market by selling at that price that equates aggregate production to the amount demanded by consumers in the market. Thus, Cournot stays as close as he can to the spirit of competitive economics while still taking account of the strategic linkages between firms – the fact that the choice of any one firm has discernible effects on the profits of the other firms. Second, it is the prototype of nearly all other noncooperative (noncollusive) equilibria in oligopoly and other noncompetitive economic situations. The key element of noncooperative equilibria is that each economic agent has the opportunity to choose a plan (i.e., a policy or strategy), and, in equilibrium, the choice of each agent maximizes the profit (or utility) of that agent, given the plans made by the remaining agents. The relationship among Cournot equilibrium, competitive equilibrium, and the number of firms in the market is examined following the work of Ruffin (1971).

Two elements left unexplained by the Cournot model are dealt with in Chapter 3. One is the mechanism of price formation, and the other is the modeling of markets in which firms produce similar, but nonidentical, products. Most products we see are easily identified as to what they are, but they are not identical from one firm to another. For example, anyone can recognize a television set, but two television sets from two different firms are not exactly the same. And, as the grocery store illustration suggests, the location at which a product is sold can be an aspect of the product itself. Rather than being identical (*homogeneous*), such products are *differentiated*. Based on the pioneering work of Hotelling (1929), Chamberlin (1933), and later writers, Chapter 3 contains an exposition of models in which the firms in a market produce differentiated products.

The mechanism of price formation is troublesome in the Cournot model because, on the one hand, it is not plausible that consumers set prices, but on the other hand, if firms set them, then the model differs greatly from Cournot's description. Consumers are assumed to be numerous and to be price takers, and it is assumed that their behavior can be summarized by a conventional demand function. If the firms were thought to set prices with no collusion, then price, rather than output, would be a firm's decision variable. Consumers would buy from the firm charging the lowest price, and the whole analysis would differ markedly from what Cournot described. By contrast, in a differentiated products model it is quite natural to have the various firms selling at different prices and to have price be the firm's decision variable. Even if output were retained as the decision variable, it would be possible to explain a mechanism of price formation under which firms select prices.

Throughout Chapter 3 the nature of the product of each firm is fixed. Product choice, however, is an interesting and important topic, and in recent years some significant progress has been made in the formal economic explanation of it. Some of these models and results are contained in Chapter 4. The underpinnings of this work stem from two sources: the spatial model of Hotelling (1929) and the "characteristics" approach of Lancaster (1966; 1979). In the simplest models, each firm's product is physically identical with that of every other firm, but each firm is at a specific location. Consumers are spread among various locations. They must pay the cost of transporting the good from the seller's location to their locations, and they wish to minimize their total cost, which is purchase price plus transport cost. As an illustration, imagine dry cleaning establishments under the assumption that they all do equally good jobs of cleaning clothes. They are at several distinct locations in a city, and the consumers are spread throughout the city. Product choice for the dry cleaner means choice of location. A consumer will typically use the nearest cleaner if all charge the same price, but he will go to another if its price is sufficiently less than that of the nearest to pay for the extra transportation cost.

Many characteristics of products other than location of seller can be quantified and are of importance to a consumer. The size of a television screen, the capacity of a refrigerator, the weight per yard of a fabric, and the thickness of a sleeping bag are examples. In the models of Chapter 4, the profit-maximizing efforts of a firm lead it to choose both the character of its product and the price (or output level) offered.

In many areas of economics, questions arise that cannot be easily discussed within the confines of static, single-period models. This is especially true of oligopoly, and the material of Chapters 5 through 8 is aimed at providing the kind of solid theoretical framework needed to put discussion of such questions on a firmer analytical footing. Much of the oligopoly literature written prior to the formal development of dynamic (i.e., multiperiod) models contains extensive discussion of the intertemporal relations of firms, even though the formal models in the same articles and books are strictly single-period (static). An important line of research in oligopoly during the past twenty years or so has been the development of explicitly dynamic models of oligopoly.

The earlier chapters of this book provide required building blocks for the multiperiod models appearing later. Furthermore, it can be seen that the basic approach supplied by Cournot remains valid and useful in these more general models. This is not to say that the Cournot equilibrium itself is particularly interesting in the multiperiod setting, but a suitably generalized version of it is useful. That generalization, called the *noncooperative equilibrium,* clearly retains the spirit of Cournot in a more sophisticated setting, and it has been introduced into game theory by Nash (1951).

Chapter 5 is devoted to reaction function models and variants of them. A *reaction function* is a policy for the firm under which the price or output chosen during a time period depends on the prices or quantities chosen in the preceding period. In this and subsequent chapters the aim of firms is assumed to be maximization of discounted profits over an infinite horizon. Reaction functions can be traced back to Cournot, who seems to have an informal dynamic structure in part of his oligopoly discussion. Much of the chapter is concerned with elaborating and making explicit the line of development he started.

Advertising is incorporated into various models in Chapter 6. It seems plausible that the effects of advertising on the sales of a firm depend on advertising from the past as well as advertising during the current period. That is, advertising probably is like capital goods in providing a stream of benefits over time. This theme, found in the work of Nerlove and Arrow (1962), is developed in Chapter 6. Another aspect of advertising is that the advertising of one firm may affect the demand curves of all other firms in the market. The effect can be either beneficial or deleterious, depending on the nature of the good. This, too, is incorporated into some of the models that are presented.

It is difficult to think of firms operating over extended time horizons without contemplating the investment decision that a firm faces. The models of Chapter 7 have capital stocks incorporated into them, with the firms having to make investment decisions. The models from this chapter are used in Chapter 8 to study the entry process. Another intertemporal phenomenon whose study has been actively advanced in recent years is the entry of new firms into a market. Until very recently the formal models of entry were static and did not even incorporate the potential entrants as rational decision-making economic agents. It was assumed, for example, that if prices in a market were above a particular level, new entry would occur. Yet there was no attempt to show that an entrant's decision should be related to the prices observed in the market prior to entry, nor was the entrant seen to be making decisions in its own best interest. More recently, multiperiod models have been formulated in which the potential entrants are rational, profit-maximizing economic agents. Some of this work is covered in Chapter 8.

The final chapter makes explicit a connection that is implicit throughout the earlier chapters. The models of oligopoly presented throughout this volume are applications of the theory of noncooperative games, and the equilibrium concept generally used is the Nash (1951) noncooperative equilibrium. A reader of the first eight chapters will have received an introduction to and extensive applications of noncooperative game theory; therefore, it is worthwhile to discuss the basics of noncooperative games and then show how several of the oligopoly models can be explicitly interpreted as games. This is the task of Chapter 9.

1.4. Further comments

The purpose of the chapters that follow is to present a readable survey of the present state of oligopoly theory. Models and important results are explained carefully in words, and the mathematical structure is also given in symbols. There are three ways in which this work falls far short of being a treatise. First, for some models, certain assumptions are not stated in the text. The omitted assumptions are always of a highly technical nature, lacking particularly interesting economic content, and they are omitted to improve the exposition of the fundamental economics of the model. Second, proofs of results are rarely provided; however, I have tried to be meticulous in noting results that are known to be correct (i.e., that have been formally proved), as compared with conjectures. Proofs are omitted in order to make this volume accessible and readable for a wide audience. The student who wishes to delve more deeply is always provided with references to original sources where any results claimed herein have been proved. Third, I make no claim to completeness. Undoubtedly there are topics that have been omitted and that could reasonably have been included, and there will surely be readers who would opt for a different menu of topics. But I believe that the bulk of the material included falls into the main body of oligopoly theory and provides a useful and broad survey.

The existence of equilibrium receives attention in nearly every chapter. Some readers may wonder why and may question the usefulness of this preoccupation. For many readers there is much greater interest in various qualitative and comparative static aspects of equilibrium, such as these: Are equilibrium profits on the profit possibility frontier? Will established firms pursue policies that keep new firms from entering the market? If the government increases the cost of advertising to firms or forbids them access to certain media, how will industry output be affected? These are interesting and important questions, and they are addressed later. Surely everyone will agree that they must be asked within the framework of economically interesting models if the answers are to be valid. But it is also important that equilibrium exist for the models under study, for if equilibrium is not known to exist, the derived properties of the model may be meaningless. For example, characteristics of equilibrium may be found that prove to be incompatible with the very existence of equilibrium itself. Or perhaps equilibrium cannot exist in a given model. Then the investigation of equilibrium conditions that, of course, cannot all be fulfilled could lead to the proclaiming of supposed aspects of equilibrium behavior that cannot occur.

But what constitutes an economically interesting model? Here the views of reasonable people may differ. Koopmans (1957) counsels us to base our models on reasonable assumptions and warns that patently absurd assumptions will yield unsatisfactory models. In his conception of the nature of scientific progress in economic theory, theory consists of a collection of models that explain various economic phenomena. Over time, this collection is improved as some models are replaced by others of greater generality. Set against this is the view of Milton Friedman (1953) that models should be judged by their predictive accuracy. If model A yields better predictions than model B, then model A is superior even if its underlying assumptions are ridiculous and those of model B are sensible.

Both views, at their most extreme, are difficult to accept in total, and each has at least a kernel of value. On the one hand, the reasonableness of some assumptions is extremely difficult to verify; on the other hand, testing and comparing the predictive accuracy of many models is virtually impossible. The reader is entitled to know that my view is more closely aligned with that of Koopmans.

Returning specifically to the meaning of an economically interesting model, the first priority is that the assumptions be plausible. When they are clearly untrue, they should be near enough to being correct that the models based on them will provide insight into economic behavior. Reading through the various assumptions stated in this book and looking at the results obtained must raise certain questions in the minds of many readers. First and foremost is whether or not the many assumptions made about the structure of demand and cost are reasonable in the sense of being representative of the conditions of actual firms. They do not represent the full complexity and richness of markets, of course, for they leave entirely out of account many variables that affect demand and cost; however, it is enough if they are reasonable assumptions given the level of abstraction of the models under study. Unfortunately, good data are lacking for a definitive answer. My own intuition suggests that the models are reasonable for their level of abstraction in the sense that some markets (a significant number) probably are enough like those portrayed here that the models can provide some insight.

All policy discussions take place within the context of models and abstractions, although very often the models are not explicitly stated, and as discussion proceeds, the models implicitly in use may be changed. Perhaps two discussants have in mind two different models, although each thinks the other person is staying within the same framework that he is. Because the models are not explicit, when someone shifts ground from one set of assumptions to another he may not be aware he is doing so. We think in terms of abstractions and simplified situations in the first place because we lack the mental equipment to keep the whole of a complex situation before us. In economics, the conclusions a person comes to often are those dictated by some simple models that long ago became part of that person's intellectual equipment.

The point of these observations is to stress that even those who disdain formal models make unconscious use of them. Models organize and, partly, direct our thoughts and judgments. I believe it is better to be explicit about what models one uses and to understand as well as possible the characteristics of those models. Often those models do not go very far, or they may require restrictive assumptions, but they are far better than no models at all, and they are improving with time.

A case in point about models and attitudes concerns the uniqueness of Cournot equilibrium. Many economists are impatient, not to say intolerant, of models in which equilibrium is not unique. Perhaps this is because uniqueness is such a comfort or because, knowing that the economy has at any one moment of time a particular configuration of prices, output levels, and so forth, they suppose that uniqueness is natural. It may well be that equilibrium in most economic processes is not unique; if so, it is very important for us to find out. We need to better understand what forces cause particular equilibria to be realized. The first part of such studies involves determining the conditions for the existence and uniqueness of equilibrium.

Because this book deals with oligopoly theory, empirical work and empirical issues are left aside. I believe that theoretical economics is interesting, indeed fascinating, in its own right. At the same time, empirical implementation of theory is quite important; however, the concept of division of labor can be profitable in economics as elsewhere, and the task of applying oligopoly theory to empirical and policy questions is best left to hands more practiced than mine. For the reader mainly interested in oligopoly theory, I hope the following chapters provide a clear and useful survey, along with appropriate further references. For the reader mainly interested in policy or empirical applications, I hope the theoretical structure provided here proves an aid to clearer understanding and to delineation of interesting issues.

2

The Cournot model of oligopoly

Of all oligopoly models, Cournot's is both the first and the most famous. Virtually any price theory textbook includes a discussion of it, even if nothing else is presented on the subject. Apart from historical interest, the model provides an excellent, simple vehicle for the understanding of important basic principles of oligopolistic behavior. The remainder of this chapter, which opens with a historical note, is written to draw as many insights as possible from Cournot's model of oligopoly and to lay foundations for all later chapters.

Section 2.2, which follows the historical note, contains a simple duopoly (i.e., two-firm oligopoly) example that is used to introduce the Cournot equilibrium and show some of its properties. In Section 2.3 a large class of n-firm oligopoly models is described for which it is known that the Cournot equilibrium exists. Examples are presented to illuminate the roles of various assumptions in assuring that there is an equilibrium. Conditions guaranteeing the uniqueness of the equilibrium are also stated, and an example illustrates the way uniqueness is attained. The fourth section takes up the relationship between Cournot equilibrium and the competitive (price equals marginal cost) equilibrium. Examples are used to show the convergence of Cournot equilibrium to the competitive equilibrium and to show why this convergence might, sometimes, be impossible. Section 2.5 contains a brief look at the stability

19

analysis made by Cournot and the beginnings of reaction functions. In Section 2.6 the remarks of Cournot's early critics are mentioned, particularly the famous comments of Bertrand. Finally, in Section 2.7 the main lines of the chapter are summarized.

Throughout this volume it is usually assumed that any single firm knows the cost and demand conditions faced by every firm in its industry. Any exceptions to this assumption of *complete information* are noted as they occur.

2.1. A historical note

Augustin Cournot, a noted French mathematician, was born in 1801. In addition to his great contribution to economics, *Researches into the Mathematical Principles of the Theory of Wealth,* published in 1838, he is also remembered for his contributions to philosophy. Cournot's work (1838) is remarkable and important for the development of economics in two respects. It is the first publication in economics to use mathematical models without specifying precise functional forms. This practice is commonplace now, because it is universally recognized that we do not know whether demand functions are linear or quadratic or yet something else, and similarly with most other mathematical functions arising in economics. Cournot's practice, like the modern practice, was to write a general function such as $Q = F(p)$ for market demand and then state some qualitative restrictions on the domain of the price variable p and on the nature of the function $F(p)$. The second and more commonly remembered contribution is his oligopoly theory, contained in Chapter 7 of his book. Its most astounding characteristic is its complete originality. Usually, such a field of study develops through a series of stages, one shading into another, at the hands of a succession of writers. These stages commence with a vague awareness of a concept or model and proceed to clearer and clearer formulations over time. Had this happened with oligopoly, there would be writings prior to Cournot pointing toward his work by discussions suggestive of his concept of equilibrium. None, however, is known. Until recently, the word "monopoly" was used for oligopoly and monopoly. A market with three sellers would be said to have "three monopolists." Chamberlin coined the word, although he then discovered (1933, p. 8) that a German economist, Karl Schlesinger, had invented it twenty years earlier.

The core chapters of Cournot (1838) contain a mathematical exposition of demand (Chapter 4), monopoly (Chapter 5), the effect of a tax on equilibrium under monopoly (Chapter 6), oligopoly (Chapter 7), and competitive markets (Chapter 8). Apart from the oligopoly chapter there is nothing conceptually new, although all topics are handled with precision and clarity that had not previously been attained.

Oligopoly can be approached from either of two directions: *cooperative* and *noncooperative*. The former is based on the assumption that the oligopolists will collude and that they will be able to make legally binding agreements. There are two main questions to be answered under this approach: (a) What coordinated policy will get the most profits for the oligopolists? (b) What division of profits will be agreed on? Under the noncooperative approach the oligopolists act independent of one another in the sense that they do not collude; however, they do each choose their policies taking into account the behavior they expect from their fellow oligopolists. It can be seen in the later chapters of this volume that the distinction between the cooperative and the noncooperative is easily blurred in dynamic models.

A famous passage from Adam Smith (1766, p. 145) illustrates that the cooperative approach goes back at least two hundred years and that it developed in the more usual gradual manner: "People of the same trade seldom meet together, even for merriment and diversion, but the conversation ends in a conspiracy against the publick, or in some contrivance to raise prices." Cournot was aware of the cooperative approach, but he made a deliberate decision to take the complementary path. His chapter arrangement, moving from markets of one firm to markets of several firms and finally to markets of many firms probably led him to his great discovery. In opening Chapter 7 he states that he will deal with firms that act "independently," for if the firms collude, the outcome "will not differ so far as the consumers are concerned" from the monopoly outcome. Apparently he wanted his analysis of several-seller markets to avoid being a repetition of his monopoly analysis.

2.2. Cournot's model: a two-firm simple example

Imagine an isolated coastal village in which there are two commercial fishing firms. Each firm has one fishing boat, and each day both boats set out at 3:00 a.m. to catch fish for sale that day. Fishing is perfectly reliable in the sense that each captain knows exactly how many pounds of fish he will catch. The haul depends on three things: the nature of the fishing boat, the number of crew members on board, and the number of hours the boat stays out. Boiling this information down into cost functions, the first firm's cost function is

$$C_1(q_1) = 6000 + 16q_1 \qquad (2.1)$$

and that of the second firm is

$$C_2(q_2) = 9000 + 10q_2 \qquad (2.2)$$

where q_1 is, of course, the harvest of fish, or output level, for firm 1, and q_2 is the analogous variable for firm 2. Firm 1 uses a less capital intensive and less highly automated fishing boat than the other firm, which accounts for its lower fixed cost of 6000 and its higher marginal cost of 16.

The day's catch of fish is brought into port by 9:00 a.m. and must be sold the same day. Each day is taken to be entirely separate in the sense that the two firms concern themselves with the profit of only the current day and engage in no longer-term planning at all. When they set sail, each has already decided on the catch to bring back that day, and neither knows what the other has decided. Perhaps each has an educated guess, but neither has spies in the other's camp or any source of factual knowledge of the other's commitments. Each of them, however, does know both cost functions, as well as the market demand function. Letting p denote market price,

$$q_1 + q_2 = 1000 - 10p \qquad (2.3)$$

There is a single market price because the catches of the two firms are identical, and with each firm deciding in advance on its output (catch) for the day, the market price will be adjusted to perfectly clear the market. With the decision variables of the firms being their output levels, the market price is dependent on them, and it is convenient to write demand in the form of an *inverse demand function:*

$$p = 100 - 0.1(q_1 + q_2) \qquad (2.4)$$

The two firms' profit functions are

$$\pi_1(q_1, q_2) = pq_1 - C_1(q_1) = 84q_1 - 0.1q_1^2 - 0.1q_1q_2 - 6000 \qquad (2.5)$$

$$\pi_2(q_1, q_2) = pq_2 - C_2(q_2) = 90q_2 - 0.1q_2^2 - 0.1q_1q_2 - 9000 \qquad (2.6)$$

Note again the character of the decision each firm must make. The individual day is taken as an isolated occurrence; hence, there is neither a future to consider nor a past from which to obtain guidance. Each firm makes its decision on output in a once-for-all way without knowing what the other firm will choose. In effect, they select output levels simultaneously and independently in the sense that they cannot communicate or coordinate.

Firm 1 wishes to choose q_1, its output level, to maximize its own profit, π_1, and firm 2 has a parallel objective. The *Cournot equilibrium* is the pair of output levels (q_1^c, q_2^c) that simultaneously achieves both maxima. That is to say, q_1^c is the profit-maximizing output level for the first fishing firm, given that $q_2 = q_2^c$, and q_2^c is the profit-maximizing output level for firm 2, given that $q_1 = q_1^c$. Thus, (q_1^c, q_2^c) is the simultaneous solution to the equations

$$\frac{\partial \pi_1}{\partial q_1} = 84 - 0.2q_1 - 0.1q_2 = 0 \qquad (2.7)$$

$$\frac{\partial \pi_2}{\partial q_2} = 90 - 0.1q_1 - 0.2q_2 = 0 \qquad (2.8)$$

The equilibrium can be viewed as a consistency condition in which no firm has ex post regret after observing the choice of the other firm. That is, seeing the chosen outputs to be (q_1^c, q_2^c), firm 1 notes that it could not have obtained greater profit by having selected differently from q_1^c, nor could firm 2 have done better by selecting differently from q_2^c. For any other output pair, (q_1', q_2'), at least one of the firms would not be maximizing its profit, given the output choice of the other. In considering whether or not to expect $q_2 = q_2'$ and to choose $q_1 = q_1'$, firm 1 will easily have cause to reject (q_1', q_2'). On the one hand, q_1' may not maximize the profit of firm 1, given $q_2 = q_2'$, in which case firm 1 will not choose q_1'. On the other hand, if q_1' does maximize the profit of firm 1, then q_2' cannot maximize the profit of firm 2 (by hypothesis that (q_1', q_2') is not a Cournot equilibrium); therefore, firm 2 cannot be expected to choose q_2'. *Only at the Cournot equilibrium will the firms have expectations that are correct and with respect to which they will each have maximized their own profits.*

It is interesting to look further at the structure of the market of these two fishing firms. If we ask the hypothetical question "What profit possibilities are technically attainable in this market?" we find that the Cournot equilibrium is a distinctly inferior outcome with respect to what would be attainable if the firms could cooperate. Solving equations (2.7) and (2.8), the Cournot equilibrium output levels are $q_1^c = 260$ and $q_2^c = 320$. From equation (2.4), price is 42, and, using equations (2.5) and (2.6), profits are 760 for firm 1 and 1240 for firm 2. A *profit possibility frontier* can be found by selecting profit levels for firm 1 and then maximizing the profits for firm 2 with respect to q_1 and q_2, while requiring that the profit for firm 1 be held at the preassigned level. For each preassigned profit level for firm 1, and associated maximum profit for the second firm, one point on the frontier is found.

An alternative procedure for finding points on the frontier is by maximizing a weighted sum of π_1 and π_2 with respect to q_1 and q_2. The meaning of a point on the frontier is that there is no other pair of output levels that can result in higher profits (simultaneously) for both firms. The profit possibility frontier for the fishing example is shown in Figure 2.1, and the point labeled C in the figure is the Cournot equilibrium. To see more exactly how to find points on the

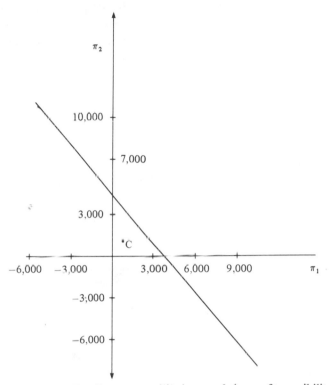

Figure 2.1 The Cournot equilibrium and the profit possibility frontier.

frontier, let k be between zero and one, and maximize $k\pi_1 + (1 - k)\pi_2$ with respect to q_1 and q_2. The first-order conditions are

$$84k - 0.2kq_1 - 0.1q_2 = 0 \tag{2.9}$$

$$90(1 - k) - 0.2(1 - k)q_2 - 0.1q_1 = 0 \tag{2.10}$$

Solving equations (2.9) and (2.10) for k gives

$$k = \frac{q_2}{840 - 2q_1} \tag{2.11}$$

from equation (2.9) and

$$k = \frac{900 - 2q_2 - q_1}{900 - 2q_2} \tag{2.12}$$

from equation (2.10). Equating these to eliminate k leaves an equation depending on q_1 and q_2. This equation can be written

$$(378{,}000 - 1{,}320q_1 + q_1^2) - (1{,}290 - 2q_1)q_2 + q_2^2 = 0 \tag{2.13}$$

If a particular value for q_1 is chosen, there remains a quadratic in q_2 that can readily be solved. Where there are two roots, the smaller is the correct one. The values of q_1 and q_2 found in this way are then substituted into equations (2.5) and (2.6) to obtain a profit point on the profit possibility frontier.

Returning to Figure 2.1, it is clear that collusion would allow both firms to simultaneously obtain much higher profits than they achieve at the Cournot equilibrium. But can the firms successfully collude? Under the conditions postulated in the model, definitely not. Suppose the two heads of the firms met to make an arrangement. For example, if they agreed on $q_1 = 195$ and $q_2 = 240.5$, then the market price would be $p = 56.4$, and their respective profits would be 1,887 and 2,172. The reason this agreement would not hold up is that it would not be in the interest of either firm to keep its word, and there would be no enforcement mechanism to coerce them into sticking by the agreement. After agreeing, each would actually be free to choose any output level, just as before. Consider the situation from the vantage point of firm 1. If firm 1 thought that firm 2 would live up to the agreement and choose $q_2 = 240.5$, then, from equation (2.7), it would maximize its profits by selecting q_1 to satisfy $84 - 0.2q_1 - 0.1 \cdot 240.5 = 0$, or $q_1 = 299.75$. Profits would be 2,985 instead of 1,887. But undoubtedly firm 1 would realize that firm 2 faced parallel incentives; therefore, firm 1 would not expect firm 2 to choose 240.5. After thinking the whole situation through, only the Cournot outcome would remain as believable.

Recall that throughout this discussion the fishing market is treated as a single-period situation. Other possibilities open up if the firms take account of their being in the same market in many future periods. Such considerations arise in Chapter 5, but for the time being they are suppressed. There is much to learn from the static, single-period oligopoly models covered in Chapters 2 and 3, and so the unrealistic single-period assumption is maintained throughout them. At bottom, the same principles are used by optimizing firms whether the market is a single-period market or has an infinite horizon, and it is important to see how to correctly formulate and apply those principles.

2.3. Cournot's model: the general case

In presenting the Cournot model, there are some minor details in which the version that follows differs from the original. This is to facilitate handling questions that Cournot did not raise, such as the following: (a) Under what conditions does the Cournot equilibrium exist? (b) What conditions ensure that, in equilibrium, each firm chooses to produce a strictly positive level of output? In this and all later chapters, unless the contrary is expressly stated, all functions are differentiable up to any desired order.

Specification of the model

The basic setting for the Cournot model is an industry with a fixed number, n, of firms. There is neither entry of new firms nor exit of existing ones, although any firm may choose to produce nothing and, consequently, to have a profit level equal to the negative of its fixed cost. The firms should be imagined to be in a single-period, or one-shot, market in which they make their decisions simultaneously. The good they produce is perfectly homogeneous, and consumers have no costs in going to a seller or transporting the good. Therefore, any consumer will, if faced with more than one price, choose to buy from a producer offering the lowest price in the market. Price competition does not enter the Cournot world, being ruled out by the expedient of assuming that each firm chooses an output level and that the market price is determined from the demand function as the price that equates the amount demanded by consumers to the amount produced by the industry.

Letting q_1 denote the *output level of the ith firm*, $Q = \sum_{i=1}^{n} q_i$ the *total output of the industry,* and *p* the *market price,* the *inverse demand function* is written $p = f(Q)$ and obeys the following conditions: (a) $f(0)$ is greater than zero. (b) If $Q > 0$ and $f(Q) > 0$, then $f'(Q) < 0$. (c) If $Q > 0$, then $Qf(Q) \leq M$, where M is some finite number. Condition (a) ensures that there are positive prices at which some amount of the product can be sold (i.e., there is a demand). Condition (b) is the common assumption that the demand curve slopes downward, and condition (c) stipulates that total revenue for the industry can never exceed a finite amount M. A more restrictive alternative for condition (c) is that the demand curve cuts both axes. These conditions are illustrated in Figure 2.2. The purpose of condition (c) is to eliminate any chance for the firms to have infinite profits.

Denoting the firm's *total cost function* $C_i(q_i)$, the conditions put on costs are that total cost be strictly positive for all output levels $[C_i(q_i) > 0$ for $q_i > 0]$, that marginal cost be positive $[C_i'(q_i) > 0]$, and that fixed cost be nonnegative $[C_i(0) \geq 0]$.[1] The *profit function*

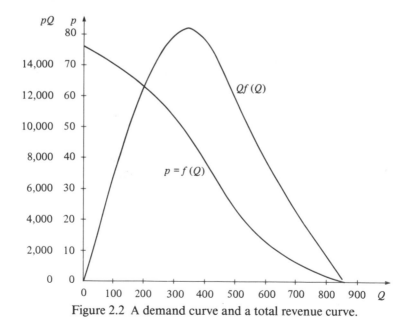

Figure 2.2 A demand curve and a total revenue curve.

of a firm may now be written, letting $q = (q_1, \ldots, q_n)$ be the *output vector*,

$$\pi_i(q) = q_i f(Q) - C_i(q_i) \tag{2.14}$$

Cournot equilibrium and some of its characteristics

The *Cournot equilibrium* is a collection or vector of output levels $q^c = (q_1^c, \ldots, q_n^c)$ having the property that no single firm i can increase its profit by choosing an output level different from q_i^c, given that the other firms are choosing q_j^c $(j \neq i)$. That is, each firm is maximizing its own profit with respect to its own output level, and all are accomplishing this simultaneously, which means that q_i^c maximizes $q_i f(q_i + \Sigma_{j \neq i} q_j^c) - C_i(q_i)$. $Q^c = \Sigma_{i=1}^n q_i^c$ is the Cournot equilibrium level of industry output. For a Cournot equilibrium at which all output levels are strictly positive, the following system of simultaneous equations is satisfied:

$$\pi_1^1(q^c) = f(Q^c) + q_1^c f'(Q^c) - C_1'(q_1^c) = 0$$

$$\vdots \tag{2.15}$$

$$\pi_n^n(q^c) = f(Q^c) + q_n^c f'(Q^c) - C_n'(q_n^c) = 0$$

In one sense this equilibrium fails all tests of efficiency that might be put to it. From the economywide standpoint, price clearly exceeds marginal cost, and so presumably the economy cannot be at a Pareto optimal point if there is an industry at a Cournot equilibrium embedded within it. Furthermore, the industry itself is at a profit point that is not on the firms' profit possibility frontier. As the fishing example illustrates, if the firms could collude, they could find a way to simultaneously increase the profits of all firms, as illustrated in Figure 2.1. Letting $\pi = (\pi_1, \ldots, \pi_n)$ denote a point in the profit space, the *profit possibility frontier* can be defined in relation to the set of *attainable profit points* H, given by

$$H = \{\pi(q)|q \geq 0\} \tag{2.16}$$

and the profit possibility frontier H^*, given by[2]

$$H^* = \{\pi \in H | \pi^0 \not\succ \pi \quad \text{for all } \pi^0 \in H\} \tag{2.17}$$

That is, a profit vector is in H if there is some feasible vector of output levels that attains the profit vector, and a profit vector is on the frontier if it is feasible and there is no feasible profit vector for which all firms have higher profits.

From the standpoint of the economy, the absence of Pareto optimality provides an argument for breaking large firms into sufficiently small units that they will be competitive. Set in opposition to this is the possibility that there are significant economies of scale to offset the oligopolistic inefficiency. If the consumers in an economy have higher real incomes under the low costs and inefficient pricing of oligopolies, then the obvious challenge is to find a way to induce better (i.e., nearer to marginal cost) pricing while preserving the large scale of firms.

That the Cournot equilibrium is inside, rather than on, the profit possibility frontier raises a different sort of objection to it, namely, that the firms might possess the power to do better. If collusion could yield higher profits, then surely wouldn't the firms collude? This issue receives considerable attention at various points in this volume and is of great practical importance in relation to the antitrust laws of the United States and other countries.

Before moving to a discussion of the fundamental role of Cournot's discovery, a word is needed on conditions that ensure both the existence of the Cournot equilibrium and its uniqueness. Existence is ensured if each firm's profit is a *concave function* on its own output. That is, for any output vector for which $f(Q) > 0$, $\pi_i^{ii}(q) < 0$. This is illustrated in Figure 2.3. All three functions in Figure 2.3 are concave. Their common feature is that the slope of each function never increases, going from left to right. Uniqueness of the Cournot equilibrium is guaranteed by two conditions that themselves imply concavity: For Q and q_i such that $f(Q) > 0$, it is required that $f'(Q) - C_i''(q_i) \leq 0$ and $f'(Q) + f''(Q) \leq 0$, with strict inequality holding for at least one of these two expressions. These conditions guarantee that the marginal revenue curve of the firm will rise slower or fall faster than its marginal cost ($\partial MR_i/\partial q_i < \partial C_i'/\partial q_i$). For any particular output levels of the other firms, it is always possible to find the profit-maximizing output level for firm i; the concavity

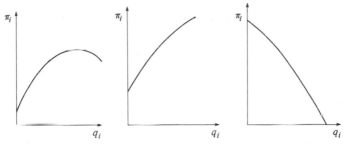

Figure 2.3 Three concave functions.

condition ensures that the profit-maximizing output for firm i is a continuous function of the output levels of the other firms. This condition has been essential in proving the existence of the Cournot equilibrium.[3]

Proof of the existence and uniqueness of the Cournot equilibrium may be found in the work of Friedman (1977) or Szidarovsky and Yakowitz (1977). Szidarovsky and Yakowitz provide an insightful proof of uniqueness by linking the firm's profit-maximizing output level to the total industry output, showing the optimal q_i falls as Q rises. This proof can be illustrated using the fishing example. Equations (2.7) and (2.8), which characterize the Cournot equilibrium, can be rewritten as follows: For firm 1, $84 - 0.2q_1 - 0.1q_2 = 84 - 0.1q_1 - 0.1(q_1 + q_2) = 84 - 0.1q_1 - 0.1Q = 0$, or

$$q_1 = 840 - Q \tag{2.18}$$

Repeating the same procedure for firm 2,

$$q_2 = 900 - Q \tag{2.19}$$

Adding equations (2.18) and (2.19),

$$q_1 + q_2 = 1,740 - 2Q \tag{2.20}$$

Obviously, at equilibrium, $q_1 + q_2$ from the left-hand side of equation (2.20) must equal Q from the right-hand side. Solving equation (2.20) for this common value gives $3Q = 1,740$, or $Q = 580$. Using

$Q = 580$ in equations (2.18) and (2.19) returns the equilibrium output values of $q_1 = 260$ and $q_2 = 320$. Looking again at equation (2.20), notice that $q_1 + q_2$ falls as Q rises; therefore, it is impossible to have more than one value of Q for which $Q = 1,740 - 2Q$.

An example showing the connection between concavity and the existence of equilibrium is provided in Chapter 3. Other facts that are proved by Friedman (1977) are that if $f(0)$ exceeds $C_i'(0)$ for at least one firm, then $Q^c > 0$, and if $Q^c > 0$ the Cournot equilibrium is not on the profit possibility frontier. The reason that Cournot equilibrium output for the industry is strictly positive when $f(0)$ exceeds $C_i'(0)$ for at least one firm can be seen by imagining the situation if all firms were to produce zero. Then any firm satisfying the condition $f(0) > C_i'(0)$ could increase its profit by increasing its output above zero because its marginal revenue $[f(0)]$ would exceed its marginal cost $[C_i'(0)]$.

The significance of Cournot's insight

Several questions can be raised about the Cournot equilibrium: Is it convincing? What significance does it have for more general models? Is it realistic? All these questions are elaborations on the issue of whether or not the Cournot equilibrium is convincing; however, consider that question first from a narrow point of view based solely on a single-period complete-information quantity model of the class specified in the preceding section. By *complete information* is meant that each firm knows the market demand function and knows the cost functions of all firms in the market. Furthermore, explicitly assume that the Cournot equilibrium is unique and that the firms are prohibited from making binding agreements. That is, they cannot meet, make an agreement concerning their output levels, write a legal contract embodying the agreement, and then go to the courts if someone among them does not carry out his part of the agreement. Therefore, an agreement lacking an enforcement mechanism would have to be *self-enforcing* in order to be honored. It would need to be in the interest of no single firm to break the agreement, if the agreement were to be kept. By the very definition of the Cournot equilibrium, no output vector could be agreed to and honored except a Cournot equilibrium.

So, in a situation that is single-period, with each firm simultaneously making an output decision and with binding agreements ruled out, the Cournot equilibrium is convincing and is the only equilibrium that is convincing. As for realism, the very restrictive circumstances that the market be single-period is surely grossly unrealistic, and it is definitely important to the conduct of firms in the economy that they interact with one another for long stretches of time.

Yet the Cournot equilibrium has a basic lesson to teach in markets where binding agreements cannot be made. That lesson concerns the fundamental nature of a noncooperative equilibrium. Any firm possesses certain information and can choose from a particular set of actions. If the firm is in a many-period market where, in each period, simultaneous output decisions are made, and if a firm always learns what its rivals chose in past periods prior to selecting its current-period output level, then the firm gathers additional information over time and must contemplate its present choice in the light of the way it expects that choice to influence its future circumstances. In fact, at any time, it needs to select its present action as part of a larger plan in which it decides a policy for present and future output choices. Such a plan is termed a _strategy_. Each decision maker will realize that its rivals, the other decision makers with whom it interacts, will think and plan in the same way.

In this expanded, more general setting a noncooperative equilibrium is analogous to the Cournot equilibrium in the one-period model, for, in equilibrium, each firm should be using a strategy that maximizes its objective function (e.g., discounted profits), given the equilibrium strategies of the others. So, in any particular model there is an appropriate way to state the consistency requirement that is embodied in the Cournot equilibrium. How this is done inevitably depends on the exact nature of the model under discussion. It was Cournot's great discovery to see this consistency requirement in the context of single-period oligopoly. Prior to Cournot, no writer on economics had dealt from a strategic point of view with economic situations involving only a few decision makers.[4]

In judging Cournot's equilibrium it ought to be borne in mind that nearly the whole of economic theory was static, single-period equilibrium theory until the middle of this century. The major exception to this was capital theory, and even in recent years capital theorists have led the way in developing multiperiod models. In oligopoly it is quite natural to discuss the intertemporal relations among firms, and many writers have done this while using a single-period model as a vehicle. Confusions, errors, and valuable insights have resulted from this practice, as the remainder of this volume should make clear. Multiperiod oligopoly models are, of course, analyzed in many of the later chapters.

The study of single-period models is important for several reasons. There is, first, the basic point made in the preceding paragraph that a noncooperative equilibrium, an equilibrium of the general sort discovered by Cournot, is characterized by each firm having a plan of action (strategy) that is best for it given the plans of the other firms. The exact meaning of the terms *best* and *plan of action* must be determined by the context of the model. Two examples: (a) In the single-period Cournot model, *best* would be *profit-maximizing,* and *plan of action* would be *output level.* (b) In a multiperiod extension of the Cournot model, *best* would mean *discounted profit-maximizing,* and *plan of action* would be *an overall plan that indicates which output level will be chosen in each time period.* The basic feature of noncooperative equilibrium is most easily learned in the simple setting in which Cournot discovered and formulated it.

The second reason for studying single-period models is that they provide the basis for multiperiod models; hence, they must be understood before they can properly be put to use. Finally, a better understanding and appreciation of oligopoly can be achieved if one has some sense of its historical development and, as noted earlier, most of the early development was essentially single-period in nature.

2.4. Cournot and competitive equilibrium

Suppose the cost structures of the fishing firms in the example in Section 2.2 were symmetric; that is, the firms have identical cost functions, which are

$$C_i(q_i) = a + 5q_i + q_i^2 \tag{2.21}$$

The fixed cost, a, is left as a parameter of the model so that its effect on equilibrium behavior can be observed. Likewise, the number of firms is n rather than two. The questions to be addressed with this example are the following: Is the Cournot equilibrium close, in some reasonable sense, to the competitive equilibrium? Will the Cournot equilibrium become more like the competitive equilibrium as n, the number of firms, increases? Will the two equilibria coincide as the number of firms goes to infinity? These questions are interesting from two points of view. First, there is the welfare question concerning whether or not society loses much by the presence of oligopolistic markets. This question will not be answered in a precise way, partly because doing so would require a general equilibrium model. The models under study here and elsewhere in this book are partial equilibrium models; however, where Cournot equilibrium and competitive equilibrium differ, one can gain an intuitive grasp of whether or not they are close by merely inspecting the numbers. The second question concerns whether or not Cournot equilibrium and competitive equilibrium differ by so little that one can as well study oligopoly under the assumption that the firms behave as if they were competitors. If I thought the differences were trivial, there would be little excuse for writing this book; however, this is a serious question that deserves some attention. There are economists who think that assuming competitive behavior will always suffice, because noncompetitive markets are rare and, where they occur, the behavior in them is only negligibly different from competitive behavior. Clearly, the truth of these assertions is an empirical matter for which definitive evidence is not available (at least, to my knowledge). It is possible to gain an appreciation of the issues involved through examination of the examples presented next.

By assuming the firms to all have the same cost functions, it is possible to examine symmetric equilibria. This greatly simplifies the exposition and brings into sharp relief the things on which we should concentrate. The profit function of a firm, using the cost function in equation (2.21) and the inverse demand function

$p = 100 - 0.1Q$, is

$$\pi_i(q) = pq_i - a - 5q_i - q_i^2 = 95q_i - 1.1q_i^2 - q_i\sum_{j\neq i}q_j - a \qquad (2.22)$$

The firm's first-order condition for profit maximization as a Cournot player is

$$\frac{\partial \pi_i}{\partial q_i} = 95 - 2.2q_i - 0.1\sum_{j\neq i}q_i = 0 \qquad (2.23)$$

But because it is known that the equilibrium is symmetric, $q_i = q_j$ for all i and j; so equation (2.23) can be written $95 - 0.1(21 + n)q_i = 0$. Solving for q_i yields

$$q_i = \frac{950}{21+n} \qquad (2.24)$$

Total industry output is $Q = nq_i = 950n/(21 + n)$, market price is $p = 100 - 95n/(21 + n)$, and profit for the ith firm is

$$\pi_i = 11\left(\frac{95}{21 + n}\right)^2 - a \qquad (2.25)$$

A glance at these equations reveals that q_i must fall as n, the number of firms, increases, but at the same time, Q increases. With total industry output rising as n rises, market price falls. It also appears that Q goes to 950 as n goes to infinity, with price going to 5; however, the presence of the fixed cost, a, implies an upper limit to the possible value of n. Presuming that equilibrium profits must be greater than or equal to zero, for each value of a, there is a maximum associated n for which equilibrium profits will be non-negative.

Table 2.1 gives summary information on the model. For the value of a shown in the first column, column 2 gives the largest sustainable value of n. Thus, for example, with $a = 500$, profits will be negative at any Cournot equilibrium with $n > 23$ and will not be negative for $n \leq 23$. The remaining three columns give market price (p), the output of a single firm (q), and the output of the whole market (Q) at Cournot equilibrium when n has the value shown in

Table 2.1. *Cournot equilibrium for various fixed costs and levels of* n

a	max n	p	q	Q
2,000	1	95.68	43.18	43.2
1,800	2	91.74	41.30	82.6
1,600	3	88.13	39.58	118.8
1,500	4	84.8	38.0	152.0
1,400	5	81.73	36.54	182.7
1,000	10	69.35	30.65	306.5
500	23	50.34	21.59	496.6
200	49	33.5	13.57	665.0
100	78	25.15	9.6	748.5
10	294	11.33	3.02	886.7
1	975	7	0.95	930
0.1	3,129	5.63	0.3	943.7
0.01	9,942	5.2	0.095	948

column 2. Comparing the data in Table 2.1 with competitive equilibrium presents a small problem: Strictly speaking, competition requires that n be infinite, and with each firm sustaining a fixed cost, there cannot be an infinite number of firms unless that cost is zero. The appropriate way out of this problem is to examine the equilibrium Shubik (1959) calls the *efficient point*. The efficient point is found by supposing that each firm maximizes profits subject to the condition that price equals marginal cost. Thus, the equilibrium condition will be $p = 5 + 2q_i = 100 - 0.1nq_i$. Output for each individual firm will be $q_i = 950/(20 + n)$. For the market $Q = 950n/(20 + n)$, market price will be $p = 100 - 95n/(20 + n)$, and the profit for each firm will be $\pi_i = 100[95/(20 + n)]^2 - a$. Table 2.2 contains information parallel to that in Table 2.1 for the efficient point. Comparison of any line of Table 2.1 with the line in Table 2.2 corresponding to the same level of fixed cost shows that market price and total industry output are very nearly the same.

Should the result of the comparison lead one to conclude that treating oligopolists as if they are competitive will be nearly correct? Not necessarily. As the next example makes clear, the sort of comparison just made could go either way. A further consideration,

Table 2.2. *Efficient point equilibrium for various fixed costs and levels of* n

a	max n	p	q	Q
2,000	1	95.48	45.24	45.2
1,800	2	91.36	43.18	86.4
1,600	3	87.61	41.3	123.9
1,500	4	84.17	39.58	158.3
1,400	5	81	38	190
1,000	10	68.33	31.67	316.7
500	22	50.24	22.62	497.6
200	47	33.36	14.18	666.4
100	75	25	10	750
10	280	11.33	3.17	886.7
1	930	7	1	930
0.1	2,984	5.63	0.316	943.7
0.01	9,480	5.2	0.1	948

beyond the scope of the present chapter, but taken up in Chapter 8, is whether or not the number of firms in the market need be the maximum that the market can sustain. Say, for example, that $a = 100$. Then a Cournot market could sustain 78 firms, and they would reach an equilibrium that would differ little from the efficient point. But need there be 78 firms? If there were only 10 firms, the market price would be 69.35, which is quite different from the efficient point price of 25. This raises the question of entry, of course. It is seen in Chapter 8 that a firm may be free to enter a market, and if the firm were actually already in the market it would be profitable, but the firm cannot enter the market profitably because of some kind of start-up cost. The nature and size of these start-up costs can be influenced by firms already operating in the market. For example, if advertising creates brand loyalty on the part of consumers and if this brand loyalty slows the acceptance of a product from a new firm, then established firms can advertise more than they would if there were no possibility of a new firm entering the market. This extra advertising may increase brand loyalty to the point that the entrant cannot come in profitably, even though the equilibrium that would eventually obtain would eventually become

Table 2.3. *Cournot and efficient point equilibria for various fixed costs and levels of* n

	Cournot				Efficient point			
a	max n	p	q	Q	max n	p	q	Q
10,000	1	56.82	431.8	431.8	2	13.64	431.2	863.6
6,000	2	40.63	296.9	593.8	3	10.94	296.9	890.6
4,000	3	32.14	226.2	678.6	4	9.52	226.2	904.8
700	10	15.18	84.8	848.2	11	6.7	84.8	933
10	98	6.15	9.58	938.5	94	5.2	10.08	948
1	313	5.36	3.02	946.4	300	5.06	3.16	949.4
0.1	995	5.11	0.95	948.9	949	5.02	1	949.8

profitable. Admittedly, this example presumes differentiated products; however, a similar example can be described using firms' capital stocks when higher capital stocks bring about lower marginal costs of production.

The second example is a simple variant of the first. The same demand function is retained, but the cost functions are

$$C_i(q_i) = a + 5q_i + 0.01q_i^2 \qquad (2.26)$$

The information in Table 2.3 repeats, for this example, the facts parallel to Tables 2.1 and 2.2. Note that for $a = 700$, the divergence between the efficient point and the Cournot equilibrium is still great. The Cournot price is more than double, with the maximum numbers of firms being nearly the same in the two cases (10 and 11). At $a = 10$, the maximum number of firms rises to nearly 100, and the two equilibria become much closer.

These examples suggest the following: (a) Cournot equilibrium is quasi-competitive. That is, total industry output rises and market price falls as the number of firms in the market increases. (b) As the number of firms goes to infinity, Cournot equilibrium converges to the competitive equilibrium. (c) The number of firms cannot go above a finite upper bound if the firms have a positive fixed cost. (d) The output level of an individual firm falls as the number of firms increases. Ruffin (1971) presented analytical results that confirm (a) through (d) and provide more detail on when they hold. For markets in which the marginal cost of the firms is nondecreasing as output rises, and in which marginal revenue is always below market price, (a) and (c) always hold. Conditions (b) and (d) depend, in general, as in the examples, on the nature of the cost function. When there is a positive fixed cost, the average total cost curve is U-shaped, and the number of viable (profit-making) firms in the market is limited. In such a case it is not meaningful to speak of the number of firms going to infinity, and convergence of Cournot equilibrium to competitive equilibrium cannot occur. As the first example shows, however, it can get very close. Cournot price will, for any *n*, always be above the efficient point price because the oligopolist's marginal revenue will, by assumption, always be lower than market price.

2.5. Cournot's stability analysis and the genesis of the reaction function

It has been common in economics to investigate the stability of static models. Cournot probably was the first to do this in a formal way. Walras (1874) followed in his footsteps, and the study of Walrasian stability of static general equilibrium systems has been a considerable cottage industry during the past several decades. Such analysis inherently involves a logical contradiction, because stability is a dynamic property. Therefore, it cannot actually be studied in a static setting. This problem is dodged by the unsatisfactory expedient of grafting ad hoc dynamic assumptions onto the static model and examining the stability properties of the resulting ill-formed dynamic model. There are several reasons for devoting time and effort here to the exposition of this material. First, in discussions of oligopoly, a great deal of confusion and error is generated by treating static models in an ad hoc dynamic fashion. By seeing precisely why the ad hoc dynamics are faulty, it will be easier to avoid this pitfall. Second, many people note the inconsistencies inherent in thinking of Cournot's stability analysis as a genuine dynamic model and then proceed to dismiss all of Cournot's oligopoly theory. This throws out the baby with the bath water, for there is great insight in the static Cournot model and associated equilibrium. Third, stability analysis can be used to determine whether or not the static Cournot equilibrium is unique. Finally, stability analysis can be used as an introduction to more appropriate dynamic analysis.

Stability in a two-firm example

Stability is first addressed for the two-firm fishing model of Section 2.2. Following that, a more general formulation is given. The basic idea is to imagine the firms to be in a discrete time situation, as described in Section 2.2, but with two differences: In each time period each firm actually does recall the choices made in the past by itself and by its rival. Second, each firm assumes that in time t its rival will choose the same output level that it chose in time $t - 1$. Clearly, if a firm does not behave as its rival expects, the rival will see this; however, such a possibility is brushed aside. The myopia assumption is maintained; each firm chooses its output level in period t with a view to maximizing the profits of that same period. For firm 1, its objective function in period t can be written

$$\pi_1(q_{1t}, q_{2,t-1}) = 84q_{1t} - 0.1q_{1t}^2 - 0.1q_{1t}q_{2,t-1} - 6,000 \quad (2.27)$$

and for firm 2,

$$\pi_2(q_{1,t-1}, q_{2t}) = 90q_{2t} - 0.1q_{2t}^2 - 0.1q_{1,t-1}q_{2t} - 9,000 \quad (2.28)$$

In light of equations (2.27) and (2.28), the first order conditions, equations (2.7) and (2.8), are written

$$84 - 0.2q_{1t} - 0.1q_{2,t-1} = 0 \quad (2.29)$$

$$90 - 0.1q_{1,t-1} - 0.2q_{2t} = 0 \quad (2.30)$$

Solving equation (2.29) to express q_{1t} as a function of $q_{2,t-1}$ gives

$$q_{1t} = 420 - 0.5q_{2,t-1} \quad (2.31)$$

Equation (2.31) is a *reaction function* for firm 1. Its operational meaning is that the manager of firm 1 decides today on how many fish to catch by recalling the number of fish his rival caught the day before. He believes that the rival will go out and catch the same number of fish today as yesterday, and he calculates the profit-max-imizing amount for his own firm to catch in light of this assumption. Firm 2 behaves in a parallel way, using the reaction function

$$q_{2t} = 450 - 0.5q_{1,t-1} \tag{2.32}$$

With the firms' strategies given by equations (2.31) and (2.32), it is possible to trace the paths of their output levels through time starting from any initial output levels. For instance, say $q_1 = 100$ for $t = 1$ and $q_2 = 800$ for $t = 1$. Then, from equation (2.31), $q_{12} = 420 - 0.5(800) = 20$, and $q_{22} = 450 - 0.5(100) = 400$. In period 3, $q_{13} = 420 - 0.5(400) = 220$, and $q_{23} = 450 - 0.5(20) = 440$. Period 4 brings $q_{14} = 420 - 0.5(440) = 200$ and $q_{24} = 450 - 0.5(220) = 340$. As t increases, the output levels converge to the static Cournot values of $q_1 = 260$ and $q_2 = 320$.

One could say the model would be stable if he were content to *define* stability according to equations (2.31) and (2.32), and if he thought those equations had any operational economic meaning that was acceptable. Of course, as a description of behavior, the two reaction functions ignore two vital considerations. First, it is economically unreasonable that the firms would be in a dynamic environment and not care about future profits. Second, it is unacceptable to assert that a firm would expect its rival to repeat today its action of yesterday when, time after time, the other firm had systematically failed to do so.

Stability in the general model

Turning to a more general statement of the stability analysis, we begin with the first-order conditions for the Cournot equilibrium, equation (2.15). The equation $\pi_1^1 = 0$ is an implicit function of the output variables $q_1, \ldots, q_n$. If it could be solved to give q_1 as a function of $q_2, \ldots, q_n$, then, in this new form, it would directly give the profit-maximizing output for firm 1 for any particular values of $q_2, \ldots, q_n$. In the same way, $\pi_i^i = 0$ could be solved for q_i as a function of $(q_1, \ldots, q_{i-1}, q_{i+1}, \ldots, q_n)$. To make notation simpler, let $\bar{q}_i = (q_1, \ldots, q_{i-1}, q_{i+1}, \ldots, q_n)$, and denote the new form of the first-order condition by $q_i = w_i(\bar{q}_i)$ for $i = 1, \ldots, n$.

The system of equations $q_i = w_i(\bar{q}_i)$ for $i, \ldots, n$ can be turned into a system of difference equations:

$$q_{it} = w_i(q_{i,t-1}) \quad \text{or} \quad q_t = w(q_{t-1}) = (w_1(\bar{q}_1), \ldots, w_n(\bar{q}_n))$$

It is as if each firm makes a dated sequence of output decisions, seeking with each decision to maximize its current-period profit, and with each firm assuming that its rivals' current (time t) output levels will be unchanged from the previous time period ($t - 1$). As noted earlier in discussing the two-firm fishing example, the static expectations are unjustified, and the firms pay no attention to future profit when making current decisions; however, Cournot discussed the stability of his equilibrium in terms of the equation system $q_t = w(q_{t-1})$. Behavioral relations such as $q_{it} = w_i(\bar{q}_{i,t-1})$, under which the current action of a firm is a function of past actions, have come to be called _reaction functions_. These specific reaction functions, $w_i(\bar{q}_{i,t-1})$ derived from equation (2.15), are called *Cournot reaction functions.*

Now imagine that at each time t q_{it} is chosen to be $w_i(\bar{q}_{i,t-1})$ for all i, starting from some initial output vector q_0. The Cournot equilibrium is *stable* if the sequence of output vectors chosen in this way converges to q^c, the Cournot equilibrium, as t goes to infinity.[5] This stability analysis also informs us on the uniqueness of the Cournot equilibrium. If the best reply functions satisfy the contraction condition to be set forth later, there will be only one Cournot equilibrium. A differentiable function $\phi(x_1, \ldots, x_m)$ is called a *contraction* if $\sum_{i=1}^{m} |\phi^i| \le k < 1$ for any value of $x = (x_1, \ldots, x_m)$. For any x' and x'', if ϕ is a contraction, then $\phi(x')$ and $\phi(x'')$ are closer together than x' and x'', and the distance from $\phi(x')$ to $\phi(x'')$ is never greater than k times the distance from x' to x''. The same statement can be made of largest divergences:

$$\max_i |\phi_i(x') - \phi_i(x'')| \le k \cdot \max_i |x_i' - x_i''| \tag{2.33}$$

If the function w is a contraction, then the Cournot equilibrium is stable and the Cournot equilibrium is unique.

Is stability meaningful in the Cournot model?

The difference equations $q_{it} = w_i(q_{i,t-1})$, where $i = 1,$ ..., n, have come to be called reaction functions because they can be interpreted as output policies for the firms in a multiperiod market. In discussing stability, Cournot wrote as if firms were choosing output levels in a succession of periods, and in each period when a firm i would choose its output, it would select $q_{it} = w_i(\bar{q}_{i,t-1})$. Whether or not Cournot really thought he was dealing with a multiperiod market is not clear; however, certain things are clear: (a) He has been regarded by many writers as dealing with a multi-period market. (b) He has stimulated others to clearly formulate and analyze reaction functions. (c) In a multiperiod market, for firm i to choose its behavior by using $w_i(\bar{q}_{i,t-1})$ to determine q_{it} is best, or optimal, for the firm if two conditions are met: (a) that the firm is only interested in maximizing the profits of period t when q_{it} is chosen; that is, it has no interest in trading even one penny of period-t profits in order to gain thousands in the next or any later period; (b) that the firm believes all other firms will repeat in period t the same output levels they choose in period $t - 1$. In symbols, firm i expects that $q_{jt} = q_{j,t-1}$ for all $j \neq i$.

These two conditions are economically unreasonable. Surely no firm makes its decisions in a period based solely on the aim of maximizing that period's profits unless it plans to go out of business by the end of the period. Usually a firm's time horizon is indefinitely long. Usually a firm is a corporation with professional management and widely diffused ownership or it is owned and managed by one person, or it may fit somewhere between these extremes. In the first instance, it is clear that corporate managers make many decisions and expend considerable resources in order to increase profits at relatively distant points in time. Obviously, firms making computers and other sophisticated electronic equipment maintain research and development facilities whose activities range from engineering design to basic scientific research. The former activity will improve the reliability or accuracy of a product, make it easier to use or cheaper to make or repair, and will come to fruition within months or a couple of years. The outcome of the latter activity is problematic, for when a commercially usable discovery is made, it may be many years before it is sufficiently refined and developed that it can be marketed.

Even in more mundane industries, management must be constantly looking far ahead to determine the correct direction for current policies. Even though no single present stockholder plans to live forever, any stockholder is likely to care very much about the value of his investment at the end of his own life. Indeed, between a wish to leave bequests to descendants and the uncertainty about how long one will live, a stockholder tends to have an indefinitely long horizon. The same holds true for the owner of an owner-managed firm.

Oddly, it has not been the single-period horizon that has received the most criticism. Rather, it has been the static expectations. It has been correctly observed that, starting from an initial output vector q_0, different from the Cournot equilibrium q^c, if the firms all use their Cournot reaction functions, then it will never be true that $q_{it} = q_{i,t-1}$ for all firms i. If the Cournot equilibrium is stable, the output levels will converge to the Cournot equilibrium; however, for any finite time span, firms will generally be changing output levels from one period to the next. Why, it is asked, would a firm i assume $q_{jt} = q_{j,t-1}$ (for $j \neq i$) when, period after period, it is seen that this expectation is false? Furthermore, if all firms were following Cournot reaction functions, the observed deviations of present output levels from immediately past output levels would be systematic in character. Surely any observant and thoughtful decision maker would attempt to estimate the empirical relationship between its rivals' q_{jt} and the output levels of period $t - 1$, and it would use that information in making its own decisions.

It is vitally important to note that the foregoing objections are to the Cournot reaction function, not to the Cournot equilibrium. The Cournot equilibrium applies to a single-period market, whereas the objections raised earlier are for a multiperiod model and, even there, are not aimed at the Cournot equilibrium. Indeed, in a multiperiod extension of the Cournot model, if each firm had as its plan to choose $q_{it} = q_i^c$ for all firms i and all periods t, the result would be a noncooperative equilibrium. No firm could change its plan and increase the profit of any period, given the behavior of the other firms. In fact, even if the firm's objective were the maximization of discounted profits, it could not do better. Thus the Cournot equilibrium can still be an equilibrium in a multiperiod model. Reaction functions are investigated in greater depth in Chapter 5.

2.6. Cournot's first reviewer and early critics

It was not until 1883, forty-five years after its publication, that Cournot's book became the subject of a book review.[6] The reviewer, Joseph Bertrand, was also a mathematician. He is best remembered for his work in probability theory. He was quite down on the book, particularly the celebrated Chapter 7 dealing with oligopoly. First, Bertrand asserts that the obvious outcome is for the oligopolists to collude in the choice of a price, and he asserts that Cournot has rejected this outcome. He also regards price as the decision variable, as price is used in Cournot's monopoly analysis of Chapters 5 and 6. He presents an analysis of duopoly using Cournot's famous mineral spring example in which costs are zero, and he switches to price as the firm's decision variable. At the heart of his analysis is the recognition that where consumers have complete information, where the products of the firms are absolutely identical, where there are no costs of search or transport, and where the firms have virtually unlimited capacities to produce, each consumer will buy from the firm charging the lower price.

If both firms charge zero, each has zero profit, and neither can increase its profit by increasing its price. That this is equilibrium can be seen by imagining firm 1 charging $p_1' > 0$. Then, firm 2 can make a positive profit by choosing a price close to, but just slightly less than, p_1'. Firm 2 will then have all the sales; however, if firm 2 chooses $p_2' < p_1'$, then firm 1 can have higher profits by choosing p_1'' just a bit smaller than p_2'. And so it goes. Positive prices for the firms cannot be in equilibrium, and $p_1 = p_2 = 0$ is a noncooperative equilibrium. Edgeworth (1897) took up that cudgel from Bertrand and made a fuller analysis based on a variant of the Bertrand model.

Bertrand's model, as compared with that of Cournot, has an outstanding advantage and a related disadvantage. The advantage is in regarding price as the decision variable of the firm. It is difficult to see the institutional arrangements that determine prices in oligopolistic markets if it is not the firms that are setting them. On this score, Cournot leaves us hanging. If firms produce perfectly homogeneous goods, they cannot select their own prices without being in Bertrand's world. If, on the other hand, products are differentiated, so that a firm's demand is a continuous function of all firms' prices, firms can be easily imagined to choose both price and quantity. As will be argued later, either one of the two variables can have primary strategic importance.

A firm that must make both price and output decisions and that can carry inventories may be at one of two extremes. First, it may be able to quickly and easily adjust output and may alter prices infrequently while adjusting output to meet random or seasonal fluctuations in demand. For example, a firm that makes a large array of small hardware items (nuts and bolts in a bewildering array of sizes) and that produces for its customers a thick catalogue with prices may find it more troublesome to change the catalogue than to adjust output levels. Such a firm is essentially a price chooser, and it meets whatever demand is presented.

At the other extreme is the firm that must plan production far in advance (say a year or half a year) and that faces very high costs of holding inventory. Such a firm will make frequent alterations in prices in order to cause the rate of sales to approximate the rate of production. The American automobile manufacturers are examples. Although there are formal wholesale prices in effect at any time, the dealers often pay somewhat less. Toward the end of a model year, dealers usually receive rebates from the manufacturers, with the sizes of the rebates depending on the relationship among prevailing demand conditions, the production schedule, and the size of inventories. Even early in the model year, rebates may be given on models that are selling much more slowly than was anticipated. Whereas it is certainly the firms that are choosing prices, it appears to be more of a Cournot type of situation in which the firms' strategic variables are their output levels. Prices are indeed determined by market conditions in the sense that the firms constantly adjust their prices in order to match sales to production.

Returning to the merits and demerits of the Bertrand model, it was noted earlier that price formation appears explicitly in the model. It was argued earlier that some markets can be characterized as having price as the dominant strategic variable, whereas others have output play that role. There is a peculiarity in the Bertrand model that is entirely absent from the Cournot model. Because the good is perfectly homogeneous and the firms choose prices, then the amount one firm can sell, other prices being taken as fixed, is discontinuous at the lowest of the rival prices. Let the lowest announced price among a firm's rivals be p^*. At a price above p^* the firm sells nothing, below p^* it sells the total market demand, and at p^* it gets some share of total market demand. Change price from a penny below p^* to a penny above and sales plummet to zero.

Surely this situation cannot be found in the real world, or, if it can, it is exceedingly rare. What makes it virtually nonexistent is that goods are not really homogeneous; they are differentiated, which takes us to the topic of the next chapter.

2.7. Summary

Cournot oligopoly refers to a market of n firms in which the firms produce a homogeneous product, with each firm having its output level as its decision variable. Until a generation ago, nearly all formal oligopoly models were static, although dynamic issues often arose in the discussion woven around them. Formal or semi-formal treatments of stability are in a gray area in this respect; however, they may fairly be regarded as embryonic dynamic treatments.

In an effort to maintain conceptual clarity, the Cournot model is treated in all sections except Section 2.5 of this chapter as a purely static model in which each firm makes one, and only one, output choice. These choices are made simultaneously by the firms. Within this setting, the Cournot equilibrium is argued to be the only reasonable or acceptable equilibrium. It is the prototype of the Nash (1951) noncooperative equilibrium, and it illustrates that concept in the simplest oligopoly setting: Each firm has a family, or set, of strategies from which it can choose, and each has an objective function it wishes to maximize. A noncooperative equilibrium consists of n particular strategies, one for each firm, so chosen that no single firm could possibly have obtained higher profits if it, alone, had selected a different strategy. This principle is applied throughout all chapters of this book.

In addition to descriptions of the instructive and historically important Cournot model and Cournot equilibrium, the existence and uniqueness of equilibrium are discussed, and conditions assuring that Cournot equilibrium will converge to competitive equilibrium are given. Although this model is a good beginning point, it has many limitations, some of which are removed in subsequent chapters. Most immediately, firms in modern economics appear to produce products that are somewhat different from one another. Chapters 3 and 4 deal with this. Perhaps more fundamentally, the Cournot market has no dynamics; firms do not operate over time, maximizing discounted profit streams and following policies that reflect the motion of the market. Chapters 5 through 7 partially rectify this. Another static aspect of the Cournot market is the fixity of the number of firms, which is dealt with in a preliminary way in Chapter 8.

Questions remain that are not addressed at all in succeeding chapters. One is the treatment of research and development efforts. Although a literature is just beginning to emerge on this subject, I did not think it had developed to a point where I could treat it usefully here. Another question is how to model a dynamic market in which the future can bring totally unpredictable change (as opposed to a world of uncertainty characterized by states of nature whose probabilities of occurrence are known). Despite the gaps and inadequacies of oligopoly theory, it has progressed tremendously in the last twenty years, and it addresses with intelligence, precision, and insight many topics that had been touched on in only the loosest ways until recently.

3

Differentiated products models of oligopoly and monopolistic competition

The standard competitive models of economics, dealing with the consumer, producer, and individual market or general competitive equilibrium, are couched in terms of homogeneous products. That is, a fixed list of distinct commodities is assumed to exist, each commodity is produced by a multitude of firms, and, in some models, the consumer is presumed to buy and use strictly positive amounts of every good. If apples were one commodity, then no consumer could distinguish the apples grown by firm j from those grown by firm k. Chamberlin's concept (1933) of *differentiated products* starts from the position that no two firms make precisely the same thing, even when they are nominally in the same industry, and consumers have quite various tastes from one to another over the various firms' products. Thus, apples may be larger or smaller, more or less sweet, and varying in texture. Many consumers may confine their purchases to one firm's apples, and the price difference that will place the consumer on the margin between two kinds of apples may, and usually will, be quite variable among consumers.

Chamberlin's principal use of this concept is to frame an alternative to the usual competitive model in which there are well-defined industries consisting of product categories, like apples, that can be studied in isolation as legitimately as one can investigate a single market in the homogeneous goods framework. As under standard competition, no single firm's behavior has a noticeable effect on any

50

other firm, and there are many firms; however, each firm faces a downward-sloping, though very elastic, demand curve. Chamberlin also discusses oligopoly, particularly differentiated products oligopoly, in which an industry has only a few firms that produce nonidentical products. Such models are the main topic under study in this chapter, although two versions of monopolistic competition are also investigated. One is the standard Chamberlin version, and the other is a variant of it that Chamberlin mentions but does not develop, called the chain market.

In Section 3.1 the concept of differentiated products is discussed at length. There are some subtleties and difficulties that are brought out because they are important and have largely been ignored in the literature. Aside from Section 3.1, they are also largely ignored in this book. Section 3.2 contains an early differentiated products model due to Harold Hotelling (1929). A particularly interesting aspect of this model is that it shows how little is required for product differentiation. In Hotelling's model, it arises from two assumptions: that consumers must pay to move a good from the seller's location to their own locations and that sellers live at various locations. Although Hotelling published first, he and Chamberlin, working in isolation from one another, actually developed their results at about the same time. Because Hotelling's model is much narrower in scope and more fully worked out in its details, it is an ideal vehicle to introduce the subject. In Section 3.3 a more general single-period differentiated products oligopoly model is developed, and the equilibrium concept applied to it is that of Cournot (1838). Section 3.4 takes up the two variants of monopolistic competition that Chamberlin (1933) proposed. The term *monopolistic competition* refers to markets that, like competitive markets, have large numbers of sellers, but in which the firms produce nonidentical (i.e., *differentiated*) products. Thus, each firm has an interval of prices within which it can sell, although the large number of rival firms may cause that interval to be narrow. Section 3.5 returns to differentiated products oligopoly and presents a model in which firms choose output levels. Although prices can still vary among firms, prices are automatically adjusted to clear the market at the quantities that have been specified. It may be as natural to specify output levels as to specify prices as decision variables for the firms; so it is useful to see how a quantity-based differentiated products oligopoly can be formulated. Section 3.6 contains a brief summary. Throughout this chapter, the nature of a firm's product is given. In Chapter 4, models are examined in which firms can choose product specifications. Reasons for choosing quantity in preference to price as a decision variable are discussed.

As in Chapter 2, it is assumed in all following sections that the firms possess *complete information*. Each knows the profit functions of all firms in the market.

3.1. **On the meaning of differentiated products**

As a benchmark, think again about the homogeneous goods model. The products of two firms in the same industry are absolutely perfect substitutes for one another, but the product of one of them is in a relatively weak substitute or complement relationship with the product of any other industry. The basic idea here is that within an industry, one price must prevail, and between two industries the cross elasticities of demand are finite.

Now weaken the *perfect* substitutes condition to *strong* substitutes and the market is one of differentiated products. The product of each firm is unique. Say there are m firms. The *output of firm i* is denoted q_i, and its *price* is p_i. Letting the *vector of all prices* be $p = (p_1, \ldots, p_m)$, the *demand function* of the ith firm can be written $q_i = f_i(p)$. The *cross elasticity of demand* for the ith good with respect to the jth price is $\epsilon_{ij} = (\partial q_i/q_i)/(\partial p_j/p_j)$. To have a tidy grouping of firms into industries, the firms must be clustered according to the sizes of their various cross elasticities with one another, but each has a relatively small cross elasticity with any firm outside its group. Within the group, cross elasticities will be positive, denoting a substitute relationship, whereas cross elasticities with outside firms can be positive or negative. They will be small in absolute value, and so firms outside firm i's group will have much smaller effects on firm i than inside firms.

A note on the way products cluster into groups

It is an important empirical question whether or not a typical modern economy satisfies the foregoing conditions, and a little thought and a few well-chosen examples serve to raise doubts that it does so. At first, apples, hiking boots, pencils, and portable radios may appear to be likely product clusters. It seems peculiar to picture a consumer on the margin between a bushel of golden delicious apples and a pair of hiking boots, but it is equally peculiar to imagine him on the margin between a powerful, sophisticated shortwave radio and a pocket-size AM radio. Indeed, the shortwave radio may have a higher cross elasticity with a weekend vacation or a food freezer, and the pocket radio may compete more vigorously with popular music recordings. These criticisms are forcefully stated by Robert Triffin (1940). The issues raised here have not been completely settled, although the recent contribution of Nikaido (1975) moves in the right direction. In principle, of course, Triffin is correct: All goods are interconnected, and various quite surprising pairs of goods can be interconnected very strongly. But that does not invalidate a theoretical approach that assumes that certain firms have strong effects on one another and are so little affected by other firms that they can be studied in isolation. The study of such a grouping of firms, an *industry,* can yield many useful insights, and it is well to remember that all theoretical models involve compromises with reality. Even making the move to a "general equilibrium" framework does not ensure that everything is taken into account. For example, political and psychological considerations are left out of account. Many economists believe that isolating economic phenomena for study is valid, arguing that the answers obtained will remain largely valid when placed in a wider context. Often this claim is true. Isolating certain economic phenomena and concentrating on others (i.e., partial versus general equilibrium) is no different in principle than isolating economic phenomena and ignoring the political. The more the field of investigation is narrowed, the greater the depth and detail in which it can be examined. But depth and detail are obtained at the risk of ignoring fundamentally important variables, and good judgment is needed to tell when and how to simplify.

The features that cause differentiation

A final issue is the determination of which products are differentiated and which are not. This divides into (a) whether or not "objectively" identical products can be differentiated and (b) whether physically identical products obtained from different sellers should be regarded as the same or different. Regarding the former issue, it might be argued that aspirin, for example, cannot be differentiated because different brands are chemically identical or even because different brands are manufactured by a single supplier to the same specifications. The question, however, is not one of chemical analysis; it is a question of the personal tastes and perceptions of consumers. If people regard one brand of aspirin as an imperfect substitute for another, then the two brands are not identical from an economic standpoint. The converse can also be imagined: Firms produce products that are not physically identical, but the differences show up at a level too subtle for any consumer to notice. If consumers treat the outputs of various firms as perfect substitutes, they are homogeneous from an economic standpoint. Personal taste is the governing element, quite apart from whether one applauds or abhors that taste.

It can be argued that virtually all goods are heterogeneous, for even those products that are physically identical and are known to be, such as standardized industrial products, are bought from particular suppliers, who vary in terms of their credit policies, speed of delivery, and ancillary services. These are joint products that are tied to the principal commodity and that serve to differentiate it from the similar offerings of other firms.

By way of illustration, imagine a person who receives a prescription from his physician for medicine. The prescription completely specifies what sort of capsules will be in the bottle and how many there will be. Furthermore, it can be assumed that all pharmacies use identical bottles; yet, many people are not indifferent to which pharmacy fills the prescription, nor do people always go to the pharmacy charging the lowest price or to the one located nearest to home or office. Factors entering into the decision can include price, location, ease of parking, hours the pharmacy is open, whether or not delivery service is provided, and more.

As a second illustration, suppose a person wanting a loaf of a standard brand of bread, available at any food store in his city, buys it at a small grocery that charges 10¢ more than an equally near supermarket because he can get in and out of the small store faster. If the same loaf were being purchased along with a week's supply of food, he would go to the supermarket. Not only would prices be lower, but everything on the shopping list would be available, and time would be saved.

It is common for some people to buy appliances from sellers who have especially good records of providing repair service. Similarly, certain sellers will more readily accept merchandise returns. Some people will pay higher prices to obtain these advantages. The point of these examples is to stress that virtually all goods are heterogeneous. Similar illustrations can be made using standardized industrial products. Because the purchase of, say, a bag of sugar is actually the purchase of a composite good comprising the sugar, the seller's location, the ambience of the store, and so forth, it is reasonable to treat bags of chemically identical sugar as differentiated products. Perhaps these differences could be modeled in another way, with the sugar itself remaining homogeneous; however, this route need not be followed.

Firms' choices in product design

There is a related issue that is not dealt with in this chapter. A firm does decide what it will offer for sale. The pharmacist decides what hours to be open, whether or not to offer delivery service, and so forth. The appliance dealer decides whether to build an efficient service organization or to offer minimal service and, consequently, lower prices. So product design, as well as price, is a decision. This is the topic of Chapter 4.

Product design is often costly to change. The point is obvious when applied to the technical specifications of a piece of equipment, but it is also true of characteristics that can be changed quickly and easily. Capriciously changing his store hours from week to week would be bound to hurt the pharmacist. Information does not get around quickly enough for customers and potential customers to keep up with frequent changes, and many would go elsewhere rather than taking a chance on the pharmacy being open or having to call to check. Similarly, a lenient policy on merchandise returns will do no good in building clientele if it is carried out during fifteen randomly chosen weeks per year, with tougher rules obtaining the remainder of the time.

Throughout this chapter, product design is taken as given, products are differentiated, and each firm i is endowed with its own *demand function,* $q_i = f_i(p)$, where $p = (p_1, \ldots, p_n)$ is the *vector of prices* of the n firms in that market. The demand functions can vary quite considerably from one firm to another. What they have in common is that q_i ought generally to fall as p_i rises, it ought to rise as p_j ($j \neq i$) rises, and it ought to be impossible for all firms to simultaneously raise their prices and have all their demands increase. These properties are repeated and elaborated in Section 3.3.

3.2. The Hotelling model of spatial duopoly

In Hotelling's model there are two firms that produce physically identical products. Suppose them to be a pair of dry cleaners that differ only in location. Each chooses its own price and sells to all consumers at that price and at its own location. The locational possibilities for both firms and consumers are represented by a line segment, as shown in Figure 3.1, that represents "Main Street" in a one-street town. Throughout this section, the locations of the firms are taken as given and unchangeable. Hotelling was interested in determining where the firms could be expected to locate, as well as in analyzing equilibrium price policy once location is determined; however, consideration of where to locate is deferred to Chapter 4. Consumer demand is assumed to be uniformly distributed along the line segment as if each point were the location of a consumer and all consumers were identical except for

Figure 3.1. Hotelling's "Main Street."

location. Demand is also perfectly inelastic; so each consumer buys the same amount of dry cleaning no matter what prices he faces. The only decision he must make is which cleaner to patronize. On top of the product price, the consumer must pay a transport fee that is c per unit distance between him and the firm from which he buys; this can be thought of as the cost of going from home to the dry cleaning establishment.

The point marked 1 in Figure 3.1 is the location of firm 1, and the point marked 2 is the location of firm 2. The line segment has a length of $L = a + x + y + b$. Taking the level of demand to be one unit for each unit length of the line segment, the two firms between them sell $q_1 + q_2 = L$; however, the customers divide themselves between firms so that each consumer buys at the lower price (gross of transport cost). Take the consumer located at point Z in Figure 3.1. He is x units distant from firm 1 and y units distant from firm 2; so his cost is $p_1 + cx$ if he buys from firm 1 and $p_2 + cy$ if he buys from firm 2. Moving to the left of Z, it becomes steadily cheaper to buy from firm 1 and more expensive to buy from firm 2; so if Z were the consumer for whom $p_1 + cx = p_2 + cy$, then every consumer to the left of Z would buy from firm 1, and every consumer to the right of Z would buy from firm 2.

Taking the consumer at Z to be on the margin between the two firms, it is easily verified that using

$$p_1 + cx = p_2 + cy \tag{3.1}$$

$$L = a + b + x + y \tag{3.2}$$

x and y can be expressed in terms of the cleaners' prices and the parameters L, a, and b. From equation (3.1), $y = x + (p_1 - p_2)/c$, which can be substituted into equation (3.2). Then equation (3.2) is solved for x, which is

$$x = \frac{1}{2}\left(L - a - b - \frac{p_1 - p_2}{c}\right) \qquad (3.3)$$

Solving for y in a similar way gives

$$y = \frac{1}{2}\left(L - a - b - \frac{p_2 - p_1}{c}\right) \qquad (3.4)$$

Hotelling assumes that the firms have zero fixed and variable costs; hence, profit for each is its own price multiplied by its sales. The first dry cleaner sells $a + x = q_1$, and the second sells $b + y = q_2$. Thus, using equations (3.3) and (3.4), profits are

$$\pi_1 = p_1 q_1 = p_1(a + x) = \tfrac{1}{2}(L + a - b)p_1 - p_1^2/(2c) + p_1 p_2/(2c) \qquad (3.5)$$

$$\pi_2 = p_2 q_2 = p_2(b + y) = \tfrac{1}{2}(L - a + b)p_2 - p_2^2/(2c) + p_1 p_2/(2c) \qquad (3.6)$$

With each profit function now written to depend only on the two prices and parameters of the model, Hotelling looks for an equilibrium in the spirit of Cournot, a noncooperative equilibrium that is characterized by a pair of prices (p_1^*, p_2^*) such that the profit of firm 1 is maximized using p_1^*, given that firm 2 uses p_2^*, and, conversely, the profit of firm 2 is maximized using p_2^*, given that firm 1 uses p_1^*. Consider now the best price for the first dry cleaner, supposing p_2 fixed. As an example, let $L = 100$, $c = 5$, $a = b = 10$, and $p_2 = 500$. Thus, the two cleaners are far from one another and near the ends of the village. The profit function for the first cleaner is depicted in Figure 3.2. Note that it reaches a maximum of 25,000 at $p_1 = 500$, then falls as price declines. However, at $p_1 < 100$ it approaches a secondary maximum; 100 is the price at which firm 1 is about to take over the whole market. With $p_2 = 500$, if p_1 is less than 100, then the delivered price of the first cleaner is lower for all locations than the delivered price of the second. The relative heights of these two peaks depend on the firms' locations, and if $a = b = 40$ (with all other specifications unchanged), then circumstances change significantly. As depicted in Figure 3.3, a profit maximum is again reached at $p_1 = 500$, with $\pi_1 = 25,000$; however, the first

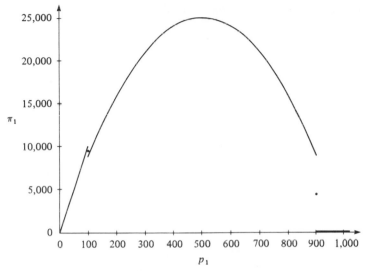

Figure 3.2. Profit for firm 1 in Hotelling's model with firms far apart.

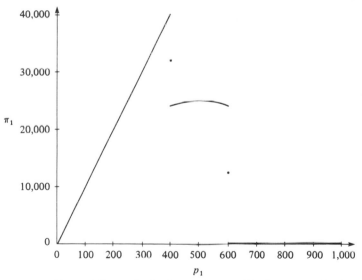

Figure 3.3. Profit for firm 1 in Hotelling's model with firms close together.

cleaner takes over the whole market at any price below $p_1 = 400$. At slightly under 400, π_1 is just below 40,000, making such a price more profitable than $p_1 = 500$. When it does not pay for either cleaner to attempt taking over the whole market, the equilibrium prices are found by solving the pair of simultaneous equations

$$\frac{\partial \pi_1}{\partial p_1} = \frac{1}{2}(L + a - b) - \frac{p_1}{c} + \frac{p_2}{2c} = 0 \qquad (3.7)$$

$$\frac{\partial \pi_2}{\partial p_2} = \frac{1}{2}(L - a + b) - \frac{p_2}{c} + \frac{p_1}{2c} = 0 \qquad (3.8)$$

The equilibrium prices are

$$p_1 = c\left(L + \frac{a - b}{3}\right) \qquad (3.9)$$

$$p_2 = c\left(L - \frac{a - b}{3}\right) \qquad (3.10)$$

and the equilibrium output levels are

$$q_1 = a + x = \frac{1}{2}\left(L + \frac{a - b}{3}\right) \qquad (3.11)$$

$$q_2 = b + y = \frac{1}{2}\left(L - \frac{a - b}{3}\right) \qquad (3.12)$$

A lesson that Hotelling seeks to teach from this model is that goods must be perfectly homogeneous if the sort of situation described by Bertrand (see Chapter 2) is to obtain. Merely because of the introduction of spatial differentiation – two firms selling physically identical products at different locations, coupled with transport costs for the consumers – the demand facing one firm is a continuous function of the two prices, as is seen from equations (3.3) and (3.4). Then, converting these equations to demand functions,

$$q_1 = a + x = \frac{1}{2}\left(L + a - b - \frac{p_1 - p_2}{c}\right) \qquad (3.13)$$

$$q_2 = b + y = \frac{1}{2}\left(L - a + b - \frac{p_2 - p_1}{c}\right) \qquad (3.14)$$

for $c(L - a - b) > p_1 - p_2 > -c(L - a - b)$. One firm does not obtain all the sales if it prices itself just a hair beneath the other firm. Likewise, equilibrium prices and profits are not zero, but are strictly positive, as can be verified from equations (3.9) through (3.12).

Hotelling developed the equilibrium conditions shown in equations (3.7) through (3.12) as if they would hold for all fixed values of a and b; however, as some of the preceding analysis has suggested, there may be values of a and b for which an *interior* equilibrium (i.e., an equilibrium with both firms producing at positive levels) is ruled out. D'Aspremont, Jaskold Gabszewicz, and Thisse (1979) have pointed out that with locations fixed, there are two categories of equilibria. The first obtains when the two firms share the same location and the equilibrium is that of Bertrand, with both prices equal to zero.

The second requires that the two firms be sufficiently far apart. In particular, if the two firms are not at the same location (i.e., $a + b < L$), equilibrium exists if and only if

$$\left(L + \frac{a - b}{3}\right)^2 \geq \frac{4}{3} L(a + 2b) \tag{3.15}$$

$$\left(L + \frac{b - a}{3}\right)^2 \geq \frac{4}{3} L(b + 2a) \tag{3.16}$$

in which case equilibrium prices are given by equations (3.9) and (3.10). To see the significance of equations (3.15) and (3.16), recall that as the price of firm 2 falls, with that of firm 1 remaining constant, the point Z in Figure 3.1 moves leftward. Point Z is the location of that consumer who is indifferent between buying from firm 1 and firm 2. As p_2 continues to fall, it eventually reaches the value $p_2 = p_1 - c(L - a - b)$ at which the marginal consumer is precisely at the location of firm 1. With a further slight decrease in p_2, firm 2 captures the whole of firm 1's market. If a is too large, then firm 2 may find it more profitable to choose a price that just barely freezes firm 1 out of the market, rather than choosing a price satisfying equation (3.8). If $a = b$, equations (3.15) and (3.16) reduce to $a \leq \frac{1}{4}L$.

As to equilibrium locations, Hotelling argued that both firms would locate exactly at the center of the market, because every other possibility could be ruled out. From equations (3.10) and (3.12) it is seen that equilibrium profits for firm 2 with given locations would be $C[L + (b - a)/3]^2/2$ if they located so that equilibrium were not Bertrandesque. Differentiating with respect to b, the parameter that indicates the location of firm 2, it is seen that $\partial\pi_2/\partial b = C[L + (b - a)/3]/3$, which is positive for all values of a and b. Thus, the optimal location is the location that makes b as large as possible, suggesting that firm 2 should locate very close to firm 1 and on the side of firm 1 containing the center point of the interval. But, because firm 1 will wish to do likewise with respect to firm 2, there can be no equilibrium with a firm located away from the center of the market. On the other hand, if one firm were at the center, the other would not locate there, for, as D'Aspremont, Jaskold Gabszewicz, and Thisse (1979) proved, equilibrium profits would be zero. The other firm could locate elsewhere and make positive profits. Thus, there is no locational equilibrium for the celebrated Hotelling model. It remains to use the foregoing information to develop a full equilibrium in which the two cleaners decide where to locate their shops as well as what prices to charge. This is carried out in Section 4.4 of Chapter 4.

3.3. A more general model of differentiated products oligopoly

The modeling of demand in this section can be regarded as a generalization of the Hotelling model and also as a way of making more precise the verbal and graphical analysis of Chamberlin (1933). The fundamental feature in modeling Chamberlinian demand is that the sales of one firm *always* vary continuously with the prices of all firms. There is no special price for a firm at which another firm abruptly (discontinuously) gains its customers. As an example that modifies the Hotelling village-on-a-line model, suppose the transport cost for a customer is cd^2, where d is the distance from consumer to dry cleaner. The marginal cost of going an additional mile increases with distance. Imagine that p_1 is just enough below p_2 to cause the consumers exactly at the location of the second dry cleaner to patronize the first cleaner. Still, the consumers to the right of firm 2 will continue to purchase from firm

2. A slight lowering of p_1 will shift the location of the marginal consumer only a little farther to the right.

If product design is fixed, demand can be stated as a relationship determining the amount a firm can sell as a function of its own price and the prices of the other firms in the market. Reasonable qualitative conditions are as follows: At a price vector for which the ith firm's demand is strictly positive, an increase in its own price will cause a decrease in the amount it can sell. If, in addition, the demand of some other firm j is also positive, an increase in p_j will cause an increase in the amount demanded. If j's demand is zero, an increase in its price ought not affect any firm, for, effectively, it is out of the market. These boundary conditions, relevant when one or more firms have zero demand, make the complete specification of demand quite cumbersome; however, everything can be put quite clearly by considering the demand conditions in several distinct steps: (a) For all nonnegative price vectors ($p \geq 0$), $f_i(p)$ is a finite-valued, nonnegative, and continuous function. (b) For any $p \geq 0$ such that $f_i(p) > 0$, f_i is twice continuously differentiable with respect to p_i. If, in addition, $f_j(p) > 0$ for some other firm j ($\neq i$), then f_i is twice continuously differentiable with respect to (p_i, p_j). These conditions establish some regularity properties (i.e., those conditions concerned with continuity and differentiability) and two properties of economic significance (demand cannot be infinite or negative). For the remaining three conditions, p is always chosen so that $f_i(p) > 0$. (c) $f_i^i(p) < 0$. (d) If $f_j(p) > 0$ for some $j \neq i$, then $f_i^j(p) > 0$; however, if $f_j(p') = 0$ for p' close to p (i.e., in a neighborhood of p), then $f_i^j(p) = 0$. (e) Suppose that $f_k(p) > 0$ for a subset of firms, A. A can be all firms and always includes firm i. Then, for some $\epsilon > 0$, $\Sigma_{k \in A} f_i^k(p) \leq -\epsilon$. Condition (c) is the usual downward-sloping demand assumption. As a firm lowers its price, other prices remaining unchanged, its sales increase. Condition (d) stipulates two things about the effect of a change in one firm's price (p_j) on the demand of another firm (f_i). First, if the firm is *in the market* [i.e., if $f_j(p) > 0$], then an increase in its price will cause the demand for the other firm to rise. The two firms' products are gross substitutes. Second, if it is out of the market, meaning that its sales are zero and a small price decrease will not bring positive sales, then it has no effect on the other firm's demand. Small alterations in p_j will leave $f_i(p)$ unchanged. The economic import of condition (e) is that equal increases in the prices of all firms will cause a decrease in the demand facing each of them. This condition implies that there is a special price vector p^+ that is the largest price vector that need be considered. First, $f_i(p^+) = 0$ for all i; however, for any $p < p^+$ there is at least one firm having strictly positive demand. And, of course, if $p_i \geq p_i^+$, then $f_i(p) = 0$, irrespective of the values of the other prices. Proofs of the statements concerning p^+ can be found elsewhere (Friedman, 1977, p. 55).

The basic idea underlying this demand structure is that consumers' tastes are diverse, and the n products offered by the firms of the industry differ in various qualitative dimensions. Some of these aspects of design may be the sort for which more is always better, but others may not. For example, making a radio lighter in weight probably will displease no one, other things being equal, but the amount a person is willing to pay for a given reduction in weight will vary greatly from one consumer to another. Some will pay nothing, but an affluent backpacker may be willing to pay a large amount. If the case of the radio is bright red, instead of a sedate dark blue, some may like it better, and others less. There may be no price difference between them at which a very high fraction of consumers is just on the margin. These considerations are intended to justify a demand function for each firm characterized by great regularity. For two prices to be equal is of no special significance. Making a small change in a price, other prices being fixed, will never cause a huge change in demand for the firm whose price is changed or for any other firm.

Using the cost function from Chapter 2, the profit function of the ith firm is

$$\pi_i(p) = p_i f_i(p) - C_i[f_i(p)] \tag{3.17}$$

The Cournot concept of equilibrium applied to this single-period differentiated products model is a price vector, p^c, such that no firm *i* can increase its profit by choosing a price different from p_i^c, given that all other prices are $\bar{p}_i^c = (p_1^c, \ldots, p_{i-1}^c, p_{i+1}^c, \ldots, p_n^c)$. Symbolically this can be expressed

$$\pi_i(p^c) = \max_{p_i} \pi_i(p_i, \bar{p}_i^c) \qquad (i = 1, \ldots, n) \qquad (3.18)$$

Although the *Cournot equilibrium* is, properly speaking, defined for a homogeneous goods model, it is so near in spirit to a noncooperative equilibrium for any single-period model that it is used here in this broader way. And if the Cournot equilibrium has strictly positive output for all firms, equation (3.18) is equivalent to

$$\pi_1^1(p^c) = 0$$
$$\vdots$$
$$\qquad\qquad\qquad\qquad\qquad\qquad\qquad (3.19)$$
$$\pi_n^n(p^c) = 0$$

supposing, of course, that second-order conditions $[\pi_i^{ii}(p^c) < 0]$ are met. As with the Cournot quantity model, the equilibrium is characterized by prices having an internal consistency property. If a single firm imagined that the others would choose $\bar{p}_i^c$, then it could do no better than p_i^c, and putting itself into the position of any of its rivals, clearly it would regard no firm j as having an incentive to choose differently from p_j^c.

Likewise, if the firms were to have a meeting to attempt collusion, in the absence of binding agreements, no firm would have an incentive to do as it had agreed if the price vector agreed on were not a Cournot equilibrium. Thus, when the Cournot equilibrium is unique, it is an obvious outcome, even if the firms are unable to carry on any negotiations. In contrast, if there were several Cournot equilibria, none of which would give more profit to one firm than (*Pareto dominates*) to all the others, it would not be obvious how the firms would behave. If they could communicate with one another, either through conversation or written messages, it would be possible for them to choose one among the equilibria. Any Cournot equilibrium agreed on in this way constitutes a *self-enforc-*

ing agreement. It is self-enforcing because, being a Cournot equilibrium, no firm has an incentive to deviate from what it agreed to do, nor does it have any reason to suppose its rivals will deviate.

It remains to note four additional characteristics of the Cournot equilibrium, for which proofs can be found elsewhere (Friedman, 1977, Chapter 3):

(a) As in the Cournot quantity model, the Cournot equilibrium in the price model is not on the profit possibility frontier. The reason for this is that at Cournot equilibrium, a slight increase in the price of one firm will benefit each of the other firms while hardly costing any lost profits to the firm that changes price. Should all firms simultaneously increase prices just a little, then all will increase profits. To see this more precisely, note that $\partial \pi_i / \partial p_i = 0$ at Cournot equilibrium, whereas $\partial \pi_i / \partial p_j > 0$, because the cross derivative in demand (f_i^j) is positive and price exceeds marginal cost $(p_i - C_i' > 0)$. Loosely speaking, if a firm charges slightly over the Cournot price, its own profits are unaffected, but all others' profits rise.

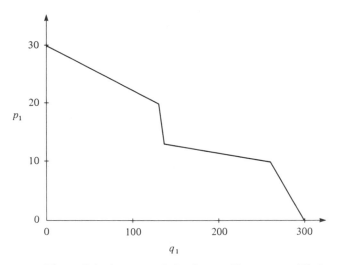

Figure 3.4. An example having no Cournot equilibrium: demand for firm 1.

(b) If $\pi_i(p)$ is concave with respect to p_i (i.e., $\pi_i^{ii} < 0$) for all price vectors satisfying $f_i(p) > 0$ and $p_i > C_i'[f_i(p)]$, then a Cournot equilibrium exists. To see how the absence of concavity can lead to there being no Cournot equilibrium, consider the following example: For the first of two firms, suppose demand to be

$$
\begin{aligned}
q_1 &= 240 - 4p_1 + 4p_2 \quad \text{for} \quad 0 \le p_1 < 10 \\
&= 610 - 41p_1 + 4p_2 \quad \text{for} \quad 10 \le p_1 < 13 \\
&= 90 - p_1 + 4p_2 \quad \text{for} \quad 13 \le p_1 < 20 \\
&= 330 - 13p_1 + 4p_2 \quad \text{for} \quad 20 \le p_1
\end{aligned} \tag{3.20}
$$

with the additional proviso that q_1 is always nonnegative. This demand function is continuous and is drawn in Figure 3.4 for $p_2 = 15$. Costs are nil; so $\pi_1 = p_1 q_1$, and Figure 3.5 shows the profit function for $p_2 = 15$. For firm 2, demand is given by

$$
\begin{aligned}
q_2 &= 300 - 5p_2 + \frac{p_1 - 17}{p_2^2 - 17^2} \quad \text{for} \quad 0 \le p_2 < 8 \\[2mm]
&= 732 - 59p_2 + \frac{p_1 - 17}{p_2^2 - 17^2} \quad \text{for} \quad 8 \le p_2 < 10 \\[2mm]
&= 162 - 2p_2 + \frac{p_1 - 17}{p_2^2 - 17^2} \quad \text{for} \quad 10 \le p_2 < 16 \\[2mm]
&= 290 - 10p_2 + \frac{p_1 - 17}{p_2^2 - 17^2} \quad \text{for} \quad 16 \le p_2
\end{aligned} \tag{3.21}
$$

also with the understanding that demand cannot be negative. Figures 3.6 and 3.7 show the demand and profit functions for firm 2 with $p_1 = 17$.

Now recall that the Cournot equilibrium is a pair of prices that satisfies $\pi_1^1(p) = 0$ and $\pi_2^2(p) = 0$ simultaneously. These two functions are plotted in Figure 3.8, where it is seen that no pair of prices simultaneously satisfies both equations. In particular, $\pi_1^1(p) = 0$ is satisfied by $p_1 = 10$ when $p_2 \le 15$ and by $p_1 = 20$ when $p_2 \ge 15$. That is, $p_1 = 10$ maximizes profit for firm 1 for any p_2 less than or equal to 15, and $p_1 = 20$ maximizes π_1 for $p_2 > 15$. Similarly, π_1 is maximized when $p_2 = 8$ if $p_1 \ge 17$ and when $p_2 = 16$ if $p_1 \le 17$. As

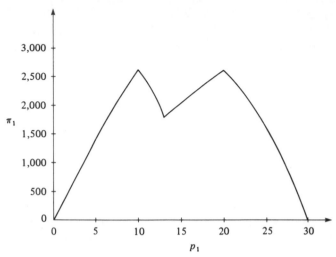

Figure 3.5. An example having no Cournot equilibrium: profit for firm 1.

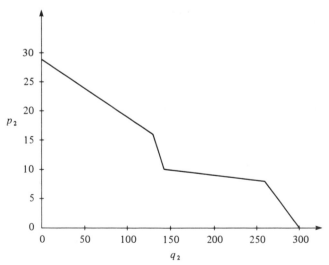

Figure 3.6. An example having no Cournot equilibrium: demand for firm 2.

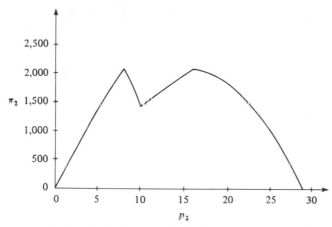

Figure 3.7. An example having no Cournot equilibrium: profit for firm 2.

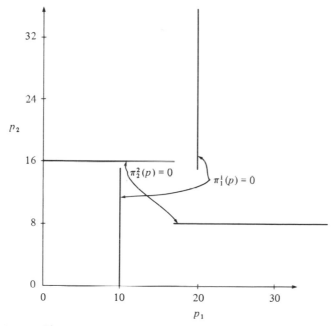

Figure 3.8. An example having no Cournot equilibrium: the Cournot reaction functions of the two firms.

Figure 3.8 demonstrates, if π_1 and π_2 are not concave (strictly speaking, quasi-concave) in p_1 and p_2, respectively, then the functions $\pi_1^1(p) = 0$ and $\pi_2^2(p) = 0$ can, as in the example, be discontinuous and fail to intersect. When this happens, there is no Cournot equilibrium.

(c) The condition that follows guarantees that a Cournot equilibrium is always associated with strictly positive output for every firm: There is a price $p_i^0 > C_i'(0)$ such that $f_i(p_i^0, 0) > 0$. This condition asserts that at p_i^0 the firm will face positive demand, no matter what prices are chosen by the other firms, and that p_i^0 exceeds the firm's marginal cost at zero output. Thus, no matter what $\bar{p}_i = (p_1, \ldots, p_{i-1}, p_{i+1}, \ldots, p_n)$ may be, the profits of the ith firm cannot be maximized at zero output.

(d) Uniqueness of equilibrium is assured by a condition on the second derivatives of the profit function: $|\pi_i^{ii}(p)| > \sum_{j \neq i} |\pi_i^{ij}(p)|$ for all p such that $p_i > C_i'[f_i(p)]$, where $i = 1, \ldots, n$. The role of the preceding condition can be seen by constructing a *best reply function* for each firm. This means taking the first-order condition for Cournot equilibrium, $\pi_i^i(p) = 0$, and inverting it so that it can be

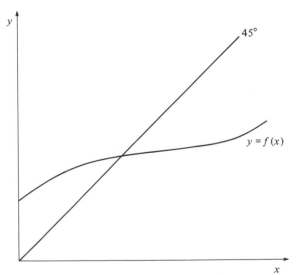

Figure 3.9. A function that is a contraction.

expressed in the Cournot reaction function form $p_i = w_i(\bar{p}_i)$ for each firm i. Condition (d) is that the best reply functions are *contractions*. That is, the sum of the absolute values of the first derivatives of w_i is less than one ($\Sigma_{j=1}^{n}|w_j^i| < 1$). It is a well-known theorem in mathematics that an equation system $\pi_1^1(p) = 0, \ldots, \pi_n^n(p) = 0$ is satisfied by no more than one vector in p when the equations are contractions. The idea is shown in Figure 3.9. The function $y = f(x)$ can cross the 45° line no more than once if f' is always less than unity in absolute value.

3.4. Chamberlin's two versions of monopolistic competition

Edward Chamberlin (1933) is much better remembered for the concept of monopolistic competition than for differentiated products oligopoly. *Monopolistic competition* centers about the concept of product differentiation coupled with markets composed of many small firms. In the version that he stressed, (a) each firm faces a downward-sloping demand curve when its own demand changes as a function of its own price, other prices constant, is contemplated, and (b) the price changes of one firm have only a negligible effect on the demand of any other firm. This can be illustrated with an example: let a typical firm face a demand curve given by $q_i = 100 - p_i + \Sigma_{j \ne i} p_j/n$, and let the firm have no costs. Its profit function is $\pi_i = 100p_i - p_i^2 + p_i \Sigma_{j \ne i} p_j/n$, and its profit is maximized with respect to its own price, given the prices of others, when

$$100 - 2p_i + \frac{1}{n} \sum_{j \ne i} p_j = 0 \tag{3.22}$$

or, solving for p_i as a function of the other prices,

$$p_i = 50 + \frac{1}{2n} \sum_{j \ne i} p_j \tag{3.23}$$

Note that the derivative of the optimal price for firm i with respect to a specific other price p_j is $1/(2n)$. It is in the spirit of Chamberlin's principal view of monopolistic competition that n be regarded as a very large number so that $1/(2n)$ is negligible. The effect of a change in firm j's price on the best price for firm i is virtually nil.

Chamberlin sought an analogue to competitive markets in which individual pairs of firms would be totally isolated from one another as in a competitive market. That is, the actions of one individual firm would have no noticeable effect on any other firm. The two types of markets would differ because the monopolistic competitor would face a downward-sloping, rather than horizontal, demand curve. In such a market there are no strategic interactions among firms, because the cross effects between pairs of firms are virtually nil. Thus, distinct individual products are allowed, but much of the analytic convenience of competition is retained.

This is fine but for one thing. To my knowledge there is no example of a market that approximates these conditions. There are markets having many small firms, each of which sells a somewhat different variant of the product, but they differ from Chamberlin's market in one crucial way: Each firm's product is an especially close substitute for those of a few other firms. The cross effects in demand between this firm and each of the several "nearby" firms are not negligible. Consider food stores before the days of the supermarket, dry cleaning establishments, gasoline stations, or restaurants. They fit Chamberlin's prescription in all ways but one. Cross effects between any two firms in such industries are not negligible. With, say, restaurants, if two were located within a mile of one another and both were relatively modest neighborhood restaurants, the cross effects between them would be large. If, on the other hand, they were located near one another, but one specialized in fine French food in an elegant setting and the other were a modest diner, the cross effects would be tiny. Or, if the two places were similar in character but were located fifty miles apart, again the cross effects would be very small.

Chamberlin suggests this, calling it a *chain market,* although he does not develop the approach. It might be modeled in either of two ways. First, there is an infinite number of firms, and for any firm i, demand is restricted by

$$f_i^i(p) + \sum_{j \neq i} f_i^j(p) \leq -\epsilon \tag{3.24}$$

where, as before, $f_i^i < 0$ and $f_i^j > 0$ for $j \neq i$. For example, imagine firms numbered with all the integers (. . . , $-3, -2, -1, 0, 1, 2,$ $3, \ldots$), and let

$$q_i = 100 - 3p_i + \tfrac{1}{2} p_{i+1} + \tfrac{1}{4} p_{i+2} + \tfrac{1}{8} p_{i+3}$$
$$+ \ldots + \tfrac{1}{2} p_{i-1} + \tfrac{1}{4} p_{i-2} + \tfrac{1}{8} p_{i-3} + \ldots \quad (3.25)$$

The cross derivatives, f_i^j, are very small for all but a modest number of firms. For example, $f_i^j > 0.01 = \delta$ for firms numbered $i - 1,$ $i - 2, i - 3, i - 4, i - 5, i - 6, i + 1, i + 2, i + 3, i + 4, i + 5,$ and $i + 6$. For all remaining firms, $f_i^j < 0.01$. A similar statement can be made for any value of $\delta > 0$. This is implied by equation (3.24) and f_i^j being bounded.

A second way of modeling demand in a chain market is to specify for each firm a few related firms for which $f_i^j \neq 0$. For all other firms, $f_i^j = 0$. This approach is a special case of the first version and is likely to be easier to work with analytically. As an approximation to reality, there is little difference. The chain market approach to monopolistic competition is eminently reasonable and mirrors very well the nature of most of the markets having a great many firms in them.

3.5. A differentiated products model with output levels as the decision variables

In the Cournot model, with homogeneous products, there is a large difference in equilibrium outcome according to whether firms choose outputs or prices. This point was made by Bertrand (1883) and emphasized by Edgeworth (1897). With differentiated products the situation changes. Although the Cournot equilibrium will differ according to which variables are used, results are similar. In particular, as Section 3.3 attests, using prices need not introduce discontinuities in demand. Firms can actually be considered to select both quantity and price, with one of them being paramount. If price is paramount, then the process will be that at the start of the market period, all firms post prices that cannot be changed. Then consumers place orders with firms, and the firms produce what has been ordered from them. If output is paramount, then firms produce prior to the start of the market price. They adjust prices through the period so that they reach its end with their stocks of output just running out. Following the presentation of a quantity choice model, the topic of price versus quantity is taken up again at more length.

To sketch the quantity model, take the demand system described earlier in Section 3.3, giving $q = (q_1, \ldots, q_n) = [f_1(p), \ldots, f_n(p)] = f(p)$. If the function f can be inverted so that demand can be written $p = f^{-1}(q) = F(q)$, then profits can be written $q_i F_i(q) - C_i(q_i)$. This inversion can be accomplished for any function that, like f, obeys the condition that the derivatives f_i^i are larger in absolute value than $\Sigma_{i \neq j} f_i^j$ (Gale and Nikaido, 1965). Knowing, in addition, that the f_i^i are negative and the f_i^j ($j \neq i$) are positive assures that $F_i^j < 0$ for all j including $j \neq i$.

The homogeneous products model is a limiting case of the demand system $F(q)$, obtained when $F_i(q) = F_j(q)$ and $F_i^i(q) = F_i^j(q)$ for all firms i and j. *Cournot equilibrium* can be defined for the differentiated products quantity model in the obvious way: q^c is a Cournot equilibrium if $q^c \geq 0$ and $q_i^c F_i(q^c) - C_i(q_i^c) \geq q_i F_i(q_i, \bar{q}_i^c) - C_i(q_i)$ for all $q_i \geq 0$ and all $i = 1, \ldots, n$.

If the firms are output choosers, then how are prices determined? To say that they can be read off the inverse demand functions does not answer this question, for the issue is to understand the mechanism by which economic agents set prices. Consulting the inverse demand functions only tells what prices must prevail in order to clear the market. As between prices and quantities, one is a natural decision variable if it is less easily changed than the other variable. Consider several illustrative examples: Imagine firms that must set production schedules several months in advance and for whom it is extremely costly to make output rate changes on shorter notice than a month or so. Assume, further, that there is no obstacle to making price changes on a weekly basis. The procedure for price changes can be to state a *book price* that is actually the highest price the firm considers charging, and then to offer some discount from this price to buyers. The size of the discount will reflect market conditions. If, also, inventory carrying costs are quite high, the firms in the market will set output levels for a several-month period and then, until output can be changed again, keep varying prices so that sales approximate output. Thus, firms are the choosers of prices; however, price choices are subordinate to quantity as the strategic variable.

Now picture the converse situation, in which it is costly to change prices, but output can be easily and quickly altered. Where a price must be individually labeled on each item of output or where a firm has an extensive product line and publishes catalogues, it may be very costly to change prices. A maker of hardware (nuts, bolts, screws, corner braces, etc., of various sizes) may be in this position. Prices are chosen from time to time; in between, the level of output is varied to approximately match demand.

The reader is likely to suggest that both output levels and prices be decision variables and that inventories be allowed. Such a model appears in Chapter 5; however, it is an exception to the usual practice of singling out one of the two as the decision variable. Later chapters use both price and quantity models for the study of dynamic oligopoly.

3.6. Summary

All models in this chapter are static, or single-period, models, as in Chapter 2. The new element is that the markets are for differentiated products. In my view, homogeneous product markets are virtually nonexistent; therefore, introducing differentiated products is an important step forward. The first model presented (as well as the first to have been published) is Hotelling's spatial model. It shows how little is needed to differentiate goods, and using the location of a firm as its product specification, it foreshadows Chapter 4. The Chamberlinian model in Section 3.3 characterizes demand in a more flexible way, but product specifications are implicit in the form of demand and are not explicitly shown. Later sections develop the concept of monopolistic competition and, finally, show that assuming differentiated products is compatible with using either price or output as the decision variable.

It is central to Chapters 2 and 3 that each firm know the profit functions of all firms and that no randomness enter the structure of the models. Probably the lack of randomness is not important, for were it incorporated into cost or demand, the firms would wish to maximize expected profits, and the results would differ little from what has been seen. Changing the information conditions so that a firm knows only its own profit function, or perhaps not even that, may present more difficulties. If a firm has a probability distribution over possible profit functions of rivals, the model reduces again to one with randomness; however, if such information is not assumed, it is not at all clear how to proceed. The Cournot equilibrium ceases to make sense, and single-period behavior reduces to shooting in the dark. Multiperiod models are easier in such a case, for if the underlying structure can be assumed stationary over time, then the firm learns more and more about it as time progresses.

Anyone familiar with general equilibrium theory must be struck by the fact that oligopoly models usually start with demand functions on the consumers' side of the market, whereas general equilibrium models customarily derive demand from preferences of consumers and from market data. Can suitable demand functions be derived from reasonable underlying preferences? It was shown by Roberts and Sonnenschein (1977) that they cannot. At least, they cannot if the usual assumptions are made about consumer preferences. Perhaps some restrictions can be put on preferences that are not too severe and that imply demand functions of the sort required for oligopoly theory.

At least the static character of this chapter is overcome when the models developed here are incorporated into dynamic models in Chapters 5 through 8.

4

Product choice and location

In a sense, people do not buy commodities for the sake of the commodities themselves; they desire one or more characteristics that each commodity provides. When two goods are close substitutes for one another, they provide similar arrays of characteristics. Imagine, as an example, a person who is on the fence between going to the opera or having a fine meal in an elegant restaurant on a given evening. Food and music are not by any means the same thing, but perhaps either choice will be "entertainment" from this person's point of view. Both will provide festive surroundings, and supposing they are to be enjoyed with another person, both will also provide companionship and the pleasure of a shared experience.

An alternative to the traditional view that utility is a function of the commodity bundle that a person consumes is the view that each good provides an array of basic characteristics, or attributes, and that a commodity bundle is best represented by the total amount of attributes in it. Utility is a function of attributes consumed. It is this approach to the analysis of market behavior that has been pioneered by Lancaster (1966; 1971; 1979) and forms the basis for this chapter. Lancaster's approach, in a strict sense, is discussed, followed by an examination of a modified version of the characteristics approach that is much closer to traditional analysis using commodities.

The remainder of this chapter is divided into five sections. Section 4.1, discussing the nature and interpretation of the characteristics space, is based largely on the pioneering work of Lancaster. Market equilibrium, following Salant's elaboration (1980) of Lancaster, is examined in Section 4.2. The third section describes a somewhat different market model due to Leland (1977), applying results of portfolio theory. In the fourth section the focus of attention is again the Hotelling model, encountered earlier in Chapter 3, this time dealing with locational choice. The final section is a brief summary. As in previous chapters, complete information is assumed.

4.1. **On the nature of the characteristics space**

The traditional approach to consumer theory uses a commodity space of finite dimension in which each coordinate corresponds to a specific good. A commodity bundle $x = (x_1, \ldots, x_n)$ denotes a consumption basket containing x_1 units of the first good, say apples, x_2 units of the second good, say tennis balls, and so forth. Each of these commodities is of interest to the consumer for its own sake. Under Lancaster's characteristics approach, there is a characteristics space of finite dimension, and a consumer derives utility from the characteristics bundle $z = (z_1, \ldots, z_s)$ that he consumes. Each dimension corresponds to a specific characteristic: comfort, nutrition, exercise, competition, intellectual diversion, warmth, shelter, social standing, elegant appearance, transportation, and so forth.

Combinable and noncombinable consumption

Ordinary goods such as apples and tennis balls enter this scheme because each good is a bundle of characteristics. An apple conveys to the person who eats it a certain quantity of nutrition, as well as certain sensations of taste, smell, and texture. A tennis ball conveys some exercise, competition, and, perhaps, social standing. Thus, a unit of good i is described by a vector $c_i = (c_{i1}, \ldots, c_{is})$ of characteristics. Of course, many of the individual entries may be zero for a typical good.

The characteristics bundle z that a person consumes is found by combining the characteristics of the specific goods consumed; however, how these characteristics are combined is not so simple. In Lancaster's terminology, consumption can be combinable or non-combinable. If all consumption were *combinable,* then a person consuming commodity bundle x would consume $x_1 c_{11} + x_2 c_{21} + \ldots + x_n c_{n1}$ units of characteristic 1, and, more generally.

$$z = \sum_{i=1}^{n} x_i c_i \tag{4.1}$$

is the characteristics bundle consumed. The relationship between food items eaten and nutrition received is a good analogy to the relationship between commodities consumed and characteristics consumed under combinable consumption. Five apples yield five times the amount of each nutrient found in a single apple. The total nutrients in a meal equal the amounts in each individual item added together. Many nutrients cannot be bought by themselves, and, likewise, most characteristics cannot be bought alone. Perhaps they are bought in bundles (called commodities) because the cost of providing them alone is prohibitive or because there are some economies in consuming them jointly.

Noncombinable consumption is related to indivisibilities. If owning a bicycle yields a particular amount of transportation and exercise, having six bicycles does not yield six times as much. Similarly, two cars that seat six passengers are not the equivalent of one car that seats twelve, nor is half of the six-passenger car equivalent to one three-passenger car. As another example, imagine a city having several golf clubs, each of which conveys a particular amount of social standing in the community. Say that clubs A and B each convey the same amount and that club C conveys twice as much as either A or B. Membership in both A and B will not convey as much social standing as membership in C; indeed, membership in both probably will convey no more than membership in either one by itself.

A critique of the characteristics approach

The examples of the preceding paragraph should make it clear that there is a conceptual problem to face concerning the nature and meaning of characteristics. Before commenting on the problem directly, note that the common way out of it is to add a restriction to the model that a single individual buys only one version of a particular type of good. That is, goods are divided into types or groups. What characterizes a group of goods is that a certain list of characteristics is available only from goods within the group. For example, exercise and competition can be obtained, say, only from sports like tennis, golf, basketball, and marathon racing. No other good provides either the one characteristic or the other, and these four goods (sports) provide them in varying proportions. It is assumed that a person consumes (participates in) only one of the four, although he can choose any quantity (hours per week of play) that does not violate a budget constraint.

This restriction is not a happy solution. Many people participate in more than one sport and, in general, buy more than one version of a particular type of good. Groups of goods would have to be defined in a very peculiar way if no one ever bought more than one member and if lightweight sweaters, heavyweight sweaters, unlined jackets, waterproof jackets, and thickly lined jackets were to be five distinct groups.

To see the conceptual difficulty with the characteristics approach, return to the bicycle example and imagine a person who owns three somewhat similar bicycles that are kept at the same location. It can be said that the characteristics bundle supplied by a first bicycle is different from that supplied by a second, and the bundle supplied by a third is distinct from the other two. Taking this view, there is pleasure in variety or pleasure from ostentation. This approach has merit, and although it seems farfetched for bicycles, it is perfectly reasonable when applied to clothing items, pottery bowls, and other items of household use. A drawback to this way of thinking of characteristics is that the characteristics bundle attaching to a particular item does not inhere in the item itself; it depends on how many others the person also possesses. Having five lightweight sweaters may afford positive amounts of some characteristics that are supplied in zero amount if only one is owned. Other characteristics may be supplied fivefold with five sweaters, and yet others may be supplied in the same amount no matter how many are owned (given that there is at least one).

Another problem related to characteristics is that of identifying them in an operational way. One advantage of traditional commodities is that, as a rule, we know what they are. Few disputes will arise about whether an object is an apple or a bicycle or a chair. Meanwhile, what are the attributes that are primary to satisfaction? How can they be defined, and how can they be recognized?

The characteristics approach can be used in a modified way to study individual markets by describing the product of each firm in terms of measurable, observable characteristics that are of concern to the consumer or that are related to unobservables of concern to the consumer. Magazines like *Consumer Reports* in the United States and *Which?* in Great Britain exist primarily for providing these sorts of measurements to their readers. The characteristics of a radio might include whether or not it operates on batteries, which bands it receives, measures of its ability to pick up weak signals, the accuracy of its sound reproduction, its physical size and weight, and its operating cost per hour. On the whole, these characteristics are not the fundamental sort that Lancaster seems to have in mind; however, it is possible to discuss preferences in terms of them.

4.2. Further elaboration of the Lancaster approach

The presentation in this section is based on Lancaster (1979) and Salant (1980). A great deal of Lancaster's recent book looks at one industry in isolation or at one industry producing a differentiated product in an economy having one other good that is homogeneous. None of the characteristics supplied by the differentiated goods is supplied by the homogeneous good. Much of what Lancaster has to say concerns single differentiated products industries, and he has many fine insights. It is in this area that his characteristics approach looks likely to bear the most fruit.

The producers

Taking the production side of the market first, imagine that the goods vary along a single attribute dimension analogous to location along a line. Such a variation can be due to the systematic changing of two technologically related characteristics. For example, a radio may have to be made heavier if it is to be more sensitive to weak signals. Everyone may prefer lighter to heavier radios and more sensitive to less sensitive radios, but if one aspect is improved, the other is necessarily made worse. Assume further that the attribute variable is normalized and can take any value from zero to one; any firm can choose to produce at any point on the interval, and all firms are restricted to one product each.

It is also assumed that the production functions are identical for all versions of the product; thus, if a bundle of inputs can produce exactly one unit of specification c, then it can produce one unit of specification c'. At a cost, this assumption can be extended to define natural units in a two-characteristics model like that of the radio in the previous paragraph, modified to allow both quality dimensions to be independently changed. Say that more input will either allow weight to be decreased or allow sensitivity to be increased while the other attribute is held constant. Then the weight–sensitivity trade-off obtainable from a specific amount of input, efficiently used, is depicted as in Figure 4.1. If production is assumed to be homothetic with regard to characteristics or, more strongly, to exhibit constant returns to scale, then this single curve carries much information. To see what is meant by saying that production is *homothetic* in characteristics, imagine any two weight–sensitivity combinations c and c' that can be produced from the same input vector y. Now suppose that some multiple of c, kc, can be produced from an input vector λy that is a multiple of y. Then kc' can also be produced from λy. Put another way, if input vector $2y$ is used, then the corresponding characteristics possibility curve is an outward radial expansion of the curve for y. Under constant returns, the expansion will be by a factor of 2, as illustrated in Figure 4.1.

Throughout this section it is assumed either that each firm has a U-shaped average total cost function or that average total costs decline as output increases. Without such an assumption, the equilibrium numbers of firms and products would not be finite. That is to say, if average total costs increased with the level of output, starting at zero output, both firms' aggregate profits and consumer welfare could be increased by adding new firms. Equilibrium in the numbers of firms and goods would occur when there

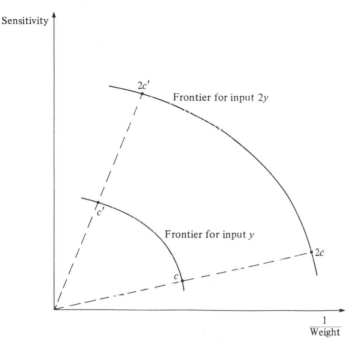

Figure 4.1. Characteristics possibility frontiers.

was an infinite number of infinitesimal firms arrayed across the quality interval, with each consumer able to buy that product variant he likes best.

Such an outcome is no problem to handle analytically; however, it does not correspond to what is observed in the economy. We must conclude that firms' cost functions do not show increasing average total cost throughout, for we see limited, rather than limitless, product variety, and the scale of many manufacturing plants and distribution facilities suggests the existence of important economies of scale. Empirical evidence can be found in the work of Bain (1956).

Consumers and market equilibrium

The following method of modeling consumers is due to Salant (1980), and it offers some improvement over that of Lancaster, although it is certainly an extension and generalization of the latter. There are n firms, each of which produces a specific version of the differentiated product. Consumption is noncombinable; hence, each consumer buys one version. The consumers' incomes are in the form of an endowment of a second good, different from the differentiated product and called the outside good. Letting i denote a firm, q_i is the output of producer i. The producer can locate at any point between zero and one; so $0 \leq i \leq 1$. Thus, i denotes the producer and the variant of the good that the producer makes. Similarly, a consumer j is identified by his most favored version of the good. The index j can take any value between zero and one, and it represents the version that the consumer will buy if all varieties in the interval $[0, 1]$ are available and all are sold at the same price; j can be referred to as the consumer's "location." The amount purchased by consumer j from firm i is q_{ij}. The variable x_j is the quantity of the outside good consumed by j, and R_j is his income measured in units of the outside good.

Recalling that a consumer buys only one version of the differentiated good, the utility of consumer j depends on x_j, q_{ij}, and $|i - j|$. Because the firm is identified by the specification of the good it produces and the consumer is identified by his favorite version of the product, $|i - j|$ is the distance between the output type of firm i and j's most preferred version of the good. The satisfaction obtained from a commodity bundle (x_j, q_{ij}) is measured by the utility function $u_j(x_j, q_{ij}, |i - j|) = u_j(x_j, q_{ij}, \delta)$, where $\delta = |i - j|$.

Say there are n producers of the differentiated product, the set of producers is $\{i_1, \ldots, i_n\} = I$, and their respective prices are $p_{i_1}, \ldots, p_{i_n}$. The outside good, x, is taken as numeraire; hence, it has a price of unity. With an income of R_j, the consumer has a straightforward two-stage utility maximization problem. In the first stage he must find, for each $i \in I$, (x_j^i, q_{ij}^*) that maximizes $u_j(x_j, q_{ij}, |i - j|)$ subject to the budget constraint $R_j = x_j + p_i q_{ij}$. This gives him the best consumption bundle, should he choose good i. In the second stage he compares the n utility maxima and selects the one yielding the highest utility. All consumers are assumed to have identical utility functions, except for differences in

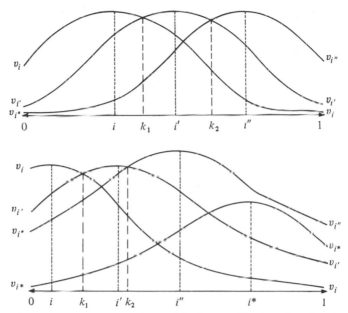

Figure 4.2. Two illustrations of indirect utility functions for the Lancaster-Salant model.

most preferred locations, and they are assumed to have identical money incomes.

By solving the first maximization problem of the preceding paragraph, which yields (x_j^i, q_{ij}^*) for a given p_i and i, an indirect utility function $v_i(j, p_i)$ is obtained; $v_i(j, p_i)$ is the maximum utility obtainable by a consumer who purchases from firm i, as a function of the consumer's location (j) and the firm's price (p_i). Various examples are illustrated in Figure 4.2, where the vertical axis measures utility with j, and i is represented on the horizontal. Prices are suppressed; however, they are implicitly present. In Figure 4.2 (top) the curve v_i is the indirect utility function associated with a firm located at i. Similarly for the curves $v_{i'}$ and $v_{i''}$. The three curves reach their maxima at the same height, which indicates that $p_i = p_{i'} = p_{i''}$. In Figure 4.2 (bottom), four firms are represented, and the firm located at i'' charges the lowest price, which can be seen by noting that curve $v_{i''}$ reaches a higher maximum than any of the others. Similarly, firm i^* has the highest price. From these diagrams it can be seen how the consumers divide themselves among the firms. In Figure 4.2 (top), any consumer to the left of k_1 is best off buying good i, any consumer j for whom $k_1 < j < k_2$ is best off buying good i', and any consumer to the right of k_2 is best off buying good i''. Consumers for whom $j = k_1$ are indifferent between goods i and i', whereas those at $j = k_2$ are indifferent between i' and i''. Precisely the same statements can be made about Figure 4.2 (bottom); however, there is a fourth firm located at i^* that has a sufficiently high price in relation to $p_{i'}$ that any consumer will prefer to buy good i'' rather than i^*. Intuitively, the expected relationship between adjacent goods is that the marginal consumer is located somewhere between them. As the price of the firm on the left falls (or that on the right rises), the marginal consumer is located farther to the right, until eventually he is virtually at the location of the firm on the right. An additional price change in the same direction then causes all the remaining consumers of the firm on the right to switch to the firm on the left, Bertrand style.

Salant's firms are output choosers. Market equilibrium occurs when no firm can alter output or location or both and increase its profit. It has long been thought that monopolistic competition naturally encourages too many firms and too much capital investment; however, as the following paragraphs show, this need not be true.

The efficiency of monopolistic competition

A fundamental point emerges from Lancaster's analysis concerning the efficiency of monopolistic competition. An assertion found in the literature is that monopolistic competition is necessarily economically inefficient, and Lancaster shows that the argument that supports this contention is faulty, because it ignores the beneficial effects of product variety. The basis of the claim of inefficiency lies in the following facts: (a) Each firm has a downward-sloping demand curve. (b) If positive profits are being made, entry will occur. (c) Hence, long-run equilibrium must occur at a point of tangency between each firm's demand function and its average total cost curve to assure zero profits. These three facts imply that average total cost is falling for each firm at the point of equilibrium and therefore has not yet reached its minimum. Holding the total expenditure of consumers constant, it will be possible to decrease the number of firms and increase the amounts produced by the remaining firms so that the total number of units produced will be increased, prices will be reduced for the remaining firms, and the profits of all remaining firms will be increased.

The preceding can be illustrated with the aid of a simple example. Imagine there are 100 firms making ice cream. Each firm makes one flavor, and their demand and cost functions are

$$q_i = 103 - 100p_i + \sum_{j \neq i} p_j \qquad (4.2)$$

and

$$C_i = 100 + 2q_i \qquad (4.3)$$

If all firms charge a price of $p_i = 3$ per quart, the market is at a Cournot equilibrium in which all firms have exactly zero profits. The average total cost is 3 (equal to price), and the output of each firm is 100 quarts. To verify that this is a Cournot equilibrium, note the situation for firm i when all other firms choose $p_j = 3$. Then $q_i = 400 - 100p_i$, and $\pi_i = -900 + 600p_i - 100p_i^2$. Differentiating π_i with respect to p_i yields the first-order condition $600 - 200p_i = 0$, which implies $p_i = 3$, $q_i = 100$, and $\pi_i = 0$ at equilibrium. In the aggregate, consumers are spending 30,000 and obtaining 10,000 quarts of ice cream. Now reduce the number of firms to half and suppose demand is $q_i = 157.53 - 24.97p_i + \sum_{j \neq i} p_j$. If each firm produces 220 quarts and sells them at 2.6 each, consumers will pay 28,600 in return for 11,000 quarts. Thus, they will pay 1,400 less and receive 1,000 additional quarts; meanwhile, the profit of each firm will rise from zero to 32.

It is argued that everyone can be made better off, as in the preceding example, by reducing the number of firms. A key element that this argument ignores is that the consumers are not necessarily better off merely because they are getting more units at a lower price per unit. Variety is decreased, and all those consumers who were buying the fifty flavors that were eliminated from the market must now make do with flavors they like less. They pay a bit less to receive a few more quarts of a less satisfactory ice cream. The remaining consumers are better off, for they continue to buy their old flavors, getting more quarts for less money. Lower production cost is achieved in return for reduced variety, and the effect on economic welfare is indeterminate. It could rise or fall, changing in a way that benefits some persons and hurts others.

Lancaster gives a fine example that makes the point. Say that a town is strung out along a road with constant population density from one end of the town to the other, and there is a fire station every mile. The quality of fire protection afforded to a person is measured by his distance to the nearest station, because the time it takes for the fire department to reach a house is proportional to the distance. Now imagine an innovation that can cut response time to fires in half, and say that the town can obtain and operate the new system at precisely the same cost as the old system, using a fire station every two miles. The average response time in the community will be the same under the new system as under the old, and costs will be unchanged; however, some people in the community will be receiving better service and others worse. Houses within $\frac{2}{3}$ mile of a firehouse under the new system will be better off after the change, and those farther than $\frac{2}{3}$ mile will be worse off. No unambiguous welfare statement can be made in this case in comparing the two situations. More generally, Lancaster has proved the existence of a Pareto optimal configuration of goods, outputs, and prices and has shown that at a Pareto optimum, firms must be producing in a range where average total cost is declining. Essentially, it is declining at a rate that just offsets the gains to consumers from additional variety in the product mix.

The essence of the cost-versus-quality trade is, of course, that having a larger array of goods allows consumers to obtain, on average, a more nearly ideal version of the product. If the number, locations, and output levels of firms are so constituted that each firm is producing at the minimum of its average total cost function, then increasing variety may be accompanied by only small increases in cost and price. Assuming that the firms are all optimally placed after their numbers are enlarged, it is quite possible that welfare can be increased.

The following example may be helpful. Imagine that the quality variable is measured by a point on the circumference of a circle. This could correspond to location on a ring road around a city or to a product that has two quantifiable characteristics that must be combined in proportions corresponding to points on a circle. Say the circle has a circumference of 100 units, that there are 100 firms, that each firm has a total cost function of $100 + 5q + q^2$, that consumers are evenly distributed around the circle, and that, except for location, consumers have identical tastes. If consumer j buys y_j units from firm i, his utility is $y_j(2 - |i - j|)$, where j and i are their respective locations and $|i - j|$ is the distance between them, measured along the circumference of the circle. To illustrate Lancaster's result in the easiest possible way, assume that each firm is producing at the minimum of its average total cost curve, all firms are equally spaced, price equals average total cost, and each consumer is obtaining exactly the same utility as any other consumer.[1] Then output is 10 units per firm, price is 25, and the 10 units produced by a firm are distributed among the consumers located within a half unit on either side of it.

This exercise is aimed at illustrating a point about economic welfare; hence, it is enough to show that if there are more firms and the total resources used by the industry are unchanged, then consumers can be made better off, with firms being no worse off. First, however, the utility of consumers must be calculated for the original regime. To do this, note that 5 units go to consumers on one side of a firm. Because all firms and segments of the circle are identical, let $i = 0$, and let j range from 0 to 0.5. Then $u_j = u_{0.5}$ for all $0 \leq j \leq 0.5$ means $u^{100} = y_j(2 - j) = y_{0.5}(2 - 0.5)$, or $y_j = 1.5y_{0.5}/(2 - j)$, where u^{100} is the utility level achieved by each consumer when there are 100 firms. Total consumption of 5 units over the [0, 0.5] interval means $\int_0^{0.5} [1.5y_{0.5}/(2 - j)] \, dj = 5$, or $5 = u^{100}(\ln 2 - \ln 1.5)$, and $u^{100} = 5/(\ln 2 - \ln 1.5) = 17.38$.

Assuming that the firms are competitive buyers of inputs, then to have n firms using the same total resources as the original 100 firms means that total costs per firm are $25{,}000/n$. Keeping the zero profit condition requires that consumers pay, in the aggregate, exactly as much as previously, and with firms equally spaced around the circle, each firm supplies to consumers who are within a distance of $100/2n$ on either side. It turns out that $n = 115$ is optimal. Then each firm produces 8.6194 units, aggregate output is 991.23, which is 8.77 units less than previously, and all consumers achieve a utility level of 17.58. The utility level is found by making a calculation similar to the one made earlier. With minimum average cost occurring at 10, each firm is producing at an output level below the minimum, and average total cost is falling, as Lancaster claims.

4.3. A combinable consumption model

Looking at a model of combinable characteristics serves to focus attention on a different facet of the consumer's problem. Noncombinable consumption lends itself quite well to the study of a single monopolistically competitive market, and even when it is placed into a general equilibrium model, it is essentially partial equilibrium in nature. A model of combinable consumption in which each firm produces a good embodying a different bundle of characteristics focuses more on the consumer's conventional choice problem, although it does so from the unusual angle of a characteristics approach. Furthermore, with each firm having its own production function relating inputs to the quantity and characteristics composition of output, it may be possible to obtain an equilibrium in which implicit characteristics prices can be derived from the equilibrium goods prices prevailing in the economy. The presentation that follows is based on the work of Leland (1977).

The conditions of production

Looking first at the production side of the market, each of the n firms produces a single product, and each product embodies a specific vector of characteristics in each unit; however, the range of product choices open to a firm is parameterized by a quality variable v_i that is restricted to values in the interval $0 \leq v_i \leq 1$. The characteristics vector of the ith firm's product, $c_i(v_i) =$

$[c_{i1}(v_i), \ldots, c_{is}(v_i)]$, is a continuous and differentiable function of the quality variable. In Leland's specification the c_{il} need not necessarily rise or fall as v_i increases. Some may go up and others down; hence, it cannot be said unambiguously that quality rises or falls as v_i increases. According to the particular preferences of a consumer, an increase in v_i can make the product either more or less desirable. Of course, if all the c_{il} increase (or some rise while others remain constant), then every consumer regards quality as having increased. The firm's production function is $q_i = \phi_i(v_i, y_i)$, where v_i is the firm's (scalar) quality variable, q_i is the firm's (scalar) output level, and $y_i = (y_{i1}, \ldots, y_{ik})$ is a vector of primary goods that are used to produce the various consumption goods.

The nonproduced primary goods are initially to be found in endowments owned by consumers. Firms buy them at prices $r = (r_1, \ldots, r_k)$. From the vantage points of both firms and consumers, these prices are taken as given. Indeed, throughout the model, cross effects among economic agents are largely assumed away. Just as firms and consumers are assumed sufficiently numerous that they are all price takers in the primary goods markets, the actions of any one firm in its choice of output level or quality parameter do not affect the market conditions of any other firm in the market for its product. Thus, the inverse demand function for the ith firm is given by $p_i(q_i, v_i)$. It is a weakness of the model that the inverse demand functions are not derived from the consumers' utility functions. Instead, it is implicitly assumed that they are compatible, and, strictly speaking, they cannot be compatible if the ith firm's inverse demand function does not depend on the actions of any other firm, because the inverse demand function of each consumer will depend on all firms' quantities and qualities. The profit function of the ith firm is

$$\pi_i(v_i, y_i) = p_i(q_i, v_i)q_i - ry_i$$
$$= p_i[\phi_i(v_i, y_i), v_i]\phi_i(v_i, y_i) - ry_i \qquad (4.4)$$

where $ry_i = \Sigma_{j=1}^k r_j y_{ij}$. The first-order conditions for an interior profit maximum are found in the usual way. It is assumed that π_i is a concave function of (v_i, y_i); however, the required restrictions on the functions $p_i(v_i, y_i)$ and $\phi_i(v_i, y_i)$ that would ensure concavity are not given.

The consumers

There are m consumers; the jth consumer's characteristics bundle is z_j, and his utility function is $U_j(z_j)$. If he purchases a bundle of goods $x_j = (x_{j1}, \ldots, x_{jn})$, the characteristics bundle he consumes is

$$z_{jl} = \sum_{i=1}^{n} c_{il}(v_i)x_{ji} \qquad (l = 1, \ldots, s) \tag{4.5}$$

or, letting

$$C(v) = \begin{bmatrix} c_{11}(v_1) & \cdots & c_{n1}(v_n) \\ \cdot & & \cdot \\ \cdot & & \cdot \\ \cdot & & \cdot \\ c_{1s}(v_1) & \cdots & c_{ns}(v_n) \end{bmatrix} \tag{4.6}$$

$$z_j = C(v)x_j \tag{4.7}$$

Each consumer holds ownership shares in the various firms, with θ_{ji} being the fraction of firm i that is owned by consumer j. $\sum_{j=1}^{m}\theta_{ji} = 1$ for each i, and $\theta_{ji} \geq 0$. Consumer j's ownership in the n firms is $\theta_j = (\theta_{j1}, \ldots, \theta_{jn})$. Letting $\pi = (\pi_1, \ldots, \pi_n)$, the jth consumer's budget constraint is

$$px_j = rw_j + \theta_j\pi \tag{4.8}$$

where $w_j = (w_{j1}, \ldots, w_{jk}) \geq 0$ is his endowment of the primary goods. A consumer's income derives from his sale of his endowment and his profit share from the firms' operations. In similar fashion, conditions for budget-constrained utility maximization can be derived in the customary way.

The spanning property

Except for the derivation of market demand functions from consumers' preferences, the model is complete and closed, although the existence of equilibrium is not proved. Necessary conditions for equilibrium are easily derived, as are conditions for the Pareto optimality of equilibrium. The optimal number of products is not addressed.

What is of particular interest here is the spanning property, a concept borrowed from finance theory. There is a close analogy between a unit of a good viewed as a bundle of characteristics and "a share of stock [that] can be viewed as a vector of returns across states of nature" (Leland, 1977, p. 128). For the *spanning property* to hold means that if firms make marginal adjustments in v, the various characteristics bundles they offer, consumers can offset these changes by alterations in the x_j, so that they continue to consume the same characteristics bundles as before. That is, if initially a consumer buys x_j and obtains $z_j = C(v)x_j$ as a result, then firms change from v to v', and the consumer can find a bundle of goods x_j' such that $z_j = C(v')x_j' = C(v)x_j$. Put more formally, the spanning property holds if there exists an $n \times n$ matrix

$$H(v) = \begin{bmatrix} h_{11}(v) & \cdots & h_{n1}(v) \\ \cdot & & \cdot \\ \cdot & & \cdot \\ \cdot & & \cdot \\ h_{1n}(v) & \cdots & h_{nn}(v) \end{bmatrix} \tag{4.9}$$

such that

$$\begin{bmatrix} \dfrac{\partial c_{11}(v_1)}{\partial v_1} & \cdots & \dfrac{\partial c_{n1}(v_n)}{\partial v_n} \\ \cdot & & \cdot \\ \dfrac{c_{1s}(v_1)}{\partial v_1} & \cdots & \dfrac{c_{ns}(v_n)}{\partial v_n} \end{bmatrix} = \Gamma(v) = C(v)H(v) \tag{4.10}$$

If the spanning property holds, then a pair of consumers can engage in wholly arbitrary trades of characteristics. Two consumers, j and j', holding consumption bundles x_j and $x_{j'}$, can arrange a trade under which j gives to j' a unit of characteristic l in exchange for λ units of characteristic l'. That is, he gives j' the vector of commodities Δx_j chosen so that $C(v)\Delta x_j = \Delta z_j$. Δz_j has zero in every component except for component l, which equals one. Similarly, j' can give j commodities Δx_j, which yield exactly λ units of characteristic

l'. If there are two consumers j and j' and two characteristics l and l' such that

$$\frac{\partial U_j(z_j)/\partial z_{jl}}{\partial U_j(z_j)/\partial z_{jl'}} \neq \frac{\partial U_{j'}(z_{j'})/\partial z_{j'l}}{\partial U_{j'}(z_{j'})/\partial z_{j'l'}} \tag{4.11}$$

then a value of λ can be found for which the suggested trade will increase the utility of both consumers. Therefore, in equilibrium,

$$\frac{\partial U_j(z_j)/\partial z_{jl}}{\partial U_j(z_j)/\partial z_{jl'}} = \frac{\partial U_{j'}(z_{j'})/\partial z_{j'l}}{\partial U_{j'}(z_{j'})/\partial z_{j'l'}} \quad \text{for all } j, j' = 1, \ldots, m \tag{4.12}$$

$$\text{for all } l, l' = 1, \ldots, s$$

This is, of course, a version of the familiar argument that in equilibrium all consumers have the same marginal rate of substitution between a given pair of goods. The analogy is carried a step further by Leland. Just as the (common) marginal rate of substitution equals the price ratio, equation (4.12) defines implicit characteristics prices. If the spanning property holds, and hence equation (4.12) holds, then

$$\frac{\partial U_j(z_j)/\partial z_{jl}}{\partial U_j(z_j)/\partial z_{jl'}} = \frac{P_l}{P_{l'}} \tag{4.13}$$

where $P = (P_1, \ldots, P_s)$ are implicit characteristics prices. Equation (4.13) determines only price ratios and leaves one price free; hence, a normalization is needed to make prices fully determined. One characteristic could be forced to have a price of unity, or $\sum_{l=1}^{s} P_l = 1$ could be imposed.

4.4. Hotelling revisited

A major part of Hotelling's article (1929) is aimed at explaining firms' locational choices. This effort fails in the literal sense that his analysis is incorrect; however, his article has provided stimulus for various other interesting and successful efforts.[2] Three of these are described next. In the first subsection, Hotelling's model (1929) is examined more closely, using the work of D'Aspremont, Jaskold Gabszewicz, and Thisse (1979). They found that Hotelling's famous conclusion that the duopolists will locate at the same exact point not only was unproved by Hotelling but also is incorrect. The second subsection is based on the work of Economides (1981) and deals with the nature of equilibrium in a model that generalizes the work of Hotelling only slightly, by removing the condition that each consumer have a perfectly inelastic demand for the differentiated product. Instead, each consumer has a reservation price, and he will buy either one unit or nothing, depending on his opportunities. The model in the third subsection is due to Salop (1979); in this model, as in that of Economides, the consumers do not have inelastic demands. The firms and consumers are located on a circle, rather than on a line segment, and the number of firms can be large. Using a circle rather than a line segment removes the disparity between the firms at the ends (which have only one neighbor) and the other firms (which all have two neighboring firms).

Locational choice in the Hotelling model

Following the analysis of D'Aspremont, Jaskold Gabszewicz, and Thisse (1979), it is seen in Section 3.2 in Chapter 3 that with locations fixed, there is no equilibrium in the Hotelling model unless the firms are near opposite ends of the street. Recall that the street has length L. If the firm on the left is between 0 and $\frac{1}{4}L$ and the one on the right is between $\frac{3}{4}L$ and L, there is a pair of prices forming a Cournot equilibrium. If they are both located between $\frac{1}{4}L$ and $\frac{3}{4}L$, there are no such prices. All this, again, presumes the locations to be fixed.

Now suppose the two dry cleaners can choose location and price. At equilibrium it must be true that neither firm can alter location or price or both at once and increase profit, given the price and location of the rival cleaner. Hotelling concluded, incorrectly, that the two firms will be in equilibrium if they both locate at the center of the street ($a = b = \frac{1}{2}L$). This, of course, is impossible, because no equilibrium can occur with the firms so close to one another. Looking from the viewpoint of firm 1, it is always in its interest to price itself just below firm 2 as long as p_2 exceeds zero (i.e., exceeds marginal cost). With locations fixed at $\frac{1}{2}L$ (or, generally, with the two firms at the same spot), $p_1 = p_2 = 0$ is an equilibrium; however, if $p_2 = 0$, with both firms located at the center, firm 1 can do better by charging a higher price and moving some distance away from its rival.

D'Aspremont and associates have proved that no equilibrium is possible in the Hotelling model when location is taken into account. This is because each firm will wish to locate nearer the center of the street than its rival. Only at $a = b = \frac{1}{2}L$ can both be satisfied on this criterion, and here no equilibrium is possible.

The Hotelling model with a small modification

Economides (1981) examines a two-firm market just like that of Hotelling except that each consumer has a reservation price for each of the two firms' products. He also generalizes his results to n firms; however, the following exposition deals only with the two-firm version.

The line segment where firms and consumers are located is taken to have one unit of length and is represented by the unit interval [0, 1]. Consumers are uniformly distributed along the interval, and each consumer buys either one unit of the differentiated product or none. Except for location, all consumers are identical, and each is endowed with M units of money, which would yield M units of utility if the differentiated good were not purchased. Thus, implicitly there is an outside good in the model. Were the consumer i to purchase a unit of good j at a price p_j, his utility would be $M - p_j + k - \lambda|i - j|$. In this linear utility function, $M - p_j$ measures the satisfaction received from the outside good, and $k - \lambda|i - j|$ measures the satisfaction received from the unit purchased from firm j.

Denoting the locations of the two firms x and y, and letting their prices be p_x and p_y, the consumer i achieves the maximum of

$$M \tag{4.14}$$

$$M - p_x + k - \lambda|i - x| \tag{4.15}$$

$$M - p_y + k - \lambda|i - y| \tag{4.16}$$

Figure 4.3 completely depicts the consumers' choices for specific

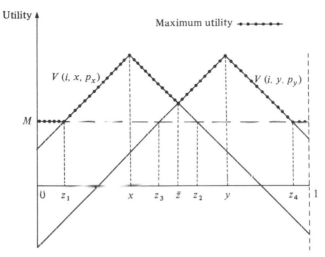

Figure 4.3. Indirect utility in the Hotelling-Economides model with markets touching each other.

values of x, p_x, y, and p_y. The horizontal line at the utility level M indicates that any consumer, irrespective of location, receives utility of M if he buys neither product. The curve consisting of two linear segments with a kink at x shows the utility a consumer will receive, depending on his location, if he buys a unit from producer x. This curve is marked $V(i, x, p_x)$. The curve marked $V(i, y, p_y)$ is an analogous curve for purchase from y. The highest utility obtainable for each value of i is shown as the curve with the dots along it, and the points on the horizontal axis labeled z_1, $\bar{z}$, and z_4 show how consumers are divided into different groups according to their optimal purchase plans. Consumers from the interval $[0, z_1]$ will purchase neither good, those in the interval $(z_1, \bar{z})$ will purchase x, those in $(\bar{z}, z_4)$ will purchase y, and those in $(z_4, 1)$ will purchase neither good. Consumers at z_1 are indifferent between purchasing x and buying nothing, whereas those at $\bar{z}$ and z_4 are, similarly, indifferent between two alternatives.

The value of z_1 is found by solving the equation

$$M = M - p_x + k - \lambda|z - x| \tag{4.17}$$

Equation (4.17) has two solutions. The smaller is z_1 and the larger is z_2. Their values are

$$z_1 = \frac{\lambda x + p_x - k}{\lambda} \quad \text{and} \quad z_2 = \frac{\lambda x - p_x + k}{\lambda} \quad (4.18)$$

Analogously, z_3 and z_4 are the solutions to the equation formed by equating (4.16) and M. Their values are

$$z_3 = \frac{\lambda y + p_y - k}{\lambda} \quad \text{and} \quad z_4 = \frac{\lambda y - p_y + k}{\lambda} \quad (4.19)$$

The value of $\bar{z}$ is found by equating the utility associated with buying x [equation (4.15)] to the utility associated with buying y [equation (4.16)]. The result, for $x < y$, is

$$\bar{z} = \frac{\lambda(x + y) - p_x + p_y}{2\lambda} \quad (4.20)$$

The outcome associated with the Hotelling model, found in the preceding subsection, obtains when k is sufficiently large that $z_1 \leq 0$ and $z_4 \geq 1$.

Imagine the situation shown in Figure 4.3, and consider what happens as p_y is reduced, all else remaining unchanged. The $V(i, y, p_y)$ curve rises, and $\bar{z}$ moves leftward, approaching x. When $\bar{z} = x$, which occurs when $p_x = p_y + \lambda(y - x)$, there is a discontinuity in each demand function. Both firms now share equally the consumers in the interval $(z_1, \bar{z})$, and, if p_y were lowered any more, x would sell nothing, and y would sell to all consumers in the interval (z_1, z_4) [or $(z_1, 1)$ if $z_4 \geq 1$]. An analogous discontinuity occurs if $\bar{z}$ moves rightward to y, which corresponds to $p_x = p_y - \lambda(y - x)$.

In Figure 4.3 the markets of the two firms touch one another. Compare this with Figure 4.4, where they do not touch. Economides proves that a noncooperative equilibrium in which the firms choose both price and location is impossible where the firms' markets touch. Whether or not equilibria exist depends on the size of the ratio k/λ, and as a rule, when there are equilibria, there are many such. In particular, the equilibrium prices are $p_x = p_y = k/2$, and it is required that $y - x > k/\lambda$. The latter condition is that the

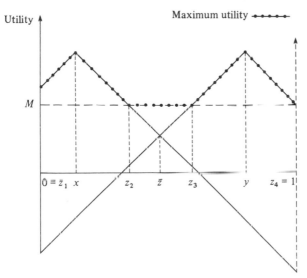

Figure 4.4. Indirect utility in the Hotelling-Economides model with markets separated.

firms be separated by a distance greater than k/λ. Clearly, if $k/\lambda > 1$, this is impossible, although even more is really required. Imagine prices and locations for which the two markets do not touch, but for which $z_1 < 0$. Then x can move a bit to the right without touching the market of y, and, at the same time, increase profit. Thus, it is also required that $z_1 > 0$ and $z_4 \leq 1$. Equilibrium profits are $k^2/(2\lambda)$.

A model of location on a circle

Salop (1979), following the suggestion of Lerner and Singer (1937) that the buyers of the differentiated product ought to have a second good available also, has modeled a market in the spirit of Hotelling, with the market being a circle of unit circumference. The essential difference between Hotelling's line segment and Salop's circle is the absence of endpoints on the circle.

The circle has unit circumference, with a total of L consumers located evenly around it, as illustrated in Figure 4.5. Each consumer buys one unit of the differentiated product from only one seller, or he buys none. In a fashion similar to the Lancaster-Salant model, a

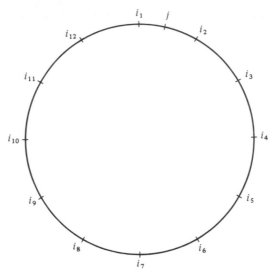

Figure 4.5. Spatial location on a circle.

consumer located at position j, where $0 \leq j \leq 1$, will obtain a utility level of $u - c|i - j| - p_i$ if he buys one unit from a supplier located at position i at a price p_i. Say there are n producers whose locations are $i_1, \ldots, i_n$. The best producer to buy from, of course, is that for which $u - c|i - j| - p_i$ is maximized over $i \in N = \{i_1, \ldots, i_n\}$; however, the consumer buys from no one if he cannot at least reach a utility level of u^*, which is what he can achieve if he uses all of his income to purchase the outside good. To simplify notation, let $v = u - u^*$, and note that a consumer buys a unit of the differentiated product if and only if there is some firm i for which $v - c|i - j| - p_i \geq 0$.

Looking at the demand function for a firm, given the prices of the other firms, there are several distinct regions. First, clustered around the firm's location there may be some consumers for whom $v - c|k - j| - p_k < 0$ for all $k \neq i$. These consumers will not buy from any firm except firm i, and whether or not they buy from firm i depends, of course, on p_i. Demand in this region, supposing it extends on both sides of location i, is $q_i = (2L/c)(v - p_i)$. This demand function is found by noting that the distance from i to the marginal consumer, x, is given by $v - cx - p_i = 0$. Solving for x yields $x = (v - p_i)/c$. On a segment of arc length $2x$, centered about i, the firm sells $2Lx$, whence the demand function given earlier.

Moving away from point i, eventually a consumer j is reached to whom the neighboring firm k can also sell. The location of j is given by $v - c|k - j| - p_k = 0$. Such a point is reached on each side of i; however, the two points need not be equidistant from i. Demand for firm i in the two adjacent regions where consumers will consider buying from it or its immediate neighbors is given by $q_i = (L/2)[|k - i| + |k' - i| + (p_k/c) + (p_k/c) - (2p_i/c)]$, where k is the neighboring firm on one side and k' on the other. This demand function is found in a way parallel to the technique used to find the first demand function. If all other firms are using the same price p' and the firms are evenly spaced at a distance of $1/n$, the preceding demand function will simplify to $q_i = (L/c)[(c/n) + p' - p_i]$.

As p_i drops further, it is possible to reach a price at which a consumer located at the same location as a neighboring firm k is indifferent between buying from i and from k. A further reduction in p_i will cause firm i to capture the whole remaining market of firm k. Under the symmetry conditions that all other firms charge p' and all are located at intervals of $1/n$, firm i will capture two adjacent markets simultaneously.

Figure 4.6 illustrates the demand function for firm i under the symmetry conditions. Price p_i^1 is the price at which consumers first find two firms offering prices low enough that buying from either one is better than not buying at all. Over the price interval p_i^0 to p_i^1 the firm is a local monopolist in the sense that the customers to whom it sells at these prices will not buy any version of the product if they do not buy from firm i. Over the interval p_i^1 to p_i^2 the firm is locally competitive in the sense that marginal consumers can buy from two firms; p_i^2 is the price at which the firm appropriates the whole of its immediate neighbors' markets. Having eliminated them, it has a local monopoly again from another price segment. Eventually, at a price of zero, no more can be sold.

Assuming a constant marginal cost of m and fixed cost of F for all

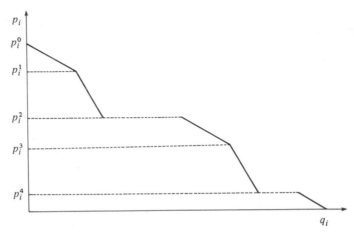

Figure 4.6. The demand curve of a firm located on a circle.

firms, Salop demonstrates the existence of a Cournot equilibrium in which no firm can, even costlessly, change its location or price and increase its profit, and at which the addition of one more firm will cause profits to be negative for all firms.

4.5. Summary

The first attempt to cope analytically with product choice was that of Hotelling. Despite great interest in differentiated products markets following his article and Chamberlin's book (1933), study of the topic made little headway until quite recently. Brems (1951) made a major effort that did not take hold. Lancaster's ambitious work (1966; 1971; 1979) undoubtedly inspired and aided the recent developments, even though Lancaster's effort to recast general equilibrium theory along characteristics lines has not progressed far. It is also notable that the characteristics work of many writers (e.g., Salant, Salop, and Economides) remains very near in spirit to Hotelling.

Except for Leland, the work reviewed in this chapter remains in a one- or two-characteristics setting. Where two characteristics are handled, it is done in a limited way, with the two characteristics varying in a special fashion together.

This work requires much further development to become very useful. One limitation to be overcome is the restriction to the setting of one characteristic or two tightly related characteristics. Another limitation in the work reviewed earlier (except that of Leland) is the strict noncombinability assumption. That is, each consumer buys from, at most, one firm. The other extreme, perfect combinability, found in the work of Leland, also goes too far. A way must be found to put these together flexibly. When we eat only to obtain nutrients, we are in Leland's world, but what good examples of this extreme combinability are there? Most people have only one home, which corresponds to the noncombinability extreme, but how many commodities fall into this category? Even homes fail if a hotel room, rental cottage, camping trailer, or tent is regarded as home while in use.

Without being overly ambitious and calling for immediate solution of all difficulties, the topic of product choice and location would be well advanced if the gaps in Leland's work could be filled and if Salant's model could be generalized to deal with two characteristics that can take on any pair of values (a, b), with $0 \leq a \leq 1$ and $0 \leq b \leq 1$, and do so in a way allowing a thorough characterization of consumer behavior and market equilibrium.

Additionally, if the characteristics approach to product choice could be placed effectively in a dynamic model, it might prove possible to explain changing tastes over time by linking the development of tastes to the consumer's previous pattern of consumption. Of course, common patterns of taste changes among consumers might well be exploited by firms that could change product designs to conform to taste changes.

The investigation of product choice and location appears to be at a beginning now. The area is promising and interesting, perhaps as much for what remains to be done as for what has been accomplished to date.

5

Reaction functions

The reaction function stems from the realization that an oligopolist is aware of the presence and activities of other firms in the market and the realization that, over time, changes in the behavior of a firm are likely to induce changes in the behavior of its rivals. At first it may seem impossible to discuss the behavior of a small number of interacting decision makers without talking in terms such as these: If A does a, then B will do b; but if B does b, then A will do a'; but if A does a'; then B will do b', and so forth. Such discussion is carried out within the framework of single-period models, where often it is logically inconsistent or is based on economically untenable assumptions, by writers going back to Cournot. The reason for persisting in this vein is that what is most fascinating about oligopoly is the intertemporal interaction of the firms in a market. What we most wish to understand is how the firms behave in their own best interests, taking into account rival actions, and it seems impossible to do this unless each firm's plan of action (strategy) prescribes what to do in each time period as a function of the recently observed choices of rival firms.

If this has often been done in the past, and to some extent still is done, using models that formally are only single-period models, it is because many writers have found multiperiod models to be intractable. But they have not been willing to limit their considerations to a single-period framework. It should be clear from the analysis of the preceding chapters that simultaneous decisions in a single-period framework do not preclude firms making their decisions while taking their rivals' (probable) decisions into account. It is the essence of the Cournot equilibrium that each firm chooses its output or price to be best, given that others look after their own self-interests in a similar way. What is absent, of course, is a process of one firm seeing the choice of another, making a decision in light of that choice, others seeing that decision and making other decisions in light of it, and so forth. Bear in mind that complete information is assumed throughout this chapter.

In Section 5.1 the timeless reaction function analysis of Bowley and Stackelberg is discussed first. Where possible, assumptions are given that make the models logically consistent; however, this is often at the cost of being economically unreasonable. Then some very recent work that remedies one of the defects of Bowley and Stackelberg, inconsistent expectations, is sketched. Finally, a single-period model of Marschak and Selten is examined that is designed to have an elaborate decision procedure. This model is the only generalization of the Bowley-Stackelberg approach that is entirely consistent internally and economically reasonable in a single-period framework. In Section 5.2 the Bowley and Stackelberg approaches are recast into multiperiod models. These models have some peculiar characteristics that it is important to see, for they make clear how reaction functions should be formulated if they are to be reasonable and also in the spirit of the Bowley-Stackelberg efforts. Various reaction function models are the subjects of the remaining sections. Section 5.3 contains a discussion of traditional reaction function models set into a properly formulated multiperiod model. This is a natural extension of the Cournot-Bowley-Stackelberg approach. On the latter, see also Fellner (1949). Section 5.4 deals with a model that allows for collusion without requiring the firms to make binding agreements. Although any firm has the power to dishonor the agreement, no firm has an incentive to do so. The equilibrium developed here can be called a reaction function equilibrium; however, it is not in the traditional reaction function mold. Section 5.5 contains a summary.

5.1. **Atemporal reaction functions**

If the genesis of the reaction function does not lie with Cournot, then it probably lies with Bowley (1924). At least he proposed the *conjectural variation,* although he did not coin the name for it; the term comes from Frisch (1933). In essence, the idea is that a firm believes that the price it chooses will affect the prices selected by its rivals, and it wishes to take this into account in choosing optimally. The way that the firm thinks changes in its price will affect the other prices is the conjectural variation, and, for Bowley, this need not reflect the actual behavior of the other firms.

Bowley's conjectural variation for two firms

Stated for duopoly, the notion is that when firm 1 seeks to maximize its profit, the appropriate first-order condition is

$$\pi_1^1(p_1, p_2) + \pi_1^2(p_1, p_2)\phi_1'(p_1) = 0 \tag{5.1}$$

where $\phi_1(p_1) = p_2$ represents what firm 1 "thinks the other is likely to do."[1] Similarly, for firm 2, the first-order condition is

$$\pi_2^2(p_1, p_2) + \pi_2^1(p_1, p_2)\phi_2'(p_2) = 0 \tag{5.2}$$

By way of illustration, imagine a pair of calculator manufacturers, each of which makes one type of calculator. Suppose their demand, cost, and profit functions are

$$\begin{aligned} q_1 &= 100 - 5p_1 + 4p_2, & q_2 &= 80 - 3p_2 + 2p_1 \\ C_1 &= 10q_1 + q_1^2, & C_2 &= 7q_2 + q_2^2 \end{aligned} \tag{5.3}$$

$$\pi_1 = -11{,}000 + 1{,}150p_1 - 840p_2 - 30p_1^2 + 44p_1p_2 - 16p_2^2 \tag{5.4}$$

$$\pi_2 = -6{,}960 + 581p_2 - 334p_1 - 12p_2^2 + 14p_1p_2 - 4p_1^2 \tag{5.5}$$

The first firm chooses its price according to equation (5.1), which is

$$1{,}150 - 60p_1 + 44p_2 + (-840 + 44p_1 - 32p_2)\phi_1' = 0 \tag{5.6}$$

and, expressing p_1 in terms of p_2,

$$p_1 = \frac{1{,}150 - 840\phi_1' + (44 - 32\phi_1')p_2}{60 - 44\phi_1'} \tag{5.7}$$

Notice that firm 1 does not use the relationship $p_2 = \phi_1(p_1)$, but only $\phi'_1(p_1)$, which expresses the way that alterations in p_1 will cause firm 2 to change its price. Corresponding to equations (5.6) and (5.7) are, for the second calculator firm,

$$581 - 24p_2 + 14p_1 + (-334 + 14p_2 - 8p_1)\phi'_2 \tag{5.8}$$

$$p_2 = \frac{581 \quad 334\phi'_2 + (14 - 8\phi'_2)p_1}{24 - 14\phi'_2} \tag{5.9}$$

The Cournot equilibrium corresponds to $\phi'_1 = \phi'_2 = 0$ (zero conjectural variation). Table 5.1 shows equilibrium values of prices, output levels, and profits for several values of ϕ'_1 and ϕ'_2.

Consider this model from the standpoint of Chapter 3, where the two firms are assumed to make their price decisions simultaneously. It is not possible for p_2 to be a function of p_1, and it would be ridiculous for firm 1 to think that. Such a situation would imply that as firm 1 contemplated various prices for itself, it would expect various possible p_2 according to the relation $p_2 = \phi_1(p_1)$. Hence, at the level of simultaneous decisions in a single-period model, conjectural variation is not meaningful. In fairness to Bowley, he probably intended to capture a dynamic process by means of the conjectural variations terms. Imagine a firm in a multiperiod market thinking that its price choice today will affect its rival's price choice in the next period according to the relation $p_{2t} = \phi_1(p_{1,t-1})$ and asking itself what the best p_1 will be after mutual price adjustments have ceased. A simultaneous solution to equations (5.1) and (5.2) is the answer if both firms think this way. This approach is discussed more fully in the next section.

The Stackelberg leader-follower model

Stackelberg (1934) is another example of someone attempting to capture the equilibrium conditions associated with a dynamic phenomenon within an essentially static model. Starting from the widely held belief that in many industries there will be one firm that is a market leader, with the other firms being followers, he modeled a duopoly. In price terms, the idea is that followers change

Table 5.1. *Conjectural variation equilibria*

ϕ_1'	ϕ_2'	P_1	P_2	q_1	q_2	π_1	π_2
0	0	64.519	61.845	24.8	23.5	736.95	736.64
0.5	0.5	65.579	62.929	23.8	22.4	756.50	750.73
1	1	68.909	66.045	19.6	19.7	771.17	774.75
0.8	1.25	69.811	68.114	23.4	15.3	852.06	700.30
1.25	0.8	75.452	69.315	0	23.0	0	903.57
0.592	0.738	66.243	63.712	23.6	21.4	770.66	754.98
0.583	0	65.111	62.190	23.2	23.7	740.37	745.93

their prices in response to the initiatives of the price leader, and the leader chooses his price knowing that the followers will quickly adjust theirs afterward in a predictable way.

This can be accommodated in a single-period model if it is assumed that firm 1, say, is the leader and firm 2 is the follower. It is then understood that firm 1 announces its price first, and after hearing the price of firm 1, firm 2 chooses its price. Both know that this sequence will be played out. Then, clearly, firm 2 maximizes its profit by behaving Cournot fashion and choosing $p_2 = w_2(p_1)$, where $w_2(p_1)$ is the price model Cournot reaction function and is analogous to the Cournot reaction function of Chapter 2, Section 2.4. Firm 1 realizes how firm 2 will behave and can use this information; hence, it maximizes $\pi_1[p_1, w_2(p_1)]$ with respect to p_1. The first-order condition is $\pi_1^1 + \pi_1^2 w_2' = 0$. In terms of the example of the two calculator manufacturers, firm 2 has zero conjectural variation; so $\phi_2' = 0$, and equation (5.9) reduces to $p_2 = (581 + 14p_1)/24$. Firm 1, as leader, supposes that $\phi_1(p_1) = (581 + 14p_1)/24$, which makes firm 2's conjectural variation term $\phi_1' = 14/24 = 0.58333$. The outcome for this situation is shown in the bottom row in Table 5.1. If both firms are Stackelberg followers, then $\phi_1' = \phi_2' - 0$, and the model is just Cournot again.

Critique of conjectural variation in static models

The description of Stackelberg's work in the preceding paragraph begs an interesting and important question that Stackelberg sought to address: Will a given firm choose to be a leader or a follower? His own conjecture was that it will be common for more than one firm to choose leadership. Of course, with the sequence of decision making fixed as in the preceding discussion, it is clear that firm 1 is leader and firm 2 is follower because the information flow forces it. It is equally true that leadership is meaningless if decisions are simultaneous; so a discussion of leadership is meaningful only within a dynamic model. Again, this is examined in the following section.

Bowley and Stackelberg are clearly concerned with dynamic phenomena, and as a result, they can be faulted on three counts: (a)

Their models are not actually dynamic. That is, time makes no explicit appearance. (b) The firms are assumed to maximize current-period profits, rather than discounted profits over some horizon of time. (c) Firms have expectations about how their rivals will behave that need not be correct. Over time, they will receive information, and even if it contradicts their expectations, they will go on believing as before. Bowley, for example, makes no requirement that the conjectural variations be correct. In terms of the calculator example, consistency means that $\phi_1'(p_1)$, the behavior attributed to firm 2 by firm 1, must be equal to $\partial p_2/\partial p_1 = (14 - 8\phi_2')/(24 - 14\phi_2')$, which is the derivative of equation (5.9). Equation (5.9) is the actual behavior rule followed by firm 2. Also, it is necessary that $\phi_2'(p_2) = \partial p_1/\partial p_2 = (44 - 32\phi_1')/(60 - 44\phi_1')$. These two conditions are satisfied for $\phi_1' = 0.592$ and $\phi_2' = 0.738$, and the associated values are in Table 5.1.

Recently, several writers have turned their attention to the consistency of conjectural variations [condition (c)] while otherwise staying in a static framework (e.g., Kamien and Schwartz, 1981; Bresnahan, 1982). Had there not been considerable progress in economics (oligopoly included) in analyzing dynamic models, this would seem a valuable development. Earlier work on dynamic oligopoly (e.g., Friedman, 1968; Cyert and DeGroot, 1970; Prescott, 1973; Kirman and Sobel, 1974) was concerned with the consistency issue while using explicitly dynamic models and endowing firms with appropriate (discounted profit-maximizing) objective functions. It remains possible that examining consistency in the absence of a dynamic model [i.e., ignoring (b) and (c)] will lead to insights that may prove valuable in dynamic models.

A one-period model with an elaborate decision process

There is a fourth single-period model with multiperiod overtones, due to Marschak and Selten (1977; 1978), that I wish to examine. Their focus is different from that of Bowley and Stackelberg, because they formulate two distinct models that they carefully relate to one another. One is a single-period model with an unusual decision structure, and the other is a multiperiod model. They then proceed to show that the two models can be made formally equivalent. The value of the single-period model is in providing a single-period framework in which the equilibrium is actually an interesting equilibrium for a multiperiod model. This shows up in two ways. First, as Marschak and Selten are at pains to prove, there is an equivalence between their static equilibrium and an interesting dynamic equilibrium. Second, their decision process, in which firms announce provisional prices, learn the provisional prices of rivals, and then are able to revise prices, is just the right decision process to make conjectural variations meaningful within a single-period model. And they do require consistency of conjectural variations; the behavior one firm expects from others is correct.

As in the Bowley-Stackelberg approach, each firm reacts to its rivals; however, unlike the earlier writers, Marschak and Selten are explicit on the form of the decision-making process, and they remain consciously and explicitly in a single-period situation. Decision is a many-stage process. Firms first, and simultaneously, announce prices; however, these prices are tentative rather than final. After the first-round prices are stated, each firm knows whether or not it is content to leave its price unchanged and have the announced vector of prices become the prices of the industry. To determine if any changes are to be made, each firm is given a chance, in turn, to change its price. The changes take place thus: The first firm is asked if it wishes to change its price. If no change is made, then the next firm is asked. However, if a change is made by the first firm, it states the new price, after which all other firms simultaneously choose new prices in reaction to the altered price of the first firm. These new prices for the $n - 1$ remaining firms are announced, and the first firm is again asked if it wishes to make a change. If it does not, then it becomes the turn of the next firm. But if the first firm wishes to change again, it announces another change, whereupon the others react to this new change. This process keeps on going until the first firm is content. Then, on to the second firm, to repeat the same procedure. Prices are final when the price vector stabilizes, that is, when there is a price vector that no firm wishes to change.

The strategy of the ith firm consists of four elements: (a) an initial price p_i^0, (b) a *response function* $\phi_i(p^0, p_j^1)$, (c) a specification of which price vectors p^0 it is content to leave unchanged, and (d) for each p^0 not in (c), what changes it wishes to make in p_i^0. The response function gives the price that firm i will choose if the current price vector is p^0 and firm j announces a change to p_j^1. Thus, if p^0 is the price vector first announced, firm 1 is first asked if it wishes to make a change; suppose it changes to p_1^1, then the next price vector in effect is $p^1 = [p_1^1, \phi_2(p^0, p_1^1), \ldots, \phi_n(p^0, p_1^1)]$. If firm 1 wishes to make a further change and chooses p_1^2, then the new price vector in effect is $p^2 = [p_1^2, \phi_2(p^1, p_1^2), \ldots, \phi_n(p^1, p_1^2)]$. The process can be iterated any finite number of times before passing on to firm 2. When the next firm has its turn, the price vector in effect is the one that the prior firm was finally content to leave alone.

It is convenient to define $\phi_i(p^0, p_j)$ for all possible p_j. The preceding discussion describes $\phi_i(p^0, p_j)$ for p_j different from p_j^0 and for j different from i. The natural meaning when $p_j = p_j^0$ is $\phi_i(p^0, p_j^0) = p_i^0$. That is, if the new price of firm j is the same as the old price, then the "response" of firm i is to keep its price unchanged. The natural meaning for $j = i$ is $\phi_i(p^0, p_i) = p_i$. That is, when firm i changes its price, its "response" to itself is its own new price. Starting with p^0, if firm i proposes to change its price to p_i^1, the next price vector can be written as $p^1 = \phi(p^0, p_i^1) = [\phi_1(p^0, p_i^1), \ldots, \phi_n(p^0, p_i^1)]$. If a firm makes a sequence of changes $p_i^1, \ldots, p_i^k$, each of which is followed by responses by the other firms, the resulting price vector can be denoted

$$p^k = \hat{\phi}(p^0, \{p_i^1, \ldots, p_i^k\}) \tag{5.10}$$

which is defined recursively by

$$p^k = \hat{\phi}(p^0, \{p_i^1, \ldots, p_i^k\}) = \phi[\hat{\phi}(p^0, \{p_i^1, \ldots, p_i^{k-1}\}), p_i^k]$$
$$(k \geq 2) \quad (5.11)$$

and

$$\hat{\phi}(p^0, \{p_i^1\}) = \phi(p^0, p_i^1) \tag{5.12}$$

where $\hat{\phi}_i$ is called an *extended response function*.

The *noncooperative equilibrium* for this model is defined by two conditions: (p^0, ϕ) is a noncooperative equilibrium if

(a) $\pi_i(p^0) \geq \pi_i[\hat{\phi}(p^0, \{p_i^1, \ldots, p_i^k\})]$ for any $\{p_i^1, \ldots, p_i^k\}$

and

(b) $\pi_i[\hat{\phi}(p^0, \{p_j^1, \ldots, p_j^k\})]$
$$\geq \pi_i[\hat{\phi}_i'(p^0, \{p_j^1, \ldots, p_j^k\}), \hat{\phi}_i(p^0, \{p_j^1, \ldots, p_j^k\})]$$

for all sequences of price changes $\{p_j^1, \ldots, p_j^k\}$ $(j \neq i)$ for all extended response functions ϕ_i' and all $i - 1, \ldots, n$. In condition (b), $\hat{\phi}_i$ is $(\phi_1, \ldots, \phi_{i-1}, \phi_{i+1}, \ldots, \phi_n)$. Condition (a) states that no firm i can increase its profit by deviating from p_i^0, given that the other firms will respond to any other price by using their response functions. Condition (b) states that for any sequence of deviations by firm j, for the given initial prices p^0, and for the given response functions of all other firms, the response function of firm i will yield at least as much profit as any other response function.

With this elaborate procedure for determining prices, a Cournot equilibrium in the narrow sense of a price vector such that no single firm can change its own price and increase its profit does not make sense. It would be shortsighted and unreasonable for a single firm to choose a price and stick by it, giving up its freedom to change its commitment, when all other firms could change from their provisional prices and respond to changes by other firms. The Marschak-Selten equilibrium is an equilibrium of the Cournot sort, adapted to the strategic possibilities that are available. For each firm, a *strategy* consists of its initial price choice and its response function. Equilibrium satisfies the same general kind of condition that is satisfied by the Cournot equilibrium: that no firm can change its strategy and increase its profits. Furthermore, it is an equilibrium in which the conjectural variations of the firms are consistent. That is, ϕ_i, the response function of firm i, shows how p_i will be changed if some other price is changed; however, ϕ_i is the rule that all other firms believe will govern the price variations of firm i.

The key feature of the Marschak-Selten intertemporal model is that once a firm has chosen an initial price, it faces a large adjustment cost if that price is to be changed. Generally, if a firm makes a price change that is unanticipated by the other firms, it has an interim period between the time its new price takes effect and the time the other firms announce new prices. The adjustment cost is so large that it is impossible in this interim period to gain enough extra profit to cover it. Therefore, a price change is advantageous only if it will bring higher profits over the long run, commencing after rival firms have adjusted to the change. This is a dynamic version of the process outlined in the preceding paragraphs. Marschak and Selten have deliberately avoided the feature found in the models of Sections 5.3 and 5.4 that allows a firm to make temporary gains after a price change and before rival firms can react.

5.2. The naive extension of atemporal reaction functions into intertemporal models

In Section 2.5 in Chapter 2 there is a brief discussion of the Cournot reaction functions as strategies in a multiperiod model, and it is noted that they are optimal if each firm in each period is interested in the profit of only that period and if each firm believes in each period that its rivals will repeat the same decisions (output level or price, depending on the model) that were chosen in the previous period. To assume that the firms have only a one-period horizon in a multiperiod model is to avoid one of the most important reasons for turning to multiperiod models in the first place. Firms do look ahead; they are willing to make trades between present and future profits, and it is important to incorporate into theoretical models an objective function that recognizes this. Parenthetically, the first model I know of that did this explicitly for oligopoly is that of Smithies and Savage (1940).

The assumption that the past behavior of others will be repeated stands on a different footing. Circumstances can be imagined in which firms know so little about their rivals' past actions and objective functions that a static assumption asserting that conditions from the immediate past will repeat themselves may be acceptable. If a firm did not know its rivals' cost and demand functions and had only rough and approximate knowledge of their past choices, such a naive extrapolation might be in order. But it is not in order under the information conditions that are assumed in Chapters 2 and 3 and in this chapter. Each firm is assumed to know the demand and cost functions of all other firms and to know all past choices of all firms. Thus, when a firm is not actually repeating past decisions, it must be perfectly clear to other firms that it is not. Were each firm behaving according to a reaction function, a great deal of regularity would be observable in the past price choices of one's rivals.

These comments apply to the Bowley conjectural variation as well as to the Cournot reaction functions. Putting Bowley's notion into a multiperiod model suggests writing $p_{2t} = \phi_1(p_{1,t-1})$ to represent what firm 1 thinks firm 2 will do and $p_{1t} = \phi_2(p_{2,t-1})$ to represent what firm 2 thinks firm 1 will do. If firm 2 does not behave according to ϕ_1, then firm 1 will not have its expectations confirmed over time and will, undoubtedly, wish to revise ϕ_1 to conform with the evidence.

The Stackelberg case is a bit different, because there are two modes of behavior: leader and follower. Stackelberg's leader, in the terminology introduced in this volume, is a firm that believes that its rivals all use Cournot reaction functions and that uses that information to maximize a discounted profit stream. For duopoly, there are three possibilities to examine: (a) both firms are followers; (b) one firm is a follower, the other a leader; (c) both firms are leaders. The follower-follower situation is the straight Cournot reaction function model discussed earlier in this chapter and in Chapter 2. The leader-follower model with firm 1 as leader requires that firm 2 uses $p_{2t} = w_2(p_{1,t-1})$, that firm 1 knows how firm 2 behaves, and that firm 1 wishes to maximize

$$\sum_{t=1}^{\infty} \alpha_1^{t-1} \pi_1[p_{1t}, w_2(p_{1,t-1})] \tag{5.13}$$

where α_1 is the discount parameter of firm 1. The discount parameter is related to the discount rate, r_1, by $\alpha_1 = 1/(1 + r_1)$. For a complete analysis of this leader-follower model, see Friedman (1977) or Fellner (1949). The first-order conditions for discounted profit maximization for firm 1 are

$$\pi_1^1(p_t) + \alpha_1\pi_1^2(p_{t+1})w_2'(p_{1t}) = 0 \qquad (t = 1, 2, \ldots) \quad (5.14)$$

By solving $\pi_1^1(p_t) + \alpha_1\pi_1^2[p_{1,t+1}, w_2(p_{1t})]w_2'(p_{1t}) = 0$ to obtain $p_{1,t+1}$ as a function of p_{1t}, the optimal behavioral rule, or *Stackelberg leader strategy*, is found. Recall that in the atemporal model of Chapter 3, the first-order condition is $\pi_1^1(p) + \pi_1^2(p)w_2'(p_1) = 0$. This differs in two ways from equation (5.14). One is that the discount parameter does not enter into the second term. The other is that the atemporal condition does not allow for movement of the leader's price over time. If equation (5.14) were solved for a steady-state long-run equilibrium price, satisfying

$$\pi_1^1[p_1^*, w_2(p_1^*)] + \alpha_1\pi_1^2[p_1^*, w_2(p_1^*)]w_2'(p_1^*) = 0 \qquad (5.15)$$

then the two conditions would differ only by the presence of the discount parameter.

In this multiperiod setup, the leader is behaving in an unexceptionable way, given that his rival is a follower, but the follower can be faulted in ways that are noted in the Cournot reaction function discussion in Chapter 2, Section 2.5. Namely, the follower makes incorrect assumptions about the leader's behavior that will be contradicted by the prices that the leader chooses and the follower observes. The third case, that of the leader-leader model, poses some difficulties. According to Stackelberg, each thinks that the other is a follower and accordingly behaves as a leader. This has been said to cause a Stackelberg disequilibrium, but in fact it is just another untenable situation that cannot arise. In parallel to the Bowley situation, the firms start with incorrect assumptions about rival behavior, and the evidence they accumulate must lead to revision of their expectations. A more complete look at this situation occupies the next section.

5.3. Reasonable reaction function equilibria under complete information: the case of smooth adjustment

The usual reaction function concept is a function for firm i that gives its period-t price choice as a function of the previous-period price choices of the remaining firms, and the function is continuous, probably even differentiable. Explicitly or implicitly, each firm is considered to gauge the way its own actions enter into its rivals' decisions and then to determine a relationship, using this information, that gives its profit-maximizing price choices. Firms are assumed to act independently in the sense that they do not collude, as with the Cournot equilibrium in single-period models. The *reaction functions* studied in this section have one difference from those discussed earlier: They are in the form $p_{it} = \phi_i(p_{t-1})$. In other words, the current-period price choice is a function of all prices of the preceding period, including $p_{i,t-1}$. Heeding the lessons from the preceding section, each firm is assumed to be a maximizer of discounted profits. Also, in equilibrium the reaction function of the firm maximizes its discounted profits, given the reaction functions of the rival firms. The point here is that the strategy of the firm in this multiperiod model is its reaction function, and the strategy it chooses should maximize its discounted profits, given the strategies (i.e., the reaction functions) of the others.

The optimal reaction function for a single firm

To make the nature of equilibrium more precise, let $\phi(p_{t-1}) = [\phi_1(p_{t-1}), \ldots, \phi_n(p_{t-1})] = [\phi_i(p_{t-1}), \bar{\phi}_i(p_{t-1})]$. Say it is time $t = 1$, and a profit-maximizing behavior for firm i is sought under the assumption that the other firms choose their prices according to $\phi_j^*(p_{t-1})$ for all $j \neq i$. In other words, a hypothetical question is being asked concerning the optimal behavior for firm i when $\bar{p}_{it} = \phi_i^*(p_{t-1})$. A natural way to tackle this problem is by dynamic programming, with the firm assumed to have a finite time horizon of T periods. T is first set equal to one, and the one-period maximization problem is solved. Then T is set equal to two, and the two-period maximization problem is solved under the condition that the last period be governed by the solution to the one-period horizon problem. In general, the T-period problem is solved assuming that the previously calculated optimal plan will be followed in subsequent periods. Finally, T is allowed to go to infinity. When the horizon is finite, the firm's optimal strategy is more complicated than when it is infinite, as is shown next.

Starting first with $T = 1$, the firm's objective is to maximize the profits of a single period, given the assumed behavior of its rivals. That is, maximize

$$\pi_i[p_{i1}, \overline{\phi}_i^*(p_0)] \tag{5.16}$$

with respect to p_{i1}. The price vector p_0 is an arbitrary initial condition, and the solution that is sought should be optimal no matter what the value of p_0 may be. Assuming that equation (5.9) is maximized at a nonzero price and nonzero output level and that the usual second-order conditions are fulfilled, the maximum is attained at that p_{i1} for which

$$\pi_i^i[p_{i1}, \overline{\phi}_i^*(p_0)] = 0 \tag{5.17}$$

Equation (5.10) is an implicit function of p_{i1} and p_0. Assume that it can be inverted to express p_{i1} as a function of p_0 in the form $p_{i1} = h_{i1}(p_0)$, where h_{i1} is actually the optimal behavior any time the firm's horizon is one period. Therefore, if the horizon is, say, fifty periods, h_{i1} will be optimal in period 50. That is, $p_{i,50} = h_{i1}(p_{49})$ describes the best choice of the firm, no matter what pattern of prices has previously been seen.

Turn now to $T = 2$. The firm's objective function is

$$\pi_i[p_{i1}, \overline{\phi}_i^*(p_0)] + \alpha_i\pi_i[p_{i2}, \overline{\phi}_i^*(p_1)] \tag{5.18}$$

and it can choose p_{i1} and p_{i2}. Again assuming an interior solution to the firm's maximization problem, the first-order conditions are

$$\pi_i^i[p_{i1}, \overline{\phi}_i^*(p_0)] + \alpha_i\sum_{j \neq i}\pi_i^j[p_{i2}, \overline{\phi}_i^*(p_1)]\phi_j^{*i}(p_1) = 0 \tag{5.19}$$

$$\pi_i^i[p_{i2}, \overline{\phi}_i^*(p_1)] = 0 \tag{5.20}$$

Equation (5.20) is already known to be satisfied by $p_{i2} = h_{i1}(p_1)$; so $h_{i1}(p_1)$ can be substituted for p_{i2} in equation (5.19). Again, assuming that equation (5.19) can be inverted, p_{i1} can be expressed as a function of p_0, recalling that $p_{i2} = h_{i1}(p_1) = h_{i1}[p_{i1}, \overline{\phi}_i^*(p_0)]$. Denote the inverted equation (5.19) by $p_{i1} = h_{i2}(p_0)$. Thus, the complete strategy for a two-period horizon is to choose $p_{i1} = h_{i2}(p_0)$ in the first period and $p_{i2} = h_{i1}(p_1)$ in the second. As long as the other firms choose prices according to $\overline{\phi}_i^*$, this strategy maximizes the firm's discounted two-period profits, no matter what the value of p_0.

Continuing in the same fashion, the firm's strategy for a T-period horizon consists of prices chosen by the following rules:

$$p_{i1} = h_{iT}(p_0)$$
$$p_{i2} = h_{i,T-1}(p_1)$$
$$p_{i3} = h_{i,T-2}(p_2)$$
$$\cdot$$
$$\cdot \qquad (5.21)$$
$$\cdot$$
$$p_{iT} = h_{i1}(p_{T-1})$$

Note that the strategy is expressed as a sequence of T distinct reaction functions, each one specific to a particular remaining time horizon, and that the firm's maximization problem is not stated in a way that requires in advance that only reaction function solutions be considered. The firm's best policy turns out to be a sequence of reaction functions, even though it could have chosen policies in which a specific sequence of prices would be chosen, no matter what, or in which the price choice of each period would depend on past prices from more than the immediately preceding period, or in which prices of firms other than the ith would enter, but not that of the ith firm itself.

Under the assumptions used in Chapter 3 and some additional conditions that are given by Friedman (1977, Chapter 5) it can be proved that the sequence of single-period reaction functions, h_{iT}, converges as T goes to infinity and that the longer the horizon of a firm, the higher the price it will choose under an optimal plan. That is to say, for p_{t-1}, $h_{iT}(p_{t-1}) \geq h_{i,T-1}(p_{t-1})$, and there is a long-run reaction function $h_i(p_{t-1})$ to which the reaction functions $h_{iT}(p_{t-1})$ converge as T increases. This is illustrated in a schematic way in Figure 5.1. Among the conditions that are imposed is that all the first derivatives of the ϕ_j are positive. The intuition behind this is that when a firm charges a higher price, it tends to benefit its rivals, and if all firms charge higher prices, all firms tend to gain; therefore, any one firm ought to be willing to use a higher price, the higher are the prices being chosen by the others.

The limiting reaction function $h_i(p_{t-1})$ is the discounted profit-maximizing strategy, or policy, for firm i if it has an infinite time

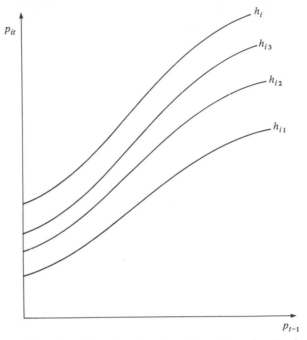

Figure 5.1. Reaction functions for various time horizons.

horizon and if its rival firms are using the policies $\phi_j^*(p_{t-1})$ for all $j \neq i$. The firm's objective in this case is to maximize

$$\sum_{t=1}^{\infty} \alpha_i^{t-1} \pi_i(p_t) \tag{5.22}$$

Equation (5.22) is maximized by h_i for any possible p_0, subject only to the reaction functions of the others, ϕ_j^*. Again, it cannot be stressed too strongly that using h_i is absolutely unbeatable. Looking ahead slightly, if $h_i = \phi_i^*$ for all i, then $(\phi_1^*, \ldots, \phi_n^*)$ is a noncooperative equilibrium. There is no other plan of action, whether more complicated or less so, whether a reaction function or not, that will yield greater discounted profits for firm i, *given that the other firms use the ϕ_j^*.*

Market equilibrium when firms choose reaction functions

Now consider what is needed for the reaction functions $\phi_1^*, \ldots, \phi_n^*$ to be a noncooperative equilibrium. Starting with any one firm i, if it observes the other firms behaving according to the ϕ_j^*, then its discounted profit is maximized if it uses h_i. Now h_i may be identical with ϕ_i^* or it may be different. If it is different, then $\phi_1^*, \ldots, \phi_n^*$ is not a noncooperative equilibrium. It is untenable that firm i would think that firm j is using ϕ_j^* if, in fact, firm j is behaving according to some other plan. The only exception would be if ϕ_j^* and the actual plan in use (h_j) happened to cause the same sequence of p_{jt} to be chosen. Barring that, firm i cannot be misinformed for long, and if it is misinformed in this very special way, perhaps it does not matter. The upshot is that a *noncooperative equilibrium* in terms of reaction functions in a multiperiod model consists of a combination of n reaction functions $\phi_1^*, \ldots, \phi_n^*$, no one of which can be changed by a firm, with the result that the firm's discounted profit increases. Each firm has a reaction function that maximizes its discounted profit, given the (true) reaction functions of the others. No firm is making conjectures about the others that it never revises, but that prove false according to the information the firm receives.

One difficulty with this reaction function equilibrium is that its existence has not been proved, although the impossibility of its existence has not been proved either. The behavior postulated has some intuitive appeal, but because its existence has not been shown, there remains the distinct possibility that this kind of equilibrium cannot happen. The existence of a similar, though less satisfactory, equilibrium is known. This equilibrium, as described later, approximates the reaction function noncooperative equilibrium. Imagine that the ϕ_i^* are all contractions, in addition to having positive first partial derivatives. Thus, $\Sigma_{j=1}^n \phi_i^{*j} \le k < 1$. This means that a one-dollar increase in yesterday's prices for all firms will lead to an increase today of less than one dollar in the price of any firm. Under these conditions, starting from any p_0 and generating successive price vectors by $p_t = \phi^*(p_{t-1}) = [\phi_1^*(p_{t-1}), \ldots, \phi_n^*(p_{t-1})]$, the price vector p_t will converge to some steady-state price vector, p^*.

Recall that for any firm i it is possible to find the reaction function h_i that would maximize profits if the others used $\overline{\phi}_i^*$. If every firm i thought that its rivals were using $\overline{\phi}_i^*$, then the firms would actually use $h(p_{t-1}) = [h_1(p_{t-1}), \ldots, h_n(p_{t-1})]$. It can be shown that there is a combination of reaction functions ϕ^* such that the associated best reply reaction functions h have the following properties: (a) $h(p^*) = \phi^*(p^*)$, (b) $h_i^j(p) \geq 0$, (c) $\Sigma_{j=1}^n h_i^j(p) \leq k < 1$, and (d) $h_i^j(p^*) = \phi_i^{*j}(p^*)$ for all i and j. Condition (a) states that the two combinations of reaction functions have the same steady-state price vector, and condition (d) states that they are so similar near to that steady-state price vector that they have identical first partial derivatives at p^*. Conditions (b) and (c) are that the h_i are, like the ϕ_i^*, contractions with nonnegative first derivatives. It is easily shown that p^* can be a price vector that is larger in every coordinate than the single-period Cournot equilibrium price vector p^c and that each firm has larger profits at p^* than at p^c [i.e., $\pi_i(p^*) > \pi_i(p^c)$ for all i]. There appears to be no obstacle to $[\pi_1(p^*), \ldots, \pi_n(p^*)]$ being on the profit possibility frontier, in which case noncooperative behavior would lead to an outcome usually associated with collusion. Whereas such an outcome might occur spontaneously, it can be imagined as the result of an agreement by the firms. Such an agreement would need no enforcement, because, being a noncooperative equilibrium, no firm would gain by unilaterally breaking the agreement. Because this is a spontaneous noncooperative equilibrium, we lack an explanation of why one particular outcome should arise. This is a question of disequilibrium dynamics, which is in a primitive state in all branches of economics.

Reaction functions and time-dependent models

Perhaps the results of this section suggest that equilibrium in multiperiod models is rather elusive. That is actually not the case. For example, there is one equilibrium that may have occurred to some readers; it is a degenerate reaction function equilibrium. It consists of choosing $p_{it} = p_i^c$ for all i and t. In other words, each firm chooses its Cournot price in each period, irrespective of any past prices. This is a noncooperative equilibrium that consists of treating each iteration of the market as if it is completely independent of every other one. In a structural sense, the time periods are independent, for the variables of one period do not enter the cost or demand functions of any other period. It can be said that the model is *time-independent.* The converse, *time dependence,* occurs when, say, the demand for a good in period t depends on the sales of the past several periods as well as on the price vector for the current price. Consumer durables are typical examples of this. If the makers of color television sets sell immense numbers of them for two or three years, their sales in the next year are likely to be less than they would have been had the earlier sales not been so large. Buyers who might have purchased in the later time have bought earlier instead. Conversely, if a recession induces many people to wait rather than replace their old television sets (or refrigerators, automobiles, etc.), then when the recession lifts, the amounts sold at any given price configuration will be higher than they would have been if the recession had not taken place and sales had been higher during that prior time. Some models with time-dependent structure are examined in Chapters 6 and 7. In such models there is no straightforward analogue to the single-period Cournot equilibrium.

Although there is no structural time dependence in the models of this chapter, the time periods can be linked behaviorally. Such a link is present in the reaction functions, and this link means that the choices of one period will influence the profits received in the subsequent period. The next section delves into a form of time-dependent behavior akin to, but different from, the reaction functions of this section. Not only does equilibrium exist, there are too many equilibria.

5.4. Reasonable reaction function equilibria: the case of tacit collusion or self-enforcing agreements

In moving from the single-period world of Chapters 2 through 4 to the multiperiod models of this chapter, a great deal of flexibility is added to what the firms can do. Indeed, so much is added that collusion, which requires binding agreements in a single-period setting, becomes possible without binding agreements. This fact is illustrated by the equilibria that are developed in the remainder of this section. Many economists have thought that the Cournot equilibrium makes no sense precisely because it does not lie on the firms' profit possibility frontier. This view was held by Bertrand (1883) and by Chamberlin (1933), although neither of them could explain how profits on the frontier would actually be achieved. The key is to use the kind of approach pioneered by Cournot, applying it to the multiperiod model. In the next three subsections this is done for two firms in a general model, followed by an example, and then for n firms. Then there are subsections discussing the role of threats, looking at a special self-enforcing agreement, and discussing the equilibrium developed in Section 5.4.

A self-enforcing agreement for two firms

Imagine the profit possibilities for a single period to be those depicted in Figure 5.2, where the curve CBD is the profit possibility frontier. Anything below this frontier is attainable with a suitable pair of prices, and the single-period Cournot equilibrium is at A. The point B is an arbitrarily chosen outcome on the profit possibility frontier, except that it gives both firms more profits than they receive at the Cournot equilibrium. All the points in the shaded area afford more profit to each firm than the Cournot point.

Let p^* denote the price vector associated with B, and p^c that associated with A, and imagine that firm 2 will choose prices by the following policy, which is known to firm 1. Policy $T2$: $p_{21} = p_2^*$. For $t \geq 2$, $p_{2t} = p_2^*$ if $p_{1\tau} = p_1^*$ for $\tau = 1, \ldots, t - 1$. If $p_{1\tau} \neq p_1^*$ for at least one time $\tau \leq t - 1$, then $p_{2t} = p_2^c$. This policy treats p^* as if it is an agreed-on price vector. Firm 2 will commence by choosing p_2^* in the initial period. In each subsequent period, firm 2 will check to see if firm 1 has always chosen p_1^* in each past period. If firm 1 has complied perfectly, firm 2 will continue with p_2^*, but if firm 1 has faltered even one time in the past, then firm 2 will choose p_2^c. Loosely speaking, firm 2 will be cooperative in the initial period, and if firm 1 is cooperative, firm 2 will continue to be cooperative.

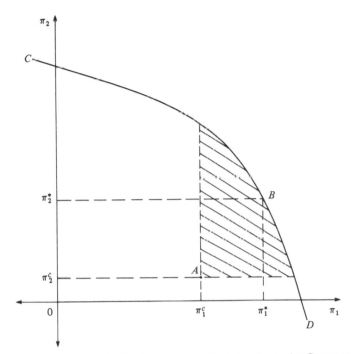

Figure 5.2. Profit outcomes that dominate the Cournot equilibrium.

Should firm 1 ever fail to be cooperative, firm 2 will switch to its single-period Cournot price and remain at it forever.

Assume that firm 1 is fully aware that policy $T2$ will be followed by its rival. What are the reasonable choices from which it might select? To simplify notation, denote $\pi_i(p^*)$ by π_i^* and $\pi_i(p^c)$ by π_i^c. First, it might use an exactly parallel strategy, call it policy $T1$, in which case its discounted profits would be $\pi_1^*/(1 - \alpha_1)$. Each would always be ready to revert to p^c, but neither would give the other cause to do so. Alternatively, say that firm 1 plans to choose p_1^* for the first t periods; then in period $t + 1$ it plans to choose some other price p_1'. Clearly, given $T2$, if it deviates from p_1^* in period $t + 1$, it can do no better than to choose p_1^c in every period following $t + 1$.

This is because firm 2 will be choosing p_2^c in all these later periods. Therefore, the discounted profits of firm 1 will be

$$\pi_1^* + \alpha_1\pi_1^* + \ldots + \alpha_1^{t-1}\pi_1^* + \alpha_1^t\pi_1(p_1', p_2^*) + \alpha_1^{t+1}\pi_1^c + \alpha_1^{t+2}\pi_1^c$$

$$+ \ldots = \frac{1-\alpha_1^t}{1-\alpha_1}\,\pi_1^* + \alpha_1^t\pi_1(p_1', p_2^*) + \alpha_1^{t+1}\frac{1}{1-\alpha_1}\,\pi_1^c \quad (5.23)$$

The only variable to be determined in equation (5.23) is p_1', which affects the profit earned in period $t+1$ and in no other period. Thus, equation (5.23) is maximized if p_1' is chosen to satisfy $\pi_1^1(p_1', p_2^*) = 0$, which means that $p_{1,t+1}'$ is chosen to maximize the profit of period $t+1$ alone, on the knowledge that $p_{2,t+1}$ will be p_2^*. Now the question arises whether the discounted profit under equation (5.23) is larger or smaller than the profit under policy $T1$. That is, when is

$$\frac{\pi_1^*}{1-\alpha_1} > \frac{1-\alpha_1^t}{1-\alpha_1}\,\pi_1^* + \alpha_1^t\pi_1(p_1', p_2^*) + \alpha_1^{t+1}\frac{1}{1-\alpha_1}\,\pi_1^c \quad (5.24)$$

which, after the π_1^* terms are consolidated, and $\pi_1(p_1', p_2^*)$ is written π_1', becomes

$$\alpha_1^t\,\frac{1}{1-\alpha_1}\,\pi_1^* > \alpha_1^t\left(\overline{\pi_1' + \alpha_1\,\frac{1}{1-\alpha_1}\,\pi_1^c}\right) \quad (5.25)$$

Equation (5.25) is equivalent to

$$\frac{1}{1-\alpha_1}\,\pi_1^* > \frac{1-\alpha_1}{1-\alpha_1}\,\pi_1' + \frac{\alpha_1}{1-\alpha_1}\,\pi_1^c \quad (5.26)$$

$$\alpha_1(\pi_1' - \pi_1^c) > \pi_1' - \pi_1^* \quad (5.27)$$

$$\alpha_1 > \frac{\pi_1' - \pi_1^*}{\pi_1' - \pi_1^c} \quad (5.28)$$

In choosing between the policy embodied in equation (5.23) and $T1$, the firm is comparing whether or not an extra gain of $\pi_1' - \pi_1^*$ in a particular period is outweighed by a decrease in profit of

$\pi_1^* - \pi_1^c$ in each succeeding period. Not surprisingly, the size of the discount parameter plays a crucial role, as shown in equation (5.28). If the discount parameter is sufficiently large, indicating a big enough weight placed on the future, the trade is not worthwhile, and *T*1 is the superior policy. If the discount parameter is too small, and the policy embodied in equation (5.23) is optimal, then it is most profitable to set $t = 1$ and choose p_1' in the first period.

A numerical example of a self-enforcing agreement

This equilibrium can be illustrated by the two calculator firms. Table 5.2 contains information on the profit possibility frontier. The column headed p gives the weight used in the expression $p\pi_1 + (1 - p)\pi_2$ to find that particular point on the profit possibility frontier. That is, for a given p, for example, $p = 0.6$, a point on the profit possibility frontier is found by solving the two equations

$$\frac{p\partial\pi_1}{\partial p_1} + \frac{(1 - p)\partial\pi_2}{\partial p_1} = p(1,150 - 60p_1 + 44p_2)$$
$$+ (1 - p)(-334 - 8p_1 + 14p_2) = 0$$

and

$$\frac{p\partial\pi_1}{\partial p_2} + \frac{(1 - p)\partial\pi_2}{\partial p_2} = p(-840 + 44p_1 - 32p_2)$$
$$+ (1 - p)(581 + 14p_1 - 24p_2) = 0$$

The meaning of the procedure is that both firms act to maximize exactly the same objective function $[p\pi_1 + (1 - p)\pi_2]$. Such behavior is efficient in the sense that it will attain profits on the frontier. The frontier is drawn in Figure 5.3, with the Cournot equilibrium also indicated. The figures for the Cournot equilibrium are from Table 5.1.

Now take $p^* = (68.852, 66.095)$, with the associated $\pi^* = (779.26, 770.49)$. Looking first from the standpoint of firm 1, what is best for it if firm 2 follows strategy *T*2? *T*2 is a policy that has $p_2 = p_2^* = 66.095$ as long as $p_1 = p_1^* = 68.852$. As soon as firm 2 detects a deviation of p_1 from p_1^*, it switches to $p_2 = p_2^c = 61.845$, its Cournot

Table 5.2. *Profit possibility frontier outcomes*

ρ	p_1	p_2	q_1	q_2	π_1	π_2
0.0911	75.451	69.315	0	22.96	0	903.55
0.1	74.516	68.777	2.53	22.70	156.78	887.06
0.15	71.507	67.092	10.84	21.74	549.04	833.72
0.2	70.153	66.401	14.84	21.10	672.38	808.21
0.25	69.440	66.104	17.22	20.57	726.94	792.60
0.3	69.053	66.020	18.81	20.05	757.04	781.29
0.35	68.866	66.077	19.98	19.50	776.91	771.77
0.357	68.852	66.095	20.12	19.42	779.26	770.49
0.4	68.822	66.249	20.89	18.90	792.33	762.53
0.45	68.897	66.529	21.63	18.21	806.14	752.32
0.5	69.086	66.928	22.28	17.39	820.08	739.67
0.55	69.399	67.469	22.88	16.39	835.57	722.48
0.6	69.866	68.198	23.46	15.14	854.13	697.23
0.65	70.540	69.193	24.07	13.50	877.86	657.39
0.7	71.522	70.593	24.76	11.26	910.27	589.43
0.75	73.011	72.672	25.63	8.01	958.10	461.70
0.8	75.452	76.033	26.87	2.81	1,036.69	185.90
0.8185	76.785	77.856	27.50	0	1,080.33	0

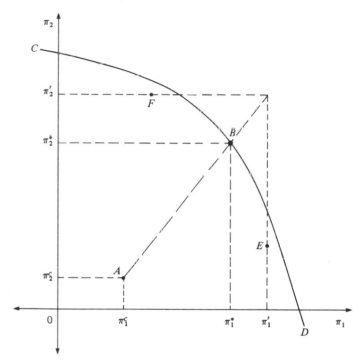

Figure 5.3. The balanced temptation equilibrium.

price. Thus, firm 1 can follow $T1$ and obtain 779.26 in each period, for a discounted profit of $779.26/(1 - \alpha_1)$, or it can maximize one period's profit while $p_2 = p_2^*$ and then receive Cournot profits of 736.95 in each later period. The price to use for this one period is found from $1,150 - 60p_1' + 44(66.095) = 0$. Then $p_1' = 67.636$, and the corresponding profit is 823.62 (shown at E in Figure 5.3). This gives discounted profits of $823.62 + 736.95\alpha_1/(1 - \alpha_1)$. The latter policy of grabbing maximum profits for one period and receiving Cournot profits thereafter is inferior to $T1$ if $823.62 + 736.95\alpha_1/(1 - \alpha_1) < 779.26/(1 - \alpha_1)$, which is equivalent to $\alpha_1 > 44.36/86.67 = 0.51$. The point F in Figure 5.3 is found by going through a parallel exercise for firm 2. Firm 2 is better off following $T2$ if $806.09 + 736.64\alpha_2/(1 - \alpha_2) < 770.49/(1 - \alpha_2)$, which is equivalent to $\alpha_2 > 35.60/69.45 = 0.51$. The numerator in the lower limit for the discount parameter (44.36 for firm 1 and 35.60 for firm 2) is $\pi'_i - \pi^*_i$, the extra one-period gain obtainable by choosing p'_i and cheating on the implicit agreement. The denominator is $\pi'_i - \pi^c_i$, the extra one-period gain plus the per period gain from using the policies $T1$ and $T2$.

Self-enforcing agreements for n firms

More generally, if there are n firms, p^* is the price vector yielding $[\pi_1(p^*), \ldots , \pi_n(p^*)] = (\pi^*_1, \ldots , \pi^*_n)$ on the profit possibility frontier, Ti is the analogue for firm i of the policies $T1$ and $T2$, and π'_i is defined by

$$\pi'_i = \max_{p_i} \pi_i(p_i, \bar{p}^*_i) \tag{5.29}$$

The policies $T1, \ldots , Tn$ are a noncooperative equilibrium if

$$\alpha_i > \frac{\pi'_i - \pi^*_i}{\pi'_i - \pi^c_i} \qquad (i = 1, \ldots , n) \tag{5.30}$$

Under Ti, firm i chooses p^*_i in time t if all other firms have always selected p^*_j ($j \neq i$) in all periods through $t = 1$.

Two outstanding features of this equilibrium are that it is not unique and that it does yield profits on the profit possibility frontier. The lack of uniqueness suggests that it would be difficult for the firms to find their way to such an equilibrium without being able to communicate. Another feature of the equilibrium that suggests the usefulness of communication is that the strategies Ti include plans for an abrupt change in behavior whenever a firm deviates from p^*_j. This part of the strategy is, so to speak, hidden from view as long as all firms are choosing the p^*_j. Under the reaction functions of the preceding section, small price changes by one firm lead to small price changes by rival firms; however, the reverse holds here. A deviation from p^* shifts all firms into a very different mode of play. The combination of profit possibility frontier profits and noncooperative equilibrium strategies makes this equilibrium a natural one to result from communication. Binding agreements are not necessary, for no one has an incentive to deviate from the agreed-on prices.[2] To see how an equilibrium like this might arise when firms cannot communicate, and when they start with arbitrary initial prices, see the work of Shapiro (1980).

Credible threats and self-enforcing agreements

The key to the self-enforcing agreement is that it does involve a noncooperative equilibrium. In effect, the threat that keeps each firm choosing the profit possibility frontier price is that all other firms are committed to reverting to single-period Cournot prices if any firm should deviate. This is a reversion to a noncooperative equilibrium that is decidedly well inside the frontier, but because it is a noncooperative equilibrium for the multiperiod game, it is a believable threat. If firm i believes that all other firms will, following any firm's deviation, revert permanently to $\bar{p}_i^c$, then firm i can do no better than to choose p_i^c.

The believability of threats is central to their usefulness. Occasionally a person will be heard to claim that a collusive agreement can be kept in force by the threats of some firms to cause large losses to the others. Even if it is possible to cause a deviating firm to suffer large losses, it may not be in the interest of the others to do so once the actual deviation has taken place. Should this be so, the threat is mere bluff and bluster, and the potential deviator is likely to see through it. Suppose firm 1 can cause a deviating firm 2 to sustain negative profits only by driving its own profits far below the single-period Cournot equilibrium profits. It is difficult to understand what will cause the more vindictive move. If firm 2 behaves rationally, then firm 1 will be able to gain higher profits by less nasty behavior. Supposing firm 1 is interested in its own profits and takes no joy in causing misery to its rival, only noncooperative behavior is tenable.

A special equilibrium on the profit frontier

The $T1$-$T2$ equilibrium for the calculator firms, illustrated in Figure 5.3, is special in that $(\pi_1' - \pi_1^*)/(\pi_1' - \pi_1^c) = (\pi_2' - \pi_2^*)/(\pi_2' - \pi_2^c) = 0.51$. In other words, the discount parameter that will place a firm on the margin between using Ti and deviating to obtain the extra one-period gain $(\pi_i' - \pi_i^*)$ is the same for both firms. Such a special profit possibility frontier outcome, called the *balanced temptation equilibrium,* where the temptation to deviate is, in a sense, equalized among firms, might be a natural outcome that the firms could think of and implement without communication.

This balanced temptation condition is not the only candidate for a natural profit possibility frontier point for the firms to select without communication. In a model in which capital stocks (K_i) enter, they might settle on that profit frontier point that equalizes the marginal rate of return to capital obtained in comparison with the single-period Cournot point [i.e., they equalize $(\pi_i^* - \pi_i^c)/K_i$ across firms]. The choice of any such outcome that is simultaneously a noncooperative equilibrium and a profit frontier point is a candidate for the concept tacit collusion.

A further look at equilibria based on self-enforcing agreements

The idea behind *tacit collusion* is that the firms in an industry can collude, or, more properly, attain the kind of outcome that is usually associated with collusion, in the absence of any kind of agreement or even discourse. Somehow, all firms know what is in their best interest, and without explicit coordination, they do the right thing. The foregoing provides a way in which this spontaneous coordination might actually take place. Note that the possibility for tacit collusion on the profit frontier is, in principle, independent of the number of firms in the market. This means that increasing the number of firms need not bring a movement of equilibrium toward the efficient point (where price equals marginal cost). This has the obvious welfare implication that merely by causing an increase in the number of firms, one cannot be assured of a move toward marginal cost pricing. Of course, as a practical matter, the fewer firms that are involved, the easier it may be to organize and sustain a profit possibility frontier noncooperative equilibrium. Because the models under study here do not include costs of organization or information gathering, such an effect will not be seen in them.

Furthermore, these equilibria depend on each firm knowing the cost functions, demand functions, and discount parameters of all other firms for the present and all future periods. They depend also on the time lag during which a firm gains from deviation being of a known and fixed duration, and, finally, each firm must be utterly convinced that the others will really follow through with Cournot prices in the event of a deviation from p_i^* by some firm.

Clearly, real life firms do not know their own cost and demand functions for all future periods, and their knowledge of them for the present may be limited. They know less about their rivals. Time is, of course, not so neatly packaged as in the models. How quickly the word gets around when prices are changed will depend on the nature of the industry. Where prices are publicly announced and adhered to until the next announcement, word will travel very fast, and the lag time may be only the time it takes for other firms to formulate and effect changes of their own. This latter time may be a random variable, and a firm may have some idea of the distribution of that variable for other firms. Where price changes show up in the form of privately negotiated rebates or discounts, word may travel more slowly, and its travel time is likely to be random.

That firms will revert quickly and unquestioningly to p^c after some firm deviates is also uncertain. Even after representatives of the several firms solemnly swear to do this, the defection of one from the ranks of the virtuous can easily bring one of several additional responses. For example, the others may consult with one another and decide that it is better for them to give the defector a second chance than to allow their very profitable arrangement to crumble. A potential defector who thinks he will surely get a second chance will be foolish not to defect, for he will not have to face an infinite future of reduced profits in payment for his defector's gain. But an assured second chance should make defectors of everyone, and all should expect universal defection. Is a second chance followed by a third? A fourth? This line of reasoning makes the kind of hard line epitomized by the $T1, \ldots, Tn$ policies look attractive. Yet everyday experience makes it clear that people often are more forgiving than that.

A second response to the deviation of one member is for the remaining $n - 1$ firms to formulate a new agreement that lies on a constrained profit possibility frontier. This is the frontier that gives the $n - 1$ firms the most they can achieve, given the behavior of the firm that can be expected to maximize its profit given what the remaining cartel members do. The weak spot in this appealing policy is similar to the weakness of giving a second chance. Rather than punishing the defector, this policy tends to reward it. It is almost in the position of getting in every period the same profits it received in its initial period of defection. And a second firm may want to defect also, believing that it might do nearly as well as the first defector. And so the agreement peels apart, layer by layer, until nothing is left.

Meanwhile, if each firm i chooses Ti and sticks to it, then no firm defects and no firm can do better. The upshot of all this is that the Pareto optimal outcomes, backed up by the promise to revert to p^c if someone deviates from p_i^*, are appealing and probably mirror some real behavior; yet such policies are not always followed when they might be. How prevalent the Ti policies are and how their prevalence varies with the variables of interest is an open question.

5.5. Summary

In this chapter the development of reaction functions is traced, starting with the static representations of Bowley and Stackelberg and ending with some explicitly dynamic models of recent origin. Several points emerge as having central importance. First, the idea of reacting to decisions of others is inherently dynamic and ought to be treated within an explicitly dynamic model. Within such a model, the firms ought to be assumed to maximize a discounted profit stream, and their expectations concerning their rivals' behavior ought to be correct if they will be receiving information that will later tell them if they were right or wrong. Although the decision process of Marschak and Selten rationalizes reactions within a single-period model, it is much more reasonable to suppose simple simultaneous actions within each period and use a multiperiod (dynamic) model.

Second, moving to dynamic models opens up the range of noncooperative behavior. In particular, collusive arrangements that require no outside enforcement become possible. Because they appear to be unrelated to the size of the market, they allow quasi-monopolistic outcomes that need not change as the number of firms in the market changes.

Three important considerations are not covered: entry, uncertainty, and incomplete information. In Chapter 8, entry is discussed, and its effect on market equilibrium is, to some extent, assessed. Uncertainty and incomplete information are beyond the scope of this book; indeed, not a great deal has been done in either direction. One wonders whether introducing uncertainty merely means that everything carries through after being restated in expected value terms or whether fundamental changes in behavior result. Some hints are found in the work of Green and Porter (1981) and Miller (1982), where previous results appear to carry through, at least approximately.

My guess is that endowing firms with little or no information about the structure of the market must lead to behavior much nearer to competitive behavior, but I know of no research that bears on this issue. For incomplete information to be persistent, and not disappear with the passage of time while firms gather information from the market, it is probably necessary to include intrinsic uncertainty in the model. Such conditions seem to me realistic and point the way toward worthwhile directions for research.

6

Oligopoly and advertising

Advertising can be viewed from any of several vantage points. In the sections that follow, the central focus is on the way in which advertising enters the demand functions of the firms in a market and, further, the effect of advertising on market equilibrium. Advertising also raises interesting and important questions touching on ethics and welfare. For example, can consumers' buying habits be so thoroughly manipulated by advertising that the large firms of the economy can virtually dictate tastes? Ought advertisers to be subject to laws that force them to be truthful, or even prevent them from making misleading claims? Can it be said that the presence of advertising increases or decreases consumer welfare in the economy?

Such ethical questions are beyond the scope of this study, and this chapter is not intended as an implicit or explicit statement concerning them. It is surely true that the amount of output a firm can sell at a given price is affected by the level of its own advertising and, often, by the advertising efforts of other firms selling similar products. Will the sales of a firm be increased or diminished by the advertising of a rival? Will the advertising expenditures of a firm in the current period carry any benefits into the future, or are they totally realized in the current period? How is the nature of market equilibrium affected by the extent to which advertising is cooperative or predatory? Will advertising expenditures rise or fall if the government places restrictions on advertising? Can firms' sales be diminished by governmental restrictions on advertising? These are the questions addressed in this chapter.

The remainder of the chapter is divided into five sections. In the first, the meaning of advertising, as used in this chapter, is discussed. The second section contains a general discussion of the ways in which advertising probably affects consumers' buying decisions. In the third section, the relationship between advertising and a firm's demand is considered. The fourth section contains formal models of oligopoly with advertising, and the fifth is a summary.

6.1. A provisional definition of advertising

Strictly speaking, the term *advertising* usually refers to paid advertisements in printed media such as newspapers and magazines, in broadcast media such as television and radio, on billboards, and by direct mail. However, these outlets are part of a broader class of expenditures aimed at selling and promoting goods. Some firms have public relations staffs who try to get regular news coverage of their products or of activities involving their products. Thus, a new line of computers might be the subject of a news story, as might an innovation in contact lenses. This is a form of "free" advertising, free in the sense that the newspaper space itself was not paid for. Yet it was not accidental that the story appeared; its appearance resulted from resources expended through the public relations staff of the firm. Likewise, products appear in television programs and films. If a scene takes place in an office, there may be a typewriter, and the particular brand that is used may be there because of public relations efforts by the manufacturer or distributor.

Salespeople are another large category of workers who are hired for the promotion of products. Examples range from automobile and home appliance salespeople to the highly trained sales staffs working for the manufacturers of complex, specialized equipment and on to the detail men employed by pharmaceutical manufacturers who visit physicians to promote their firms' drug products.

Throughout this chapter, the reader ought to think of advertising as meaning all forms of expenditure aimed at increasing sales: advertising in the narrow (usual) sense, public relations, and sales-people. Indeed, if the reader can think of a category of sales promo-tion expense that I have forgotten, that should be included too.

6.2. Advertising and the consumer

Broadly speaking, there are two ways in which advertising can affect a consumer's purchases: by providing information and by altering tastes, although it may be difficult to draw the line separat-ing them. In the traditional economic theory of consumer behavior there is no role for the provision of information, because each consumer is assumed to know all the products that exist and to know all their characteristics and uses. He can be taught nothing. In addition, his tastes are fully known to him and are immutable. In reality, consumers lack much information about goods, and if consumers know their own tastes, they know them in a less precise sense than theory presumes. Furthermore, it is clear that people's tastes evolve over time and are shaped in part by past consumption choices. In fairness to the traditional theory, it is customary to say that tastes are given at a particular moment, but might well change slowly over time. This justifies study of the consumer in a static context with tastes fixed; however, our focus here is on firms with long time horizons. They can afford some expenditures that will affect the direction of taste change, depending on the level of that expenditure and its precise direction and the amount of change.

Advertising as a means of transmitting information

The array of goods available in a modern society is vast and changing. One informational service of advertising is to alert the consumer to the existence of products he has never encountered. In recent years, rapidly developing semiconductor technology has made available very small, inexpensive, versatile calculating ma-chines, as well as digital watches and other products. When they were first available, these items cost much more than they presently do. It was necessary to advertise to reach people for whom an expense of several hundred dollars for a calculator would be worthwhile. Because these new devices were faster, smaller, and at least as capable as electromechanical calculators that cost one to two thousand dollars, there was a ready market to be tapped. This was not a mass market, but as it became clear that such calculators could be produced much more cheaply and that a mass market might be tapped, advertising became worthwhile in mass media. It is now common for calculators to be purchased for children to use in their schoolwork and for adults to use for mundane tasks like balancing a checkbook.

In addition to new products, some consumers need to be alerted to the existence of products that may have been around for a long time but that have specialized uses. At various times in a person's life, new interests emerge. Sometimes this is because the person takes an interest in a new hobby; in other cases it can stem from normal changes in mode of living. An example of the former is the person who decides to take up photography. There are many specialized items of equipment and supplies that generally will be unknown to someone who has never had an interest in photography, and for a while they will remain unknown to the novice. The novice may learn of them through ads in photography magazines or from the sales staff in a photography shop. Examples of the latter are when a person first becomes a parent, first owns an automobile, or first owns a house. All of these common events occasion interests that may not have been awakened before. The consumer may discover products that have existed for years, even centuries, but they are new to him.

A second informational aspect of advertising is that it can instruct in the uses or specifications of a product. A prospective (or, indeed, experienced) camper probably will know that sleeping bags exist, but he may not know that the insulating material used in them can be of several types, that more than one shape is available, and that sleeping bags made of any particular insulating material are available in several thicknesses. Advertising, in the form of paid advertisements, catalogues of mail order firms, or assistance from a sales staff, can provide these facts.

Third, there may be a relationship between brand identification and reliability. Some products cannot be fully judged by a consumer when he inspects them. This is most obviously true of complex durable goods such as household appliances, typewriters, clocks, and watches. If advertising helps a particular brand to become well known, and, further, if it proves reliable or unreliable, the consumer has this information to help in making later decisions. An unknown brand of an item without a brand name cannot carry with it the assurance of quality or assurance of the manufacturer's willingness to repair defects that a well-known brand may carry.

The preceding discussion is based on the implicit assumption that advertising is always truthful and reliable. Undoubtedly, this is not always the case; however, experienced consumers are likely to have a fairly good idea of which ads, at least in the printed and broadcast media, are reliable. Obviously, many ads contain vague claims of excellence or carry endorsements from well-known people who are intended to impress the consumer. Very likely, such ads do no more than remind the consumer of a product's existence. Verbal advertising, that is to say, what salespeople tell consumers, may sometimes be harder to gauge, particularly when the consumer has no prior experience with that particular salesperson.

Advertising and tastes

The usual economists' definition of tastes is, in essence, the consumer's indifference map at a particular point in time. It does not follow that a consumer is without an indifference map just because he lacks some information about certain goods. Two possibilities are easily imagined. First, the consumer may possess (or act as if he possesses) a traditional indifference map defined with respect to those commodities of which he is aware. Second, his purchases may exhibit a systematic randomness that can be interpreted to mean that his preferences are not precisely defined. Under this interpretation, one commodity bundle will be regarded as superior to another if, when the consumer is confronted with a choice between the two, he chooses the first bundle more than half the time. The bundles will be called indifferent if he chooses them equally often. Of course, this criterion is not operational if the consumer's tastes are not stationary. A second source of randomness is the consumer's desire to sample various items to acquire information. Faced with several types and brands of bread, a commodity purchased very frequently, it makes a great deal of sense to try all types that might be pleasing. And, as Scitovsky (1976) points out, the consumer may seek variety for its own sake.

For the sake of clarity, assume that the consumer does have a well-defined and precise indifference map at any instant of time. This indifference map surely changes in response to information, and advertising often provides information. In some instances the consumer will deliberately seek information before buying a good. In others he will have information thrust upon him as part of the process of buying, and in yet others he will receive information, as it were, by accident, as a by-product of other activities. An example of the first is when the consumer consults promotional material or salespeople for the purpose of acquiring information in aid of a decision. An example of the second occurs when a salesperson insists on giving the consumer information he did not request. An example of the third occurs when the consumer listens to the radio or watches television and receives information as a by-product of tuning in to a particular program. Thus, in the short run, information provided through advertising may alter the instantaneous indifference map, which is to say it may alter tastes.

It is often noted that some aspects of tastes are acquired. Many foods are found to be unpalatable when first sampled, but if a person samples such a food from time to time, he may find that he likes it after a while. It may even become a favorite. Many activities that require skill (e.g., hobbies like tennis, golf, fishing, and painting) may be downright unpleasant for a person who is a novice; however, the person may persevere in the belief that he can acquire considerable skill and that when he does, the activity will be very pleasurable. Clearly, this is often true. Equally clearly, it is sometimes false. The person may acquire great skill and never take pleasure in the activity, or perhaps he may never reach even a moderate level of skill. Likewise, a person may decide not to take up an activity that would have been very pleasurable for him had he pursued it. Apart from tastes at which the consumer must work, it remains possible that the past path of consumption will affect the present indifference map. For example, on first introduction to orchestral music a person may be pleased and at the same time may find chamber music unpleasant. Over time, after listening to the music he likes, some of the music previously disliked may come to sound better. Here the consumer is not purposely subjecting himself to unpleasant activities for the sake of future gratification, but, nonetheless, past enjoyable activities are changing his reactions to other activities.

The relevance to advertising of these aspects of intertemporal changes in tastes is that promotional efforts may affect a consumer's tastes, and hence his choices in the marketplace in the future. By vigorously promoting tennis today, the makers of tennis balls may do little for current sales, but much more for sales a few years hence.

All of the preceding discussion presumes that tastes are affected through advertising by the provision of "useful" information. Can advertising lead consumers by the nose through the provision of no information at all or of "useless" information? Consider ads that associate a particular product with elegant living or with famous and admired people. A shirt, a tennis racquet, a food item, or a vacation package may be endorsed in an ad by a well-known person or may be pictured in use in a setting many consumers might wish to copy but cannot. Does such advertising affect purchases by more than the mere reminder that the product exists? The extensive use of this kind of advertising is circumstantial evidence that it does. Some would call the information provided in such ads useless and would say that the effect is an (undesirable) distortion of preferences. Others would say that whatever results from free play in markets for goods, ideas, and persuasion is superior to whatever does not thus result. The answers are not obvious, at least to me, but it is difficult to take up the subject of advertising without touching on these issues to bring them to the reader's attention.

6.3. Advertising and its effect on consumer demand

Holding all firms' prices fixed, it is surely true that advertising expenditures increase the sales of a firm, at least up to a saturation level. Beyond this, there are two aspects of the effect of advertising to consider further. One is the interfirm effect and the other, the intertemporal.

The interfirm aspects of advertising

Taking first the interfirm effect, it is not plausible that advertising by one firm will take sales away from its rival; nor is the converse plausible, that rivals will always be helped. Some stylized examples should be illuminating. At one extreme, fresh milk appears to be a good for which advertising is close to being *purely cooperative.* That is to say, the effect of advertising on a firm's sales is more or less the same no matter which firm undertakes the advertising. Although milk is marketed under brand names, there appears to be very little brand loyalty among customers. The purchaser of whole milk, skim milk, heavy cream, and so forth, typically cannot tell one brand from another by taste and does not believe one brand can be distinguished from another. Perhaps familiarity with a brand brings an assurance of uniform, standard quality, and a totally new brand will require time for acceptance; however, once established in a locality, I conjecture that brand loyalty is not important in the choice among the established brands.[1] It follows, then, that the advertising of a firm is not going to switch consumers from one brand to another to any significant extent. If successful, the advertising of milk will increase the aggregate of consumers' milk purchases, with increased sales being distributed among firms in a way unrelated to the distribution of advertising expenditures among firms. Advertising in this situation is a pure local public good among the milk producers, and it would be natural for them to cooperate on joint advertising efforts with a single advertising campaign associated with no particular brand. In fact, this is often seen. Milk tends to be advertised jointly, and, on the whole, the advertising undertaken by individual dairy products firms is concentrated on the more highly processed, and hence more differentiated, goods such as ice cream and yogurt.

The second example is cigarettes, about which I wish to make an extreme assumption that may not be quite true, but that is convenient for illustration. Pretend that no one ever became a smoker or a heavier smoker because of advertising or promotional effort. Then, in contrast to the situation with milk, advertising cannot enlarge the size of the market as a whole, as it can with milk. If a firm's advertising is to have any impact, the impact is to take customers from rival firms. In this case, advertising can be called *purely predatory.*[2]

As a rule, the effect of advertising in an industry will lie between these two extremes. Note that advertising can be cooperative without being purely cooperative. This means that when a firm advertises, other firms are aided; however, one or both of the following conditions also hold: (a) Another firm is benefited less than if it had undertaken the advertising itself. (b) The firm that advertises is benefited more than any one of its rivals. Although the concept of purely cooperative advertising may be intuitively acceptable, it is seen in the next section that it is not easy to define with perfect clarity. Simply *cooperative advertising* is easy to define. The required condition is that advertising expenditure by one firm increase the sales of each firm in the market.

Parallel statements can be made about *predatory advertising.* If an increase in advertising by one firm causes a decrease in the sales of all of its rivals, then that advertising can be termed predatory, although the firm that advertises may gain more than the aggregate of what its rivals lose. The extreme, purely predatory advertising, is reached if, in a well-defined sense, the gain to the firm that advertises is totally at the expense of the rival firms.

Whether advertising is predatory or cooperative can, in principle, depend on both the nature of the product being advertised and the kind of advertising campaign the firm uses. The former is structural, the latter behavioral. My belief is that whether advertising is predatory or cooperative is, in practice, almost exclusively a structural characteristic, and it is taken to be entirely structural throughout this chapter. My reasons for believing the behavioral element to be unimportant are two-fold. First, I think the nature of the product is very important in determining the interfirm effects of advertising. Second, I do not think a firm ever gains by failing to center its advertising around its own brand and company names. Thus, firms do not *directly* advertise on an industry basis. They sometimes do so indirectly through trade associations, particularly when advertising is structurally very cooperative. In other words, a dairy products firm that touts its own milk as fresher and better tasting than that of its rivals will, in my view, accomplish about the same for all firms as if it were simply to praise the virtues of milk, but it has nothing to lose by tooting its own horn. The salient fact is that milk advertising is structurally cooperative.

The intertemporal aspects of advertising

It is not believable that the advertising efforts of a firm bear fruit immediately following the efforts themselves and nothing thereafter. It is more plausible that advertising creates a kind of intangible capital, which might be called goodwill, that lasts for a long time. As with the economist's conception of physical capital, if nothing is added to the stock of goodwill, it probably declines in size over time, just as physical capital depreciates. Physical capital can depreciate in either of two ways. A piece of capital equipment may function in exactly the same way for all of its lifetime, then fail completely like a light bulb. In this case, depreciation over time merely reflects that the remaining productive lifetime of the item is diminishing as time passes. The second form of depreciation stems from a decreasing rate of flow of net services as the capital good ages. Thus, a piece of machinery may spend an increasing fraction of its time being repaired as it ages. It is the latter view of depreciation that is analogous to the shrinking of goodwill over time. Goodwill can, of course, be made to grow over time by making advertising expenditures sufficiently large that depreciation is more than offset.

In practice, some advertising expenditures will have a very large immediate impact and a small effect on the subsequent size of goodwill, whereas other expenditures will have little or no extra immediate impact. An obvious example of the former is advertising that announces unusually low prices that will prevail only for a day or two. However, even this advertising can have a lasting effect if a few of the customers attracted by it are new to the establishment and become more favorably disposed toward it.

Most advertising probably is not intended to induce the consumer to run straight out and buy a good, at least as regards printed, broadcast, and direct mail advertising. A great deal of it is aimed at persuading the consumer that the given product is a little better or more desirable, so that when the consumer is actually interested in buying, the advertiser's product will receive more favorable consideration. The ads may also attempt to hasten the time when the consumer decides to buy, without attempting to propel him immediately from his chair.

Some advertising probably becomes more convincing over time. Or, more properly, the efforts of an advertiser will, in many instances, become more convincing the more previous advertising the firm has done. Claims may be more readily believed merely because they are repeated. Also, once claims are made, consumers who notice them may pay more attention to gathering evidence that will bear on their truth. For example, it has long been well known that a coat that is truly waterproof cannot "breathe." That is, it must be incapable of transmitting air, with the result that body moisture is trapped between the coat and the wearer, resulting in discomfort and, in colder weather, possibly a chilly wearer. On the other hand, a coat that can breathe will also become soaked in a heavy rain. A few years ago a fabric was first marketed that was claimed both to breathe and to be completely waterproof. Surely consumers who wanted to own completely waterproof coats must have been skeptical of the claims made, and many of them must have been on the alert for evidence. If these claims had proved true, the word would have spread, and the claims of the advertising would have been more widely believed, thus enhancing the effect of subsequent advertising.

Advertising messages and advertising expenditures

We can say that the firm buys some advertising messages when it spends on advertising, just as we can say that the firm buys some pens when it buys writing instruments. The commodity called the *advertising message* is difficult to define in practice. That difficulty is sidestepped in the next section, where a relationship between messages and expenditures is assumed; however, it is important to discuss as well as possible what is meant. As a concrete example, imagine a magazine advertisement for photographic enlargers. A message can be thought of as a minute spent looking at such an ad by a potential customer, and a potential customer can be defined as an amateur photographer who has his own darkroom or who is actively considering acquiring one.[3]

Imagine now a sum of money spent on a magazine ad in one of the photography magazines, a large number of whose readers will be potential customers. Surely, the larger the ad, the larger the number of people who will look at it, and, perhaps, the longer the average time spent looking. Beyond some critical small size, however, the number of message units from an ad is likely to rise more slowly than the cost of the ad. The cost itself will go up a little slower than the size, measured in square inches. Thus, diminishing returns is a plausible assumption, at least as applied to advertising in one place.

Compare now an ad of the same cost placed in a photography magazine and in a mass-circulation news magazine. More people will see the news magazines – so many more that the number of viewers per dollar spent probably will be higher in the news magazine than in the photography magazine. But if more potential customers see the photography magazine ad, it will produce more message units per dollar spent, because only a small fraction of news magazine readers are amateur photographers. The ads actually appearing in a news magazine are typically for products of very general interest, and those in a photography magazine are for products of narrow interest. Surely a toothpaste ad in a photography magazine will buy fewer message units per dollar spent than a similar ad in a news magazine.

But an enlarger manufacturer may find it profitable to place some advertising in magazines that have lower proportions of amateur photographers among their readers than the photography magazines. Such advertising may be more productive than spending for even larger ads in the latter. Such a firm would seek out magazines catering to interests that are common, though not universal, among amateur photographers and not too common among the whole population, so that the readership would include a moderate percentage of photographers. Perhaps travel magazines would be a suitable candidate. Whatever the right example, the point is that the firm will advertise in the most effective medium, then add to that the next most effective medium, and so on. Hence, just as ad size within one magazine is carried out to the appropriate point on the intensive margin, it is carried out among media to the appropriate point on the extensive margin.

6.4. Formal models of advertising in monopoly and oligopoly

Three models of advertising are presented in this section, one in each of the following subsections. The first two of these are for monopolistic firms. They are discussed partly because of the interest that has been taken in them and partly as stepping-stones toward the fuller model of advertising in oligopoly, which is presented last.

The ideas embodied in the last of these models have been around in some form for up to nearly sixty years. Marshall (1919) made brief reference to cooperative and predatory advertising. For a general understanding of the economic aspects of advertising, the discussions of Braithwaite (1928) and Chamberlin (1933, Chapters 6 and 7) are very good. Early models appeared in the work of Chamberlin (1933), Buchanan (1942), and Dorfman and Steiner (1954). The idea of treating advertising as creating a stock of goodwill was modeled in the frequently cited article by Nerlove and Arrow (1962), although the idea that spending on advertising is like investing in a capital good goes back further (e.g., Chamberlin). The earliest formal modeling of an oligopoly with advertising that could be predatory or cooperative of which I am aware was that of Shubik, communicated to me over twenty years ago. Such a model appeared in an unpublished working paper in 1961, and a variant has been published (Shubik, 1980). For a blend of theoretical models along with discussion of some of the empirical findings on advertising, Schmalensee (1972) is very good.

A static model of advertising for a monopolistic firm

The simple model presented here is due to Dorfman and Steiner (1954) and is attractive because of a tidy equilibrium condition. Letting p denote the price charged by a monopolistic firm, s its advertising expenditure, $q = f(p, s)$ its demand function, and $C(q)$ its total cost function, profits are $pf(p, s) - C[f(p, s)] - s = \pi$. The first-order conditions for profit maximization are

$$\frac{\partial \pi}{\partial p} = q + (p - C')f^1 = 0 \tag{6.1}$$

$$\frac{\partial \pi}{\partial s} = (p - C')f^2 - 1 = 0 \tag{6.2}$$

From equation (6.1), $p - C' = -q/f^1$, and from equation (6.2), $p - C' = 1/f^2$; hence, $-q/f^1 = 1/f^2$. If both sides of the latter expression are multiplied by q/sp, the expression can be rewritten $(q/s)[-q/(pf^1)] = (1/p)[q/(sf^2)]$. Noting that the elasticity of demand with respect to price is $-pf^1/q = \epsilon_p$ and the elasticity of demand with respect to advertising is $sf^2/q = \epsilon_s$, the expression becomes $q/(s\epsilon_p) = 1/(p\epsilon_s)$, or

$$\frac{\epsilon_s}{\epsilon_p} = \frac{s}{pq} \tag{6.3}$$

which is the main result of the Dorfman and Steiner analysis. If the two demand elasticities are constant, or at least have a constant ratio, then optimal advertising as a fraction of total revenue is constant. This is of interest because there is some empirical evidence supporting the constancy of advertising as a fraction of revenue. That fraction varies from one industry to another, but according to Schmalensee (1972), constancy of the advertising-to-revenue ratio is common.

Stepping quite far outside the models of this chapter for a moment, imagine firms operating in an uncertain world in which it is rather difficult to discern the effects of advertising. It is plausible that firms will peg the level of advertising expenditures at the fraction of total revenue that appears, on best educated guess, to be optimal. Rather than devote a large amount of executive energy and resources to a very amorphous decision problem, this rule of thumb may be allowed to stand for years, undergoing occasional review and revision when special attention is drawn to the subject. Why that particular rule of thumb? One could answer Why not? But to be less flippant, among a set of reasonable, simple rules, it has the virtue of cutting costs if the firm goes into recession or of expanding advertising effort as the enterprise grows. Such changes may not be optimal, but they may appear quite attractive if the effects of advertising are more a matter of faith than hard evidence.

There is a second explanation for the stability of the advertising-to-revenue ratio. A firm may advertise more intensively when a product is new or has been greatly redesigned, and less intensively as time goes on after that. If a firm markets a large array of products, each of which is in a somewhat different phase of the age cycle, then, on a product-by-product basis, those being newly introduced will have large expenditures relative to sales, and those that have been around for a long time will have small expenditures relative to sales. Across the firm, however, the aggregate ratio may be quite stable despite the great variation within products.

Returning to equation (6.3), although some very simple results in economics are believable, this one may be too good to be true. In addition to requiring constancy of the ratio of two elasticities, a very strong condition, it also ignores the capital good aspect of advertising.

A model of advertising for a multiperiod monopolist

A continuous-time model of a single firm with advertising expenditures contributing to a capitallike goodwill has been worked out by Nerlove and Arrow (1962). The model set forth next is a discrete-time analog to their model. Adding time subscripts to the symbols in the preceding section, and letting goodwill in period t be denoted by S_t and the depreciation rate of goodwill be denoted by $1 - \delta$, *goodwill* is given by the relation $S_t = \delta S_{t-1} + s_t$, and the demand function is $q_t = f(p_t, S_t)$ for period t. Noting that period-t advertising expenditure can be expressed in terms of current and past goodwill as $s_t = S_t - \delta S_{t-1}$, the profit of period t is $\pi_t = p_t f(p_t, S_t) - C[f(p_t, S_t)] - (S_t - \delta S_{t-1})$, and letting α be the discount parameter, the firm's *discounted profits* are[4]

$$\sum_{t=1}^{\infty} \alpha^{t-1}\{p_t f(p_t, S_t) - C[f(p_t, S_t)] - (S_t - \delta S_{t-1})\} \tag{6.4}$$

The firm can be considered to choose a plan, or *strategy,* of the form $\sigma = (p_1, S_1, p_2, S_2, \ldots)$, where any nonnegative price is admissible, and any goodwill level is admissible as long as it is nonnegative and, in addition, satisfies $S_t \geq \delta S_{t-1}$. The latter relation is based on the assumption that the firm's goodwill cannot be sold or even thrown away. If it diminishes, the fastest rate at which it can fall is given by $S_t = \delta S_{t-1}$, which requires a zero rate of advertising expenditure. To treat goodwill as a decision variable, instead of advertising expenditure, is analytically more convenient; however, it carries no different implications for the firm's behavior than if expenditure were used.

Denote discounted profits, given by equation (6.4), as $G(\sigma)$, and examine the first-order conditions for an interior maximum of discounted profits:

$$\frac{\partial G}{\partial p_t} = \alpha^{t-1}[f_t + (p_t - C_t')f_t^1] = 0 \tag{6.5}$$

$$\frac{\partial G}{\partial S_t} = \alpha^{t-1}[(p_t - C_t')f_t^2 - 1 + \alpha\delta] = 0 \tag{6.6}$$

for $t = 1, 2, \ldots$. Manipulating these two conditions for a given value of t, as done in the preceding section for the Dorfman-Steiner model, yields

$$\frac{\epsilon_S}{\epsilon_p} = \frac{(1 - \alpha\delta)S_t}{p_t q_t} \tag{6.7}$$

where ϵ_S is the elasticity of demand with respect to goodwill. Although equation (6.7) bears a strong resemblance to equation (6.3), it implies very different behavior for the level of advertising expenditures s_t. If the elasticity ratio were constant, the firm's rule would be to choose s_t, advertising expenditures, in a way that would keep the ratio of goodwill to revenue constant. Under such a policy, the advertising-to-revenue ratio would decline sharply in the downswing of a cycle and rise sharply in an upswing.

Intuitively, the Nerlove-Arrow notion of goodwill is very appealing. If it is true that empirical data support the near constancy of the advertising-to-revenue ratio, the explanation is unlikely to lie in the twin conditions of advertising having only a current-period effect (as in the Dorfman-Steiner model) coupled with constancy of the ratio of demand elasticities. Each of these conditions is implausible, but when combined they defy belief altogether. It is much more likely that the constancy of the advertising-to-revenue ratio either is not in fact true or is explained by phenomena that have not yet entered the analytical models.

A model of oligopoly with advertising

The model presented in this section carries over the Nerlove-Arrow (1962) concept of goodwill and embeds it in an n-firm oligopoly model under complete information. Two other features are prominent: Interfirm advertising effects can be either cooperative or predatory, and expenditure on advertising shows decreasing returns in ways that are made specific later. The remainder of this section is subdivided into two parts. In the first, the model is explained in relatively general terms; in the second, a special case is examined for which some specific comparative static results can be obtained. The model itself is taken from Friedman (1980).

The general model. Notation from previous sections is carried over, with the change that $p_t = (p_{1t}, \ldots, p_{nt})$ is a *price vector* for period t, and similarly with other variables such as s_t, S_t, and q_t. The cost of advertising is related to goodwill by the relationship $s_{it} = \theta_i(S_{it}, S_{i,t-1})$, and the formulation used in the Nerlove-Arrow model is a special case of this. It is assumed of θ_i that $\theta_i(S_{it}, S_{i,t-1}) = \max\{0, \theta_i^*(S_{it}, S_{i,t-1})\}$ for $i = 1, \ldots, n$, where θ_i^* satisfies (a) $\theta_i^*(S_{it}, S_{i,t-1})$ is twice continuously differentiable and convex, (b) $\theta_i^*(0, 0) = 0$, (c) $\theta_i^{*1} > 0$, (d) $\theta_i^{*2} < 0$, (e) $0 < \theta_i^*(S_i, S_i) < S_i$, and (f) $\theta_i^{*1}(S_i, S_i) + \theta_i^{*2}(S_i, S_i) > 0$ for $S_i > 0$. Going over these conditions again, the first provision is that advertising expenditure cannot be negative. Apart from differentiability, condition (a) stipulates that θ_i^{11} and θ_i^{22} are both positive, along with $\theta_i^{11}\theta_i^{22} - \theta_i^{12}\theta_i^{12} \geq 0$. The significance of condition (a) is better understood in light of (c) and (d). Condition (b) merely states that if advertising expenditure is always zero, then goodwill will always be zero. Condition (c) requires that for given $S_{i,t-1}$, the larger the firm wishes to make S_{it}, the more it will cost. That is, the marginal cost of increasing goodwill is positive. $\theta_i^{11} > 0$ means that θ_i^1 increases as S_{it} increases; hence, the marginal cost of adding a unit to goodwill rises as the amount the firm wishes to add increases. Condition (d) means that the cost of achieving a specific level of S_{it} is smaller as $S_{i,t-1}$ is larger. From condition (e), the cost of maintaining a constant level of goodwill is positive, but less than the goodwill level itself. Finally, condition (f) says that the cost of maintaining a specific level of goodwill rises as the level to be maintained increases. This goodwill investment function is a variant of the investment function used by Prescott (1973).

Rather than have goodwill directly enter the demand function, it is assumed that an *advertising effectiveness* variable $h_{it} = E_i(S_t)$ enters the demand function; h_{it} depends on the goodwill levels of all firms in the market and can reflect either cooperative or predatory advertising. More specifically, for all $S_t \in R_+^n$, $E_i(S_t)$ is continuous and twice continuously differentiable, and $E_i^i(S_t) > 0$. In addition, $E_i^{ii}(S_t) \leq 0$ (i.e., E_i is concave and S_{it}), and there exists $(\rho_1, \dots, \rho_n) > 0$ such that $\sum_{j=1}^n \rho_j E_i^j(S_t) > 0$ for all i. The conditions given earlier are really quite mild. $E_i^i > 0$ means that demand is increased for firm i whenever its own goodwill is increased. $E_i^{ii} \leq 0$ is a diminishing returns condition, which means that as S_{it} rises, the marginal benefit to demand falls. This is the second diminishing returns condition placed on advertising. The first is the convexity of θ_i, which implies that the cost of adding to goodwill tends to rise per unit added as the size of goodwill rises.

Whether advertising is predatory or cooperative is defined in terms of characteristics of the advertising effectiveness functions, E_i. If, for all firms i, $E_i^j > 0$ ($j = 1, \dots, n$), then *advertising is cooperative.* An increase in the goodwill of any one firm leads to increased advertising effectiveness for all firms. Conversely, if $E_i^j < 0$ ($j \neq i$) for all i, then *advertising is predatory.* An increase in the goodwill of one firm brings with it a decrease in advertising effectiveness for all rival firms. It is less easy to define perfectly cooperative and perfectly predatory advertising, particularly the former. Here are two candidates for *perfectly cooperative advertising:* First, $E_i^j = E_i^i$ for all i and j. Second, $E_j^i = E_i^i$ for all i and j. The first definition specifies that advertising is perfectly cooperative when a marginal increase in a firm's goodwill is precisely as potent in raising its advertising effectiveness as a marginal increase in the goodwill of some other firm. That is, whichever firm does the advertising, the influence on h_i is the same. Under the second definition, the influence of an increase in the goodwill of firm i is the same on firm i as it is on firm j.

Perfectly predatory advertising can be characterized by the condition that $\Sigma_{i=1}^n E_i(S_t)$ is the same for all values of S_t. In a sense, this says that the size of the pie is invariant to the goodwill levels of the firms. Advertising affects only the way the pie is split among them.[5]

Demand is modeled in the form of an *inverse demand function* for each firm, $p_{it} = f_i(q_t, h_{it})$, and *single-period profits* are

$$
\begin{aligned}
\pi_{it} &= q_{it} f_i(q_t, h_{it}) - C_i(q_{it}) - s_{it} \\
&= q_{it} f_i[q_t, E_i(S_t)] - C_i(q_{it}) - \theta_i(S_{it}, S_{i,t-1}) \\
&= \pi_i(q_t, S_t, S_{i,t-1})
\end{aligned} \tag{6.8}
$$

Only certain values of S_t and S_{t-1} are admissible. It is assumed that total revenue for a firm in a single period is bounded above by an amount M; therefore, a firm will never have an incentive to allow goodwill to exceed S_i^0, defined by $\theta_i(S_i^0, S_i^0) = M/(1 - \alpha_i)$. Maintaining a goodwill level of S_i^0 will assure that the firm will spend more on advertising in one period than it can receive in discounted revenue. Thus, a firm will never maintain such a high level, and S_{it} must always fall beneath this upper bound. A second admissibility condition comes from the relationship of S_{it} to $S_{i,t-1}$. S_{it} cannot be smaller than the value it will have if $s_{it} = 0$. That value is given by the condition $0 = \theta_i^*(S_{it}, S_{i,t-1})$. Conditions placed on the demand

and total revenue functions are as follows: $f_i(q_t, h_{it})$ is defined, continuous, and nonnegative for all $q_t \in R^n_+$ and $h_{it} \in R$. Additionally, (a) $q_{it} f_i(q_t, h_{it}) \leq M < \infty$ for all (q_t, h_{it}), (b) $q_{it} f_i(q_t, h_{it})$ is concave in (q_{it}, h_{it}) for any (q_t, h_{it}) at which $q_{it} f_i(q_t, h_{it})$ is positive, and (c) for all values of q_t, S_t, and S_{t-1} such that S_t and S_{t-1} are admissible and $f_i[q_t, E_i(S_t)] > 0$ for all i, $f_i[q_t, E_i(S_t)]$ is twice continuously differentiable, with $f^j_i < 0$ for all j and $f^{n+1}_i > 0$.

Condition (a) forces total revenue to be bounded. The concavity condition (b) is a part of the guarantee that the profit-maximizing strategy of a firm will change in a continuous way as strategies of other firms are changed. Condition (c) requires that a firm's price be a decreasing function of any firm's output level and that increases in goodwill lead to increases in price, all output levels remaining constant.

The cost function is subject to the same conditions that are imposed in Chapter 2: $C_i(q_{it})$ is continuous and twice differentiable for all $q_{it} \geq 0$, with $C_i(0) \geq 0$, $C'_i(q_{it}) > 0$, and $C''_i(q_{it}) \geq 0$.

A *strategy for firm i*, denoted σ_i, can be thought of as $(q_{i1}, S_{i1}, q_{i2}, S_{i2}, \ldots)$. Because S_{i0} appears in the model in the determination of s_{i1} and S_{i1}, it must be given a value, and zero is suitable if the market begins at time $t = 1$. A *strategy combination*, that is, a vector of strategies, is written $\sigma = (\sigma_1, \ldots, \sigma_n)$, and the *discounted profits of a firm* as a function of the strategies are

$$G_i(\sigma) = \sum_{t=1}^{\infty} \alpha_i^{t-1} \pi_i(q_t, S_t, S_{i,t-1}) \tag{6.9}$$

with $S_{i0} = 0$.[6] A *noncooperative equilibrium* in this model is an admissible strategy combination σ^* such that no single firm can change its strategy and increase its discounted profits, given the equilibrium strategies of the other firms. It is proved elsewhere (Friedman, 1980) that any model satisfying the conditions given earlier has such an equilibrium. Additional assumptions are provided that ensure that any equilibrium involves strictly positive goodwill, price, and output for each firm in each time period and that ensure the uniqueness of equilibrium. To gain some insight into the effects of advertising on market equilibrium, it is helpful to look at a simpler model than the one proposed earlier. This is done in the next section.

Some comparative statics in a model of oligopoly with advertising. If a special case of the model in the preceding subsection is examined, it proves possible to obtain closed-form solutions to the equilibrium conditions. This facilitates examination of the way that parameter changes affect equilibrium, and, in addition, it is possible to study the effects of government regulation, at least in a limited way. To that end, let the demand, advertising effectiveness, cost, and advertising expenditure functions be

$$p_{it} = u_0 - \frac{\lambda a}{2} q_{it} - b \sum_{j \neq i} q_{jt} + h_{it} = f_i(q_t, h_{it}) \tag{6.10}$$

$$h_{it} = S_{it} + w \sum_{j \neq i} S_{jt} = E_i(S_t) \tag{6.11}$$

$$C_i(q_{it}) = v_0 q_{it} + \frac{(1 - \lambda)a}{2} q_{it}^2 \tag{6.12}$$

$$S_{it} = \gamma_1 S_{it} - \gamma_2 S_{i,t-1} + \frac{\gamma_{11}}{2} S_{it}^2 + \gamma_{12} S_{it} S_{i,t-1} + \frac{\gamma_{22}}{2} S_{i,t-1}^2$$

$$= \theta_i(S_{it}, S_{i,t-1}) \tag{6.13}$$

Letting $u = u_0 - v_0$, the single-period profit function is

$$\pi_{it} = u q_{it} - \frac{a}{2} q_{it}^2 - b q_{it} \sum_{j \neq i} q_{jt} + q_{it} S_{it} + w q_{it} \sum_{j \neq i} S_{jt}$$

$$- \left(\gamma_1 S_{it} - \gamma_2 S_{i,t-1} + \frac{\gamma_{11}}{2} S_{it}^2 + \gamma_{12} S_{it} S_{i,t-1} + \frac{\gamma_{22}}{2} S_{i,t-1}^2 \right) \tag{6.14}$$

The parameters a, b, γ_1, γ_2, γ_{11}, and γ_{22} are all nonnegative; $a > b$; $\gamma_{11}\gamma_{22} > \gamma_{12}^2$; λ is between zero and one; w lies between $-1/(n - 1)$ and 1; and $\gamma_1 > \alpha\gamma_2$.

The parameter w should be examined closely. It characterizes the degree to which advertising is cooperative or predatory. If w is positive, then advertising is cooperative; however, as w grows closer to 1, advertising converges to being perfectly cooperative (by both of the definitions offered earlier). In the other direction, negative w corresponds to predatory advertising, and as w approaches

$-1/(n-1)$, advertising becomes perfectly predatory in the sense that at the extreme value, the sum $\sum_{i=1}^{n} h_{it}$ is constant for all values of S_t.

Under conditions stated elsewhere (Friedman, 1980), the general model described in the preceding subsection has steady-state output and goodwill vectors, q^* and S^*, to which the firms converge over time under noncooperative equilibrium behavior. These steady-state values are the same for any initial conditions S_0. It is the behavior of these steady-state values as parameters of the model are changed that is investigated next. As a first step, the equations of motion of the system are found for equilibrium behavior. Following these equations leads to the steady-state values. When equilibrium behavior implies positive output levels and positive steady-state levels in all periods, the conditions describing equilibrium are the usual first-order conditions for an interior maximum, namely,

$$\frac{\partial G_i}{\partial q_{it}} = \alpha^{t-1} \frac{\partial \pi_{it}}{\partial q_{it}} = 0 = \frac{\partial \pi_{it}}{\partial q_{it}} \tag{6.15}$$

$$\frac{\partial G_i}{\partial S_{it}} = \alpha^{t-1} \left(\frac{\partial \pi_{it}}{\partial S_{it}} + \alpha \frac{\partial \pi_{i,t+1}}{\partial S_{it}} \right) = \frac{\partial \pi_{it}}{\partial S_{it}} + \alpha \frac{\partial \pi_{i,t+1}}{\partial S_{it}} = 0 \tag{6.16}$$

for $i = 1, \ldots, n$ and $t = 1, 2, \ldots$. Equations (6.15) and (6.16), in terms of the basic parameters of the model, are, respectively,

$$u - aq_{it} - b \sum_{j \neq i} q_{it} + S_{it} + w \sum_{j \neq i} S_{jt} = 0 \tag{6.17}$$

$$(-\gamma_1 + \alpha\gamma_2) + q_{it} - \gamma_{12}S_{i,t-1} - (\gamma_{11} + \alpha\gamma_{22})S_{it} - \alpha\gamma_{12}S_{i,t+1} = 0 \tag{6.18}$$

Letting **1** be the vector whose n coordinates are all 1,

$$A = \begin{bmatrix} -a & -b & \ldots & -b \\ -b & -a & \ldots & -b \\ \cdot & \cdot & & \cdot \\ \cdot & \cdot & & \cdot \\ \cdot & \cdot & & \cdot \\ -b & -b & \ldots & -a \end{bmatrix} \quad B = \begin{bmatrix} 1 & w & \ldots & w \\ w & 1 & \ldots & w \\ \cdot & \cdot & & \cdot \\ \cdot & \cdot & & \cdot \\ \cdot & \cdot & & \cdot \\ w & w & \ldots & 1 \end{bmatrix} \tag{6.19}$$

Letting $\delta = \gamma_{11} + \alpha\gamma_{22}$ and rearranging terms, the equation system (6.17) and (6.18) can be written

$$\begin{bmatrix} A & B \\ I & -\delta I \end{bmatrix}\begin{bmatrix} q_t \\ S_t \end{bmatrix} = \begin{bmatrix} -u\mathbf{1} \\ \gamma\mathbf{1} + \gamma_{12}S_{t-1} + \alpha\gamma_{12}S_{t+1} \end{bmatrix} \tag{6.20}$$

where I is the $n \times n$ identity matrix and $\gamma = \gamma_1 - \alpha\gamma_2$. For the steady-state values, $S_{t-1} = S_t = S_{t+1} = S^*$ and $q_t = q^*$. Letting $v = \gamma_{11} + (1 + \alpha)\gamma_{12} + \alpha\gamma_{22}$, the steady-state values are the solution to

$$\begin{bmatrix} A & B \\ I & -vI \end{bmatrix}\begin{bmatrix} q \\ S \end{bmatrix} = \begin{bmatrix} -u\mathbf{1} \\ \gamma\mathbf{1} \end{bmatrix} \tag{6.21}$$

and the steady-state values themselves are

$$S_i^* = \frac{\gamma[a + (n-1)b] - 1}{[1 + (n-1)w] - v[a + (n-1)b]} \tag{6.22}$$

$$q_i^* = (a-b)[1 + (n-1)w]S_i^* + \frac{u}{a + (n-1)b} \tag{6.23}$$

if the expressions in equations (6.22) and (6.23) are nonnegative. The denominator in equation (6.22) is always negative; hence, equation (6.22) is nonnegative if $\gamma[a + (n-1)b]$ is less than or equal to one. If equation (6.22) is negative, then $S_i^* = 0$. Equation (6.23) is always positive because $a > b$, $1 + (n-1)w > 0$, $S_i^* \geq 0$, $u > 0$, $a > 0$, and $b > 0$.

Provided S_i^* is positive, it rises as advertising becomes more cooperative. As S_i^* increases with w, q_i^* increases even more quickly. Intuitively, when w rises, a firm gains more in equilibrium by purchasing an additional unit of goodwill. This is because of the positive relationship between one firm's equilibrium goodwill and that of the others. Adding a unit to S_i will induce others to increase their S_j. The higher is w, the more the ith firm gains (if $w > 0$) or the less it loses (if $w < 0$) by the consequent change induced in the other firms' behavior. Note, however, that as w approaches its lower limit of $-1/(n-1)$, the effect of S^* on q^* converges to zero. Given that advertising only shuffles an existing pool of demand among the firms when $w = -1/(n-1)$, it is no surprise that the equilibrium level of advertising does not affect equilibrium output.

In a somewhat special, but still interesting, way it is possible to examine the effect on long-run equilibrium due to a government policy of banning advertising in certain media or, alternatively, of taxing firms' advertising expenditures. Denying an industry access to a particular medium, as happened in the United States when advertising cigarettes on television was prohibited, is akin to taxing the firms' advertising expenditures, for it increases the cost of purchasing advertising messages. Modeled in the simplest way, the advertising expense functions, θ_i, can be replaced with the form $m\theta_i$, where m is a parameter set by the government and has a value greater than or equal to one. Thus, each parameter γ_i and γ_{ij} $(i,j = 1, 2)$ is multiplied by m, and the equilibrium values become

$$S_i^* = \frac{m\gamma[a + (n-1)b] - 1}{[1 + (n-1)w] - mv[a + (n-1)b]} \qquad (6.24)$$

$$q_i^* = (a-b)[1 + (n-1)w]S_i^* + \frac{u}{a + (n-1)b} \qquad (6.25)$$

On the one hand, if $\gamma > 0$, there is a bounded interval within which m can be varied without forcing S_i^* to zero. If $m \geq 1/\{\gamma[a + (n-1)b]\}$, then S_i^* is zero. On the other hand, if $\gamma = 0$, then no matter how large m is, S_i^* will be strictly positive. In any case,

$$\frac{\partial S_i^*}{\partial m} = \frac{(\gamma + vS_i^*)[a + (n-1)b]}{[1 + (n-1)w] - mv[a + (n-1)b]} < 0 \qquad (6.26)$$

$$\frac{\partial q_i^*}{\partial m} = (a-b)[1 + (n-1)w]\frac{\partial S_i^*}{\partial m} < 0 \qquad (6.27)$$

Again, as advertising approaches being perfectly predatory, the effect of changes in m on equilibrium output goes to zero; hence, increasing the cost of advertising to the firms will leave output unaffected. At the same time, the equilibrium goodwill level drops, suggesting that the firms save money on advertising and increase their profits. This latter suggestion can be checked by investigating the derivative of equilibrium advertising expenditures with respect to m. This is

$$\frac{\partial s_i^*}{\partial m} = s_i^* \frac{[1 + (n-1)w] + mv[a + (n-1)b]}{[1 + (n-1)w] - mv[a + (n-1)b]} < 0 \quad (6.28)$$

In summary, if cigarette advertising is perfectly predatory, then restricting firms' access to certain media will leave output levels unaffected. No one will quit smoking, smoke less, or refrain from adopting the habit. At the same time, the cost to a firm of coaxing consumers away from rival firms is increased for all firms, with the result that they all advertise less and, through saving money on advertising, increase their profits.

6.5. Summary

Advertising is an expense aimed at increasing demand, and, in general, the advertising efforts of one firm will affect demand for all firms in the market. Thus, advertising is a local public good among the firms of the industry. The public good externality can be either beneficial (cooperative advertising) or hurtful (predatory advertising), but whichever it is stems from the nature of the firms' products, not from how they choose to act.

From the standpoint of overall efficiency in the economy, it is plausible that there is too much advertising. A judicious reduction in the total could increase the welfare of everyone. To support this conjecture, consider first a market in which advertising is perfectly predatory. A general reduction in all firms' advertising could be made that would leave demand functions unchanged. Only advertising expenditure would be altered, and consumers would buy the same amounts at the same prices as before. Perhaps such a reduction could be effected in the manner of the $T1$-$T2$ strategies of Chapter 5, Section 5.4. Where advertising is cooperative, the industry stands to gain by large advertising expenditure, luring consumer dollars from other industries. This is an interindustry predatory effect that has consequences that are analogous to the intraindustry situation sketched earlier for markets in which advertising is predatory. Carried to an extreme, this suggests that zero advertising is optimal for society; however, such a view goes too far. With no information, consumers might choose less wisely than they would with modest amounts of advertising. Of course, this discussion leaves out of account the incentives that would be created for firms to arise that would specialize in the provision of information.

The intertemporal model described in the earlier section "A model of oligopoly with advertising" is one of structural time dependence. That is, the action of a firm today (choice of goodwill) enters directly into its profit function for the next period. Such a feature is present in the models of Chapters 7 and 8, and it is more realistic that this be so. Many decisions a firm makes will directly affect its environment in the future.

Another facet of advertising to bear in mind is that, in reality, it is not a simple number like price or quantity. The advertising decision is a complex decision involving where and when to advertise, how to design the ads visually and verbally, and so forth. In view of the multidimensionality of advertising, it cannot be easy to discern its effect on demand. From the firm's point of view, this effect must have a large random component, and that may have consequences for the way advertising ought to be analyzed.

7

Oligopoly with capital

To this point, all oligopoly models have assumed implicitly that firms have fixed capital stocks. Clearly, business enterprises make capital stock decisions, and such decisions are among the most important to be faced; thus it may seem strange that the topic has been avoided. The reason is that many important principles and results can be obtained without the introduction of capital stock decisions into the model. Inclusion of capital gives the firm some control over its cost function: In general, the larger the firm's capital stock, the lower its variable costs. However, this can be modeled in various ways, as the succeeding sections show. A second aspect of capital, shared by the treatment of advertising in Chapter 6, is that the size of the capital stock in period t affects the firm's position in period $t + 1$ and beyond. That is, the individual time periods cannot be regarded as structurally independent situations, and as a consequence, single-period Cournot equilibrium behavior cannot be equilibrium behavior for the firms. Indeed, if the investment decision of period t will not affect the cost function until period $t + 1$, single-period Cournot behavior will always imply zero investment. Such a suicidal policy will rarely be in the firm's best interest even if other firms act this way.

The purposes of this chapter are several. First, it may be interesting for the reader to see various ways that capital stock decisions might be incorporated into an oligopoly model. Any way that is chosen must be economically reasonable and also compatible with the existence of equilibrium. Second, the models yield economically interesting results, some of which may prove surprising. Third, in studying entry in Chapter 8, it is helpful to use a model having a capital stock decision. Section 7.1 contains a model due to Prescott (1973) in which capital is modeled in the same fashion as goodwill in Chapter 6. The model in Section 7.2 is from Friedman (1979), but the treatment of capital is conventional and has been used by many scholars for a long time. There may, however, be a novel element in the way that capital is assumed to affect the short-run cost function. In Section 7.3 a model is used that combines elements from the two earlier sections. The remarkable model described in Section 7.4 is due to Flaherty (1980*a*). In it, the firms are modeled to be absolutely identical with respect to their opportunities and knowledge; yet it is proved that the only interesting steady-state equilibria are asymmetric (i.e., at equilibrium the firms are not identical). In all models in earlier chapters in which asymmetric equilibria result, the firms are modeled to be asymmetric from the outset. They have different cost functions, as in the Cournot model, or both different cost and demand functions, as in the differentiated products models. The model in Section 7.5, due to Friedman (1977), is a continuous-time model in which adjustment costs must be paid if a firm is to alter the size of its capital stock. Because of the adjustment costs, firms change capital only at discrete intervals of time. In essence, then, the model is a model in discrete time, with the length of the time periods being endogenous. The results are relevant to Stackelberg leader-follower (or dominant-player) models, as is discussed later. Section 7.6 contains a summary.

7.1. Capital stock as productive capacity

In Prescott's formulation (1973) of a dynamic oligopoly market the firms are Cournot competitors in the sense that they produce identical goods, with a single market price being determined by the *inverse demand function* $p_t = f(Q_t)$ in each time period t. The *output of firm i* is denoted q_{it}, and, of course, $Q_t = \sum_{i=1}^{n} q_{it}$ is *total industry output*. Each firm i produces at constant *marginal* *cost* c_i; however, in period t the firm must restrict its production to be less than or equal to its *capacity* of k_{it}. Each unit of capital supplies a fixed amount of capacity; hence, the terms *capital* and *capacity* are used interchangeably in this section. Letting I_{it} denote the *gross investment* of the ith firm for period t, measured in dollars, $I_{it} = k_{it}g(k_{i,t+1}/k_{it})$. Writing this relationship in the form $I_{it}/k_{it} = g(k_{i,t+1}/k_{it})$ it is easy to see that gross investment per unit of existing capital depends only on the ratio of desired capital to present capital $(k_{i,t+1}/k_{it})$. For example, if capital is k^*, the desired level is k^{**}, and the cost of increasing from k^* to k^{**} is I^*; then if capital is $10k^*$ and it is desired to increase it to $10k^{**}$, the cost will be $10I^*$. The first and second derivatives of g are both positive, which implies that the greater the desired value of $k_{i,t+1}$, the more it will cost, given k_{it}, and the cost of making a given size percentage increase in k_{it} rises faster than the rise in the desired percentage. That is, the cost of a 20 percent increase in k_{it} is more than twice the cost of a 10 percent increase, starting from the same base value of k_{it}. Two additional conditions are placed on g: First there is a positive number, γ, less than one, such that $0 = g(\gamma)$. Thus, if gross investment is zero, capacity falls to a fraction γ of its previous level. Second, there is a value δ such that $\delta = g(1)$; hence, for any level of capacity k_{it}, if that capacity is to be just maintained from period to period, gross investment must be δk_{it}; δ is analogous to a depreciation parameter.

A simple example for the investment function is $I_{it} = k_{it}(k_{i,t+1}/k_{it} - 0.7)^2$. The marginal cost of increasing the capital stock, $\partial I_t/\partial k_{i,t+1}$, is $2k_{i,t+1}/k_{it} - 1.4$, which rises as $k_{i,t+1}/k_{it}$ rises. If no investment is made in period t, then $g(\gamma) = 0 = (k_{i,t+1}/k_{it} - 0.7)^2$, or $\gamma = 0.7$ and $k_{i,t+1} = 0.7k_{it}$. In other words, if investment is nil today, then tomorrow's capital is a fraction, $\frac{7}{10}$, of today's capital. The amount of investment required to keep the capital stock at a constant value is found from $\delta = g(1) = 0.3^2 = 0.09$. Therefore, $I_t = 0.09k_{it}$ maintains a constant level of capital.

The *objective function of the firm,* discounted cash flow, is

$$\sum_{t=1}^{\infty} \alpha_i^{t-1} \left[q_{it}f(Q_t) - c_iq_{it} - k_{it}g\left(\frac{k_{i,t+1}}{k_{it}}\right) \right] \tag{7.1}$$

In addition to the assumptions made concerning the firm's capacity and the function g, demand is assumed to be downward-sloping ($f' < 0$), and marginal revenue is declining ($2f' + Qf'' < 0$), and there is a finite value of capacity, $\bar{k}$, sufficiently large that $(\bar{k}) < c_i$ for all firms i. The latter condition ensures that no firm has an incentive to raise its capacity beyond k. The only incompleteness left in the model is that initial capacities, k_{i1}, must be stipulated.

For each firm, a *strategy* consists of a sequence of output and capacity levels $(q_{i1}, k_{i2}, q_{i2}, k_{i3}, q_{i3}, \ldots)$ where $0 \leq \gamma k_{i,t-1} \leq k_{it} \leq \bar{k}$ and $0 \leq q_{it} \leq k_{it}$. Capacity in period t is bounded below by $\gamma k_{i,t-1}$, the level associated with no investment, and above by $\bar{k}$, a level so high that it cannot be profitable. Output must lie between zero and capacity. Prescott proves that the model has a noncooperative equilibrium. Obviously there must be periods in which output equals capacity for a firm in equilibrium. Were this not so, the firm could reduce investment in some periods, leaving the other investment choices and all output choices unchanged. This must increase cash flow in the periods when investment is reduced, while leaving all other periods' cash flows unchanged. Of course, there may be many periods in which output is less than capacity. Before moving on to the next section it is instructive to examine the first-order condition that applies in a period when output equals capacity. This condition is derived by differentiating $\sum_{t=1}^{\infty} \alpha_i^{t-1}[k_{it}f(\sum_{j=1}^{n} k_{jt}) - c_i k_{it} - k_{it}g(k_{i,t+1}/k_{it})]$ with respect to k_{it} and setting the derivative equal to zero. After rearranging terms, this is

$$g'\left(\frac{k_{it}}{k_{i,t-1}}\right) = \alpha_i \left\{ [f(Q_t) + q_{it}f'(Q_t) - c_i] + \left[\frac{k_{i,t+1}}{k_{it}} g'\left(\frac{k_{i,t+1}}{k_{it}}\right) - g\left(\frac{k_{i,t+1}}{k_{it}}\right)\right]\right\} \tag{7.2}$$

The term on the left side of the equality is the marginal cost borne in period $t - 1$ for an increase in k_{it}. The terms on the right, which accrue in period t, and are discounted, are divided into two groups using square brackets. The first of these is marginal revenue minus marginal cost. It need not be true that marginal revenue be equal to marginal cost in the present situation. The second term is the saving that will be realized in period t because the target value of $k_{i,t+1}$ will be cheaper to attain, the larger is k_{it}. That is, it equals the rate at which investment in period $t - 1$ falls per unit increase in k_{it} (with $k_{i,t+1}$ unchanged).

7.2. Capital stock as the determinant of the marginal cost curve

The modeling of production costs described next is nearer to the spirit of neoclassical, marginalist economies than Prescott's modeling of capital stock as capacity. The following formulation relates the firm's marginal cost curve to its capital stock. The more capital the firm has, the lower its marginal cost for any given level of output. There is no upper limit to the firm's capacity, but as output rises with capital fixed, marginal cost increases.

The *total cost of production* is denoted $C_i(q_{it}, K_{it})$ for firm i in period t. I_{it} is the amount of *gross investment* undertaken by the firm in period t, and K_{it} is the *capital stock* in period t. The relationship of the investment and capital of period t to the capital of period $t + 1$ is given by $K_{i,t+1} = \delta K_{it} + I_{it}$. Thus, in contrast to Prescott's model, the firm can increase its capital stock by any number of units at a constant cost per unit. Recall that in the Prescott model the cost of adding another unit of capital increases with the aggregate amount to be added. The *rate of depreciation* is $1 - \delta$, and δ is called the *depreciation parameter*. Because the marginal cost of new capital is a constant, it is convenient to define one dollar's worth of capital to be the unit of physical capital. Using a system of inverse demand functions for firms selling differentiated products, with output levels as the primary variables, the *profit function* for the ith firm in period t is

$$\pi_i(q_t, K_{it}, K_{i,t-1}) = q_{it}f_i(q_t) - C_i(q_{it}, K_{it}) - I_{it}$$
$$= q_{it}f_i(q_t) - C_i(q_{it}, K_{it}) - (K_{i,t+1} - \delta K_{it}) \quad (7.3)$$

The firm's objective is to maximize $\sum_{t=1}^{\infty} \alpha_i^{t-1} \pi_i(q_t, K_{it}, K_{i,t-1})$.

The obvious conditions to place on the production cost function are that it be nonnegative, twice differentiable, convex, and increasing as q_i increases. The first and last of these conditions are, essentially, that one does not get something for nothing. Marginal cost is always positive, and total cost could only be zero if output were zero, although, even at zero output, there could be fixed costs. The differentiability condition, of course, is made because it makes other conditions easier to state and facilitates the derivation of some results. Convexity of the cost function is needed in proving the existence of equilibrium, and it follows from concavity of the production function. There are several remaining conditions; however, what they amount to can be easily stated in nonmathematical form prior to the more technical specification. Production cost is zero only if both output and capital are zero. As capital increases, two things happen: First, the cost incurred by the firm at zero output (i.e., fixed cost) increases. Second, the marginal cost curve falls. That is, for any fixed level of output, the larger is K_i, the smaller is marginal cost. Now imagine two different capital stocks K_i' and K_i'', where K_i' is larger. There is a critical output level, dependent on both K_i' and K_i'', at which total cost is the same for both capital stocks. Below this critical level, total cost is smaller with the smaller capital stock, K_i'', and above the critical level, total cost is smaller with the larger capital stock, K_i'.

Put mathematically, $C_i(0, 0) = 0$ states that zero cost is associated with zero output and zero capital; $C_i^2(0, K) > 0$ states that fixed cost rises with the size of the capital stock; $C_i^1(q, K) > 0$ ensures that marginal cost is always positive; $C_i^1(q, K)$ goes to infinity as K goes to zero, guaranteeing that production cannot take place if the capital stock is not strictly positive; $C_i^{12}(q, K) < 0$ assures that, for fixed q, marginal cost falls as K increases; and for $0 < K_1 < K_2 < \infty$ there is $q = \phi_i(K_1, K_2)$ such that $C_i[\phi_i(K_1, K_2), K_1] = C_i[\phi_i(K_1 K_2), K_2]$, which defines the critical output level below which production is cheaper with K_1 and above which it is cheaper with K_2.

In Figure 7.1 the cost function is illustrated. $K_1 < K_2 < K_3 < K_4$, and at the output level q^{12}, production is equally costly using K_1 or K_2; however, larger capital stocks than K_2 are more expensive. Below q^{12}, using K_1 is cheaper than K_2, and the reverse holds above q^{12}. Similarly, q^{23} is the break-even point between K_2 and K_3. At this

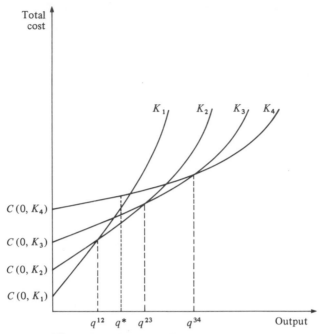

Figure 7.1. Total cost functions that depend on the capital stock.

output level, K_1 is too small and K_4 is too large. Along the vertical axis it can be seen that as the capital stock is made larger, the fixed cost $[C(0, K)]$ grows. Finally, choose a specific value of q, such as q^*, and note that the larger the capital stock, the flatter the total cost function, indicating lower marginal cost with rising capital.

An example of a cost function satisfying the conditions outlined earlier is $C_{it} = 0.05 K_{it} + (10 + 3q_{it} + q_{it}^2)/K_{it}$. Table 7.1 shows values of total cost associated with several levels of capital and output. Marginal cost of production, $(3 + 2q_{it})/K_{it}$, falls as K_{it} rises. At the other extreme, marginal cost becomes indefinitely large as K_{it} falls to zero. Production, in other words, is impossible without capital. The term $0.05 K_{it}$ is a fixed cost that is apart from the cost of actually buying capital. The latter is embodied in the investment function, whereas $0.05 K_{it}$ should be thought of as a cost of maintaining or caring for existing capital. Returning to Table 7.1, the

Table 7.1. *Total cost for various output and capital levels*

K					g			
	20.00	25.74	30.00	33.75	37.13	41.71	48.42	55.00
100	9.7	12.5	15	17.5	20	23.75	30	37
150	10.63	12.5	14.17	15.83	17.5	20	24.17	28.83
200	12.35	13.75	15	16.25	17.5	19.38	22.5	26
250	14.38	15.5	16.5	17.5	18.5	20	22.5	25.3

features of Fig. 7.1 can be seen. For each output level in the table, the lowest cost is in italics. $K = 100$ is cheapest up to $q = 25.74$, at which it is tied with $K = 150$. The latter is cheapest to $q = 37.13$, where it is tied with $K = 200$, and so forth.

As with the model in the preceding section, the most natural and easily handled concept of strategy for the firm is a sequence of output levels and capital stock values. With respect to these strategies, a noncooperative equilibrium is known to exist. This particular cost formulation is used by Friedman (1979) in conjunction with the study of entry.

7.3. A neoclassical cost structure combined with increasing marginal cost of investment

The two models presented earlier differ in the way that the firm's capital stock affects its cost of production and in the treatment of the cost of investment. These two areas of difference are separable in the sense that either way of dealing with the cost function can be coupled with either way of handling the cost of investment. Perhaps the most desirable formulation is the cost function of Section 7.2 coupled with the investment cost function of Section 7.1. The resulting single-period profit function is

$$\pi_i(q_t, K_{it}, K_{i,t+1}) = q_{it} f_i(q_t) - C_i(q_{it}, K_{it}) - K_{it} g \frac{K_{i,t+1}}{K_{it}} \tag{7.4}$$

That a noncooperative equilibrium exists for this model is a straightforward matter to prove on the basis of similar results for the preceding two models.

7.4. Natural asymmetric equilibria

In the oligopoly literature, as elsewhere in economic theory, models are often set up to be symmetric. An example of a symmetric model is a Cournot oligopoly in which all firms have identical cost functions. There is a tremendous analytical convenience to the symmetry assumption: For all practical purposes, an n-firm model collapses to a one-firm model, for it is nearly certain that if any equilibrium exists at all, then a symmetric equilibrium exists. Thus, the researcher can set out the conditions that must characterize equilibrium, impose symmetry, and then attempt to solve the system. This procedure frequently is successful and is much simpler than dealing with a more general, asymmetric model.

A natural objection arises to the use of symmetric models. There is great risk that some of the results, and perhaps the most interesting and important results, depend crucially on the symmetry assumption. To avoid this difficulty, many models are formulated with enough generality that the firm can, but need not be, symmetric. Examples abound in nearly all chapters of this volume. For example, in Cournot models where firms face a single industry demand function, it is usual to allow firms to have different cost functions, and in differentiated products models, neither the demand functions nor the cost functions need be symmetric.

In defense of these asymmetric models it is perhaps sufficient to note that symmetry is included as a special case and that observation of the empirical world reveals immediately that firms are not, in fact, identical. Yet this very observation raises a question: Why are firms not identical? On the one hand, it is customary to assume that entrepreneurs are interchangeable and that they have identical access to inputs and technologies. This assumption, if true, creates a strong presumption that firms in a market ought to be identical. On the other hand, we observe again that symmetry is not found in practice. To explain this, it is always possible to take refuge in the assertion that entrepreneurs are not really interchangeable, that, instead, each is a unique resource of his firm. Whereas believing this is not at all difficult, it is natural to wonder if this explicit source of difference among firms is a necessary condition for asymmetric equilibrium. More specifically, is it possible to formulate a reasonable and interesting model that is symmetric in the sense that the initial situation faced by the firms is identical from one to another and find that the only interesting equilibria are asymmetric?

This question has been imaginatively posed and answered in the affirmative by Flaherty (1980a). In a model that is described later she finds that both symmetric and asymmetric equilibria exist; however, only asymmetric equilibria are stable, and hence to be expected. The demand structure is identical with that of the model in Section 7.1, with *inverse demand* given by $P_t = f(Q_t)$, where p_t is the *market price* for the homogeneous good produced by the industry and Q_t is *total output*: $Q_t = \sum_{i=1}^{n} q_{it}$. As with Prescott's model (1973), Flaherty assumes demand to be downward-sloping ($f' < 0$) and marginal revenue to be decreasing for the industry ($2f' + Q_t f'' < 0$). Although firms produce at constant marginal cost within any given time period, there is no capacity constraint, and the level of a firm's marginal cost is chosen by the firm itself. Thus, to increase capital stock is to reduce marginal cost, although the relationship between capital stock and marginal cost is not made explicit. *Marginal cost* for firm i in period t is c_{it}, and the *investment function,* relating the amount spent on gross investment to marginal cost, is given by $I_{it} = g(c_{it}, c_{i,t+1})$. The *discounted cash flow of the firm,* which it wishes to maximize, is[1]

$$\sum_{t=1}^{\infty} \alpha^{t-1} \left[q_{it} f(Q_t) - c_{it} q_{it} - g(c_{it}, c_{i,t+1}) \right] \tag{7.5}$$

The investment function, $g(c_{it}, c_{i,t+1})$, is a variant of the Prescott (1973) investment function found in Section 7.1 and the advertising function governing the stock of goodwill used in Chapter 6. In addition to the strict convexity [i.e., $g^{11} > 0$, $g^{22} > 0$, and $g^{11}g^{22} - (g^{12})^2 > 0$], it is assumed that $g^1 > 0$, which means that the higher is today's marginal cost (c_{it}), the greater the expense required to achieve a given level of marginal cost tomorrow, and it is assumed that $g^2 < 0$, which means that the lower the marginal cost the firm wishes to achieve tomorrow, given the marginal cost it has today, the greater the expense; in addition, there is a floor to how low marginal cost can go. In particular, there is a level of marginal cost, c_*, that no finite investment expense can maintain [i.e., $\lim_{c_i \to c_*} g(c_i, c_i) = \infty$].[2] A concrete connection can be made between marginal cost and capital by, for example, $K_{it} = 1/(c_{it} - c^*)$.

On examining equation (7.5) it is clear that the model is symmetric, for each firm faces the same discount parameter, market demand function, and investment function. After ensuring that the model has a noncooperative equilibrium, Flaherty goes on to examine steady-state equilibria. A *steady-state equilibrium* is a noncooperative equilibrium in which each firm chooses the same marginal cost and output level in all periods. It need not be true that each firm chooses the same marginal cost and output as other firms, but only that each firm makes no changes from period to period, and, of course, the *strategy* of each firm maximizes its discounted cash flow, given the plans being followed by the other firms. Under some additional assumptions, Flaherty (1980a, pp. 1198ff.) proves that both symmetric and asymmetric steady-state equilibria exist. That is to say, there are steady-state equilibria under which all firms choose the same marginal cost and output as one another (symmetric) and steady-state equilibria under which they do not all choose identically (asymmetric). And she proves that no steady-state symmetric equilibria are stable, whereas asymmetric steady-state equilibria are stable.

This result gives the interesting and remarkable conclusion that an asymmetric outcome is to be expected in a model that is, itself, symmetric in its underlying structure. The nature of the equilibrium is described next in more detail, and the meaning of stability is precisely stated. As with many models previously encountered, a *strategy for a single firm* is defined to be a sequence of output levels and marginal costs $(q_{i1}, c_{i2}, q_{i2}, c_{i3}, q_{i3}, c_{i4}, \ldots)$. Marginal cost in period 1, c_{i1}, is an initial condition of the model. Under strategies like these, the choice of output level within any single period is the same as the choice of output level in a single-period Cournot model. The first-order conditions for a Cournot equilibrium when the optimal output levels are greater than zero are

$$f(Q_t) + q_{it}f'(Q_t) - c_{it} = 0 \qquad (7.6)$$

Whether or not each firm produces a positive amount in each period, the equilibrium output levels for the firms are unique, given the marginal costs. These optimal levels can be denoted $q_{it} = \phi_i(c_t)$, where $c_t = (c_{it}, \ldots, c_{nt})$; therefore, with the understanding that output levels will always be optimally chosen, *strategy for a firm* can be thought of as being simply a sequence of marginal costs: $\sigma_i = (c_{i1}, c_{i2}, c_{i3}, \ldots)$, and the *discounted profit* (cash flow) *streams* can be written, with $\sigma = (\sigma_1, \ldots, \sigma_n)$, as

$$F_i(\sigma) = \sum_{t=1}^{\infty} \alpha^{t-1} \left\{ \phi_i(c_t) f \left[\sum_{j=1}^{n} \phi_j(c_t) \right] - c_{it}\phi_i(c_t) - g(c_{it}, c_{i,t+1}) \right\} \quad (7.7)$$

It is understood that c_{i1} is not actively chosen by the firm in the sense that its value is a given initial condition of the model. The values of c_{it} for $t > 1$ are restricted in two ways. On the low side, there is a value of c_i greater than c_* and sufficiently close to it that the attainment of it must cost more than the maximum possible discounted revenue the firm can achieve. This is called c_{**}. On the high side, the firm will never choose a marginal cost greater than p^+, the price intercept of the demand function, and, in addition, c_{it} can never be larger than the amount defined by $0 = g(c_{i,t-1}, c_{it})$. That is, if the firm invests zero in period $t - 1$, another upper limit on c_{it} is established, and the actual c_{it} will not be above the smaller of these two limits.

Stability can now be defined. Let $\sigma^* = (c_1^*, c_2^*, c_3^*, \ldots)$ be a noncooperative equilibrium. This equilibrium *converges to a steady state* if there is some vector of marginal costs, c', to which the c_t^* converge. That is, ϕ^* converges to c' if $c' = \lim_{t \to \infty} c_t^*$; c' is associated with a steady-state equilibrium, and $\Sigma' = (c', c', c', \ldots)$ is a *stable steady-state equilibrium*. A slightly different statement of this definition is as follows: Suppose there is a c' and an $\epsilon > 0$ such that whenever $|c_{i1}^* - c_i'| < \epsilon$ for all i, c_t^* converges to c'. Then $\sigma' = (c', c', c', \ldots)$ is a *stable steady-state equilibrium*. The stability, or convergence, property is that if c_1^* is sufficiently close to c' and if σ^* is any equilibrium whose initial condition is c_1^*, then σ^* converges to c'. Flaherty proves that no symmetric steady-state equilibrium is stable, but some asymmetric steady-state equilibria are stable. The only way to attain a symmetric equilibrium is to, miraculously, start out there. Thus, the stable symmetric equilibria are the only equilibria that can be expected to be attained.

7.5. Price leadership and the timing of firms' actions

Economic agents live in continuous time, which creates a presumption that economic activity ought to be modeled in continuous time; yet, many actions people take are in discrete time. Consumers do not eat continuously. Firms do not alter prices or production rates continuously. Many decisions are made with the understanding that they will hold in force for a specified length of time, or until they are explicitly rescinded and replaced with new decisions. The usual alternative to continuous time in economic models is discrete time, with the individual time period being of an exogenously fixed length. Just as continuous time brings an unrealistic flexibility to decisions, the usual discrete time brings an unrealistic inflexibility. A firm may find it physically impossible to continuously change prices, but it need not change prices on a totally arbitrary schedule dictated, ad hoc, by a model maker.

If any insight is to be gained into leadership phenomena, one requisite is an appropriate time framework. The idea of price leadership is that a particular firm in a market, frequently the largest, is the initiator of price changes. When this firm makes a price change, the other firms in the industry quickly follow with parallel price changes. Then no further changes take place until the next occasion on which the leader makes a move. Although some observers believe they have seen price leadership empirically, sorting out the phenomenon empirically can be difficult, partly because it is difficult to define price leadership rigorously in a satisfactory way, despite a clear commonsense notion of its meaning.

What is particularly interesting is to determine the conditions under which leadership will emerge and to delineate the conditions that will determine the leader. Perhaps, in the end, leadership is merely a phenomenon in some economists' imaginations. A failed attempt at dealing with leadership is the Stackelberg (1934) leader-follower model. The failing of that model is that a firm acts as leader if it is assumed to be a leader. Leadership is not a role the firm chooses. Nor is there a reasonable modeling of the firms' behavior should more than one decide to be leader. If leadership is to have a chance to emerge, then it should be possible to take actions at any time; yet continuous adjustment ought to be ruled out. A way to accomplish this is by having a continuous-time model in which there is an adjustment cost associated with changing a variable.

Then decisions need not be made at equally spaced intervals, nor are firms assumed to make adjustments at the same times. Thus, in principle, it is possible to observe a pattern in which one firm makes a change, then all other firms quickly follow with changes, and then no further change is seen until the original firm again makes one.

Such a model has been studied elsewhere (Friedman, 1977, Chapter 6), with firms in continuous time choosing prices and capital stocks. There is no adjustment cost associated with changing prices; however, a large cost is connected with capital stock changes. It is assumed that a block of capital bought by a firm at one time consists of a complete plant that cannot be modified; so if a firm desires any alteration of its capital stock, it must discard the old plant and equipment, receiving no scrap value for it, and purchase everything new. This is an extreme version of a quite reasonable assumption. Namely, when a firm acquires some new capital, it incurs some adjustment costs in fitting that capital into its preexisting capital configuration. This is analogous to the cost of adding a room onto a house. It costs more to build the addition onto the old house than it costs to add such a room to a house being newly built. The difference between these two costs is the adjustment cost. The extreme form of adjustment cost assumed here is not crucial to the results. What is vital for the results of the model to hold is that there be some cost associated with making a change in the capital stock. If, for example, adding some new capital entails an adjustment cost of losing 10 percent (rather than 100 percent) of the value of the previous capital stock, the same qualitative results will obtain. If the adjustment cost is a flat sum of money (say $100) every time an addition is made to capital, again the same qualitative results will hold. The key element is that the size of the adjustment cost not go to zero as the size of the contemplated addition goes to zero. The extreme assumption that the old plant is entirely scrapped when new capital is purchased has the advantage that it is easy to describe and yields similar results to the alternatives noted earlier.

The model is one of price-choosing oligopolists making differentiated products with the *rates of sales for firm i* at time *t* being $q_i(t) = f_i[p(t)]$, where $p(t)$ is the *price vector* in effect at time *t*. The *rate of costs* is denoted by $C_i[q_i(t), K_i^*(t)]$, where $K_i^*(t)$ is the *capital stock* at time t, measured in efficiency units. It is assumed that newer capital is more productive than older capital; in particular, if the firm's capital was acquired at time T, then $K_i^*(t) = e^{\lambda T}K_i(T)$, where $K_i(T)$ is the number of physical units acquired at time T, measured so that one dollar buys one unit at all times. One unit of capital from time T is the productive equal to $e^{\lambda T}$ units from time zero. The firm's *rate of cash flow* at time $t > T$, when its capital stock dates from T, is

$$\pi_i[p(t), e^{\lambda T}K_i(T)] = p_i(t)f_i[p(t)] - C_i\{f_i[p(t)], e^{\lambda T}K_i(T)\} \qquad (7.8)$$

It is proved elsewhere (Friedman, 1977, Chapter 6) that, given the policies of the other firms, firm i will change its capital stock an infinite number of times, and there is a positive minimum length of time that will pass between changes. The minimum occurs because of the adjustment cost associated with buying new capital, and the number of changes is infinite because capital continually becomes more productive per unit of cost at a constant rate. The same outcome would occur if new capital were always the same but old capital was depreciating at a steady rate.

Let $Z_i = (t_{i0}, t_{i1}, t_{i2}, t_{i3}, \ldots)$ be the times at which the ith firm purchases new capital, with the understanding that $t_{i0} = 0$ and $t_{ik} > t_{i,k-1}$. Let r be the discount rate, and let $t' = t_{i,k+1}$ when $t = t_{ik}$. Then the firm's *discounted cash flow* is

$$\sum_{t \in Z_i} \left\{ -e^{rt}K_i(t) + \int_t^{t'} e^{r\tau}\pi_i\left[p(\tau), e^{\lambda t}K(t)\right] d\tau \right\} \qquad (7.9)$$

After stating conditions for the existence of noncooperative equilibrium, it is found that in equilibrium there is a specific list of times when changes in the capital stock take place. Generally, all firms obtain new capital at these times, and no firm changes capital at any other time. In between such times, prices are constant, which is not surprising, because the model is stationary over these intervals. Leadership in making capital stock changes does not emerge. That, too, makes sense within the model, for when we consider the optimal policy or strategy for a firm, given the strategies of the others, it is natural that it will want to change its capital on precisely those occasions when its rivals change theirs. Nothing will be learned by waiting a little, and it is within the nature of the equilibrium concept that each firm will exactly and fully anticipate every move made by the other firms.

This model does not provide evidence that the notion of leadership is without interest, but it does help narrow the circumstances in which leadership can make sense. My guess is that leadership requires that there be a source of uncertainty in the model. Imagine that the firms cannot be sure what will happen to demand if prices change, and, as a consequence, no firm knows, or anticipates as if it were certain, the future actions of its rivals. If the very making of changes entails costs, then gradualism will not do. On one hand, if the firm moves by inches, it will kill itself with adjustment costs by inches. On the other hand, bolder, larger changes, probably predicated on the belief that other firms will do something similar, hold the risk that the leader will not be followed, in which case a price change predicated on price changes by rival firms could be very unprofitable. Perhaps the larger a firm is, the more it has to gain, and the smaller its proportionate possible loss if it is not followed. If the leader's change should dispose other firms to change in a similar manner, then the larger is the leader relative to the market, the more its move changes the environment for the others in a way that should encourage them to change as the leader expects. Also, the larger is the leader relative to the rest of the market, the more its profit depends on its own actions, as compared with its rivals' actions.

7.6. Summary

Three ways of associating capital with cost functions are presented in this chapter: (a) constant marginal cost, independent of the amount of capital, up to a capacity limit, with capacity rising as capital stock rises; (b) constant marginal cost, with no capacity limit, with the level of marginal cost being lower, the larger is the capital stock; (c) marginal cost increases with output, but as capital increases, the marginal cost curve becomes flatter and lower. These three formulations share the feature that increasing the capital stock will reduce the marginal cost, at least for some output level. For situation (a), the marginal cost is reduced from infinity to c_i for a few additional units of output when capital is increased. These are all useful formulations, each probably having appropriate areas of application. In all three instances, capital decisions provide a structural link between time periods, especially where the Prescott investment function is employed. Investment cost incurred today will affect today's costs through the investment cost outlay and tomorrow's costs through both the production cost function faced tomorrow and the cost of attaining a given capital stock for the day after tomorrow.

A problem that has been glossed over entirely, as may have occurred to the reader, is that of measuring capital. Anyone who has studied this problem is aware that the heterogeneity of capital provides a particularly thorny aggregation problem. Capital goods of different lifetimes have their relative values changed by changes in the interest rate. Capital goods that combine differently with labor or other inputs can have their relative values changed when wage rates or other input prices change; see, for example, Bliss (1975).

The phenomenon studied by Flaherty, natural emergence of asymmetric equilibria, deserves further research. The same applies to price leadership, which needs a clear definition and requires analysis in a model in which it can reasonably emerge endogenously.

8

Entry

In the preceding chapters, the numbers and identities of the firms participating in the market are given. In this chapter, attention is turned to changes in the composition of firms selling in a new market, that is, to entry and exit. Obviously, firms enter new markets if they anticipate profits, but that leaves several questions to be answered: Will firms enter an industry whenever the previously established firms are making positive profits? If a firm would have made a profit if it had been previously established, will it necessarily decide to enter? Can established firms pursue policies that deter or prevent the entry of new firms? Are they better off pursuing such policies? Somewhat similar questions can be asked about the exit of firms: Can a firm be driven out of a market? Under what conditions will it be in the interest of the remaining firms to drive a rival firm out?

The study of entry has been done in several ways. Most familiar is what can be called static entry. The approach in *static entry* is to use a static, or one-period, model in which the number of firms in the market is a variable and examine market equilibrium as a function of the number of firms. Say that n^* is the largest number of firms that can be in the market with nonnegative profits and that for any $n < n^*$, all firms have positive profits. Under the static entry approach, the market will be in long-run equilibrium when the number of firms is n^*. If the number of firms is less than n^*, new entrants will come in, and if the number exceeds n^*, then some existing firms will leave. If adjustments by firms were instantaneous and capital were perfectly mobile, static entry would be very appealing; however, adjustments of many sorts take time, and sometimes there are costs of adjustment, and firms often have sunk costs. All these elements can cause modifications in results obtained from static entry models.

It is more natural to examine entry in the context of a multiperiod model. Even if a market is in equilibrium prior to the entry of a new firm, it is likely that a process of adjustment involving all firms and several time periods will follow the entry of a new firm into the market. If profits per period for the entrant are lower during the adjustment phase than they are following it, then it is possible that the n^* calculated from static entry considerations overstates the equilibrium number of firms, for the adjustment period may entail losses that are not offset by subsequent profits.

Strategic considerations enter into the entry process because the established firms may behave differently in a market where entry can occur than they will if entry is not possible, and their behavior may be influenced by a desire to affect the entry decisions made by their potential rivals. The potential entrants, themselves, have been handled in two distinct ways in the literature. The first is to refrain from modeling them explicitly and to assume an ad hoc rule for their decisions. The second is to model them as conscious, maximizing decision makers. Clearly the latter is the more satisfactory.

One of the oldest explanations of entry behavior is the limit price. Because of its surface appeal and wide currency, it is taken up in Section 8.1. Section 8.2 deals with models in which the cost structure of existing firms, the presence of scale economies, and the irreversibility of capital stock decisions affect the entry process. The dynamic models in the literature, reviewed in Sections 8.1 and 8.2, are mainly models with a single established firm and a single potential entrant. If there are several existing firms and many potential entrants, some interesting questions arise that are explored informally in Section 8.3. Section 8.4 is devoted to discussion of exit, and Section 8.5 contains a summary.

8.1. Limit price models of entry

Put in the simplest possible way, imagine a monopolistic firm that chooses a price for its market in a static setting. If it chooses a price in excess of p_0, then entry will occur, and its profits per period will be π^e. This critical price, p_0, is called the *limit price*. If it faces no threat of entry, it will choose the monopolist's profit-maximizing price of p_m and will attain profits of $\pi^m > \pi^e$. Supposing that p_m is larger than p_0, the largest profit it can have as a monopolist facing a threat of entry is less than π^m. This profit is found by maximizing the monopolist's profit with respect to its price, but under the condition that its price cannot exceed p_0. Call this profit π^0. In this model it is assumed that the monopolist can deter entry merely by selecting a sufficiently low price, and the only operative question is whether or not the monopolist will do so. Clearly, this rests on comparing π^0 with π^e. If the latter is higher, the monopolist will allow entry, but if it is lower, the monopolist will deter entry.

An example of the simplest limit price model

To illustrate, let the monopolist face the *demand function* $q = 100 - 2p$, and suppose costs are nil. Then, in the absence of an entry threat, the monopolist's price will be $p^m = 25$, and profits will be $\pi^m = 1,250$. Assume further that entry will mean that one firm will come into the market, and subsequently a Cournot equilibrium will prevail. Let the two firms' (postentry) *demand functions* be $q_1 = 50 - 2p_1 + p_2$ for the (former) monopolist and $q_2 = 50 + p_1 - 2p_2$ for the new firm. With costs nil for the entrant, the Cournot equilibrium occurs at $p_1^c = p_2^c = 16\frac{2}{3}$, and each firm has a profit of $\pi^e = 555\frac{5}{9}$. Then the monopolist will move to prevent entry if a price at or below p_0 will allow more than the Cournot equilibrium profit. As a monopolist, its profit will exceed $555\frac{5}{9}$ if $p > 6.366$. Thus, if the entry-preventing price, p_0, is less than 25 and more than 6.366, entry prevention is more profitable than allowing the new firm to come into the market.

The limit price idea can be found in the work of Zeuthen (1930) and Kaldor (1935); however, it is not elaborated in any detail in either source. The idea came to prominence in the work of Bain

(1949), where an insightful discussion of the entry problem is followed by a simple formal model of limit pricing. In the past decade, several articles have been published using limit pricing in much the spirit of the preceding discussion (e.g., Kamien and Schwartz, 1971; Bourguignon and Sethi, 1981). Although stochastic elements have been introduced, along with dynamic models, an essential ingredient that most have retained is that the entrant is not an explicit decision maker in the model. Instead, as described earlier, the entrant's decision on whether or not to enter and when to enter is determined by an ad hoc rule. Whether or not such a rule is consistent with optimizing behavior by the entrant is not explored, and this lack is the prime weak spot of the limit price literature. One of the most sophisticated and comprehensive treatments of limit pricing along the lines stemming from Bain is that of Bourguignon and Sethi (1981), where many additional references can be found. A notable exception, discussed in more detail in a later subsection, is the work of Milgrom and Roberts (1982), who derive limit price behavior in a model with a rational, maximizing potential entrant.

Return to the example given earlier in which there is one monopolist and one potential entrant. It is assumed that the monopolist knows the cost and demand functions it faces while in the market alone, as well as the cost and demand functions both will face if the entrant becomes active in the market. Suppose the entrant possesses the same information and attempts to maximize its own profit under the assumption that zero will be earned if the entrant stays out of the market. Then two conclusions are immediate: First, the entrant will definitely come into the market. Supposing a Cournot equilibrium to be established, the entrant's profits will be $555\frac{5}{9}$. Second, the preentry price chosen by the monopolist is totally irrelevant to the entrant's decision, because the preentry price has no bearing on the conditions that will prevail after entry.

Adjustment cost as a source of limit pricing

Then what will provide a role for the preentry price? There are two possibilities: On the one hand, the preentry price may affect the firm's price choices after entry because of a cost of adjustment. To be more specific, let $\pi_i(p_t) = \pi_i(p_{1t}, p_{2t}) = p_{it}(50 - 2p_{it} + p_{jt})$ $(j \neq i)$ for the two firms, and let them have a common discount parameter of α. If the *adjustment cost* associated with price changes is $(p_{it} - p_{i,t-1})^2$ when the period-t price is different from that of period $t - 1$, then a *firm's discounted profits* are

$$p_{i1}(50 - 2p_{i1} + p_{j1}) + \sum_{t=2}^{\infty} \alpha^{t-1}[p_{it}(50 - (p_{it} + p_{jt})) - (p_{it} - p_{i,t-1})^2] \quad (8.1)$$

Assume that the monopolist has been charging the monopoly price of 25, and then, at time t, firm 2 enters the market. Prices will not immediately be $p_{1t} = p_{2t} = 16\frac{2}{3}$, a Cournot equilibrium for both the static model and the dynamic model in the absence of adjustment costs. Instead, p_{1t} will be slightly below 25, and the entrant's price will lie between p_{1t} and $16\frac{2}{3}$. Over time, following entry, the two prices will fall to $16\frac{2}{3}$.

Can the presence of the adjustment cost affect the entrant's decision to come into the market? With the model specified precisely as it is, the answer is no, because the entrant can always make at least zero in each period no matter what prices the established firm chooses. If the profit function of the entrant is altered to allow for a fixed cost per period, then entry prevention becomes possible. Say, for example, that both firms incur a fixed cost of 555 per period and that the established firm has a preentry price of 6.4. Then, at the postentry Cournot equilibrium after all price adjustment ceases, each firm will earn a profit of $\frac{2}{3}$ per period. Note that the monopolist, alone in the market, receives a profit of 3.08 per period at a price of 6.4. Although this is much below the profit a monopolist can reap if there is no threat of entry, it is larger than $\frac{2}{3}$. A fixed entry cost can play a similar role.

With the monopolist at 6.4, if the entrant should come into the market, its equilibrium price path will begin somewhere between 6.4 and $16\frac{2}{3}$. Thus, for some periods, the entrant will be unable to escape negative profits, and, depending on the size of α, the entrant's discounted profits can easily be negative. In this situation, the established firm can prevent entry by a policy that guarantees itself larger profits than it would receive if entry occurred, and the entry-preventing policy will be credible to the entrant. That is, if the entrant came into the market, the natural, profit-maximizing policy of the established firm would entail a price path to the static Cournot equilibrium prices along which the entrant would suffer losses.

The element added to the model by a price adjustment cost is that of *structural time dependence.* The profit function for a single time period depends on certain actual past actions. The nature of the market is different at any time t according to the immediately previous price, and from the point of view of entry, the preentry price of the established firm is an initial condition that affects both firms from the moment of entry of the second firm. Therefore, speaking in terms of threats, in the absence of adjustment costs, one might imagine the monopolist threatening potential entrants by saying that it will use very low prices if an entrant comes into the market and that its price will be so low as to cause the entrant losses. But with no adjustment costs, this threat is vain posturing. Should the entrant come in, its presence is a fait accompli, and no good can arise from cutthroat pricing (assuming only one entrant can come into the market, and no more). In the presence of adjustment costs, a low price (say $p_1 = 7$) implies to the entrant that the established firm is committed to a price path rising from 7 to $16\frac{2}{3}$ over time following entry. Explicit threat, in the sense of "If you do this, then I'll get you by doing that," is not at issue. Given the low price from which the first firm starts and a will on the part of both firms to behave in a straightforward noncooperative way, the entrant is simply doomed to losses. Note, finally, that in such a case the monopoly power of the established firm is greatly attenuated by the possibility of entry. The best it can do is to pick the highest price that guarantees that the entrant cannot have positive discounted profits on entry. Such a price must be below the static Cournot equilibrium price of $16\frac{2}{3}$, for should the preentry price exceed this level, it will drift down to it after entry, and the entrant will make profits exceeding the Cournot level in the interim.

The role played by price adjustment costs can also be played by (a) irreversible capital investment, (b) output adjustment costs, or (c) demand functions in which past sales or prices affect current-period demand. In Section 8.2 a model is developed in which irreversible capital plays an entry-preventing role, and another model is discussed in which adjustment costs associated with changing output levels play a similar role.

Preentry pricing as an information source to the entrant

The second role for an entry-preventing price is in conveying information. Imagine an established firm with a cost function that is unknown to the potential entrant; however, the entrant knows that the other firm's cost function must be among a certain class of cost functions. In the simplest case, the monopolist is known to have constant marginal costs, and marginal cost is one of two values. Suppose the entrant can make a profit if the monopolist has the high marginal cost, but will be forced to suffer losses if the monopolist's marginal cost is low. Then it will attempt to infer the firm's marginal costs from its observed market behavior. If the monopolist has low marginal costs, its (monopolistic) profit-maximizing price is lower than it would be if its costs were high; however, if it has high costs, it may attempt to trick the entrant into staying out of the market by following the price policy that would be optimal for a monopolist with low costs. Although the entrant may realize this, it may not be worthwhile for the entrant to take the chance that the monopolist's costs are actually high.

Milgrom and Roberts (1982) examine a two-period model with an established firm in the market in the first period and a potential entrant that can enter the market for the second period. Limit pricing emerges naturally in the model, rather than being assumed, ad hoc, from the first. The firms produce identical products whose *inverse demand function* is $p = a - bq$. Although both firms know this demand function, and each knows its own cost function, neither knows the cost function of the other. Firm 1, the established firm, has a constant *marginal cost* of c_1, lying in the interval $[\underline{c}_1, \bar{c}_1]$ and no other cost. Firm 2, if it enters, has an *entry cost* of c_0, paid in period 1, and a constant *marginal cost* of c_2, lying in the interval $[\underline{c}_2, \bar{c}_2]$. Each firm knows the interval in which its rival's marginal cost must lie, and firm 1 knows the magnitude of c_0. Depending on the parameters of the model, it may be possible for the established firm to use to its own advantage the incomplete information of the entrant by engaging in limit pricing. The sequence of actions in the model is as follows: (a) Firm 1, the established firm, chooses its first-period output, q_{11} and receives profit of $\pi_{11}(q_{11}, c_1) = (a - bq_{11} - c_1)q_{11}$. (b) Firm 2 observes q_{11} and then decides whether or not to enter the market. (c) The entry decision is communicated to firm 1; if firm 2 enters, then both firms are assumed to know one another's true marginal costs, and they simultaneously make their period-2 output decisions. If firm 1 remains alone in the market, then it chooses its second-period output. The firms have discount parameters α_1 and α_2.

From the preceding information, discounted profit functions can be constructed, starting at the second period. If firm 2 does not enter, then firm 1 is a simple monopolist facing no entry threat in the second period, and profit for that period is $\pi_1^m(c_1) = (a - c_1)^2/4b$ at an output level of $q_1^m(c_1) = (a - c_1)/2b$. If firm 2 enters, it is assured that c_1 becomes known to it and c_2 becomes known to firm 1, and the two firms choose Cournot equilibrium output levels. Thus, their period-2 profits are

$$\pi_1^c(c_1, c_2) = \frac{(a - 2c_1 + c_2)^2}{9b} \tag{8.2}$$

$$\pi_2^c(c_1, c_2) = \frac{(a - 2c_2 + c_1)^2}{9b} \tag{8.3}$$

Therefore, once the entry decision is made, the rest of the play is determined precisely. Recalling that firm 2 will observe q_{11}, the first-period output of firm 1, prior to making its entry decision, firm 2's choice can be written $v(c_2, q_{11})$, where only two values of v are possible: $v(c_2, q_{11}) = 1$ if firm 2 enters, and $v(c_2, q_{11}) = 0$ if it does not enter.

Recalling that when firm 1 chooses q_{11} it is ignorant of c_2, and when firm 2 decides whether or not to enter the market it is ignorant of c_1, let $H_1(c_1)$ be the probability distribution that firm 2 supposes for c_1, and let $H_2(c_2)$ be the distribution that firm 1 supposes for c_2. Then, letting $\eta(c_1)$ be the choice of q_{11} made by firm 1 as a function of c_1, the *expected discounted profits* of the two firms are

$$\pi_{11}[\eta(c_1), c_1] + \alpha_1 \int_{\underline{c}_2}^{\bar{c}_2} \|\pi_1^c(c_1, c_2)v[c_2, \eta(c_1)]$$

$$+ \pi_1^m(c_1)\{1 - v[c_2, \eta(c_1)]\}\| \, dH_2(c_2) \tag{8.4}$$

$$\int_{\underline{c}_1}^{\bar{c}_1} [\alpha_2\pi_2^c(c_1, c_2) - c_0]v[c_2, \eta(c_1)] \, dH_1(c_1) \tag{8.5}$$

A *noncooperative equilibrium* is a pair of strategies, $\eta(c_1)$ for firm 1 and $v[c_2, \eta(c_1)]$ for firm 2, such that neither firm can increase its profit by unilaterally altering its strategy (taking H_1 and H_2 as fixed). Thus, $\{\eta^*(c_1), v^*[c_2, \eta^*(c_1)]\}$ is an equilibrium pair of strategies: (a) for any $c_1 \in [\underline{c}_1, \bar{c}_1]$ and any $\eta(c_1)$ with domain $[\underline{c}_1, \bar{c}_1]$ and range $(0, \infty)$,

$$\pi_{11}[\eta^*(c_1), c_1] + \alpha_1 \int_{\underline{c}_2}^{\bar{c}_2} \|\pi_1^c(c_1, c_2)v^*[c_2, \eta^*(c_1)]$$

$$+ \pi_1^m(c_1)\{1 - v^*[c_2, \eta^*(c_1)]\}\| \, dH_2(c_2) \geq \pi_{11}[\eta(c_1), c_1]$$

$$+ \alpha_1 \int_{\underline{c}_2}^{\bar{c}_2} \|\pi_1^c(c_1, c_2)v^*[c_2, \eta(c_1)]$$

$$+ \pi_1^m(c_1)\{1 - v^*[c_2, \eta(c_1)]\}\| \, dH_2(c_2) \tag{8.6}$$

and (b) for any $c_2 \in [\underline{c}_2, \bar{c}_2]$ and any $v[c_2, \eta^*(c_1)]$ whose domain is $[\underline{c}_2, \bar{c}_2] \times R_+$ and whose range is $\{0, 1\}$,

$$\int_{\underline{c}_1}^{\bar{c}_1} [\alpha_2\pi_2^c(c_1, c_2) - c_0]v^*[c_2, \eta^*(c_1)] \, dH_1(c_1)$$

$$\geq \int_{\underline{c}_1}^{\bar{c}_1} [\alpha_2\pi_2^c(c_1, c_2) - c_0]v[c_2, \eta^*(c_1)] \, dH_1(c_1) \tag{8.7}$$

An example used by Milgrom and Roberts (1982) will clarify the working of the model. Let $a = 10, b = 1, \underline{c}_1 = 0.5, \bar{c}_1 = 2, \underline{c}_2 = 1.5$,

$\bar{c}_2 = 2$, $\alpha_1 = \alpha_2 = 1$, and $c_0 = 7$. Assume that the only possible values for c_1 and c_2 are $\underline{c}_1$ and $\bar{c}_1$ and $\underline{c}_2$ and $\bar{c}_2$, respectively. Finally, let h_1 be the probability that $c_1 = \bar{c}_1$, and let h_2 be the probability that $c_2 = \bar{c}_2$. Then the following can be readily calculated:

$$\pi_1^c(\underline{c}_1, \underline{c}_2) = 12.25, \qquad \pi_2^c(\underline{c}_1, \underline{c}_2) - c_0 = -0.75 \qquad (8.8)$$

$$\pi_1^c(\underline{c}_1, \bar{c}_2) = 13.44, \qquad \pi_2^c(\underline{c}_1, \bar{c}_2) - c_0 = -2.31 \qquad (8.9)$$

$$\pi_1^c(\bar{c}_1, \underline{c}_2) = 6.25, \qquad \pi_2^c(\bar{c}_1, \underline{c}_2) - c_0 = 2 \qquad (8.10)$$

$$\pi_1^c(\bar{c}_1, \bar{c}_2) = 7.11, \qquad \pi_2^c(\bar{c}_1, \bar{c}_2) - c_0 = 0.11 \qquad (8.11)$$

$$q_1^m(\underline{c}_1) = 4.75, \qquad \pi_1^m(\underline{c}_1) = 22.56 \qquad (8.12)$$

$$q_1^m(\bar{c}_1) = 4, \qquad \pi_1^m(\bar{c}_1) = 16 \qquad (8.13)$$

It is immediately evident from equations (8.8) through (8.11) that entry is unprofitable for firm 2 when firm 1 has the low marginal cost and profitable when firm 1 has the high marginal cost.

From this example, two different sorts of equilibria exist: a *pooling equilibrium*, at which $\eta^*(\underline{c}_1) = \eta^*(\bar{c}_1)$, and a *separating equilibrium*, at which $\eta^*(\underline{c}_1) \neq \eta^*(\bar{c}_1)$. At a separating equilibrium, firm 2 can infer the correct value of c_1 by observing q_{11}; however, this is impossible at a pooling equilibrium. The strategies for the pooling equilibrium are

$$\eta^*(\underline{c}_1) = \eta^*(\bar{c}_1) = q_1^m(\underline{c}_1) = 4.75 \qquad (8.14)$$

$$v^*(\underline{c}_2, q_{11}) = 1$$
$$v^*(\bar{c}_2, q_{11}) = 0 \quad \text{if } q_{11} \geq 4.75$$
$$\qquad\qquad = 1 \quad \text{otherwise} \qquad (8.15)$$

and, for the separating equilibrium,

$$\eta^*(\underline{c}_1) = 7.2, \qquad \eta^*(\bar{c}_1) = q_1^m(\bar{c}_1) = 4 \qquad (8.16)$$

$$v^*(c_2, q_{11}) = 1 \quad \text{if } q_{11} < 7.2$$
$$\qquad\qquad = 0 \quad \text{otherwise} \qquad (8.17)$$

Note that firm 1 chooses the monopoly output of a firm with low cost in the first period of a pooling equilibrium. Firm 2 elects to enter the market if it has the low marginal cost; however, if it has the high cost, it enters only if $q_{11} < 4.75$. Expected profits from firm 1 are

$$22.56(1 + h_2) + 12.25(1 - h_2) \quad \text{if } c_1 = \underline{c}_1 \qquad (8.18)$$

$$15.44(1 + h_2) + 6.25(1 - h_2) \quad \text{if } c_1 = \bar{c}_1 \qquad (8.19)$$

and, for firm 2,

$$2h_1 - 0.75(1 - h_1) \quad \text{if } c_2 = \underline{c}_2 \qquad (8.20)$$

$$0 \quad \text{if } c_2 = \bar{c}_2 \qquad (8.21)$$

Thus, the pooling strategies form an equilibrium if $h_2 > 0.061$ and $0.273 < h_1 < 0.954$. More precisely, equation (8.18) is optimal for firm 1 if it has the low cost, but if it has the high cost, equation (8.19) is best only if $h_2 > 0.061$. Equation (8.20) is best for firm 2 if it has the low cost and $h_1 > 0.273$, and equation (8.21) is optimal if it has the high cost and $h_1 < 0.954$.

By choosing $q_{11} = 4.75$ for either cost condition, firm 1 engages in limit pricing when it has the high marginal cost. Recall that, as a monopolist, firm 1 chooses a point on its demand curve; hence, choosing q_{11} is equivalent to choosing a price, and if q_{11} exceeds the monopolist's profit-maximizing output, then firm 1 is choosing a price beneath the monopoly price. Hence, it is limit pricing. If firm 2 has the low marginal cost, the limit pricing has no effect on entry, but if its marginal cost is high, limit pricing prevents entry. Thus, from the standpoint of firm 1, limit pricing is effective with probability h_2, and from the standpoint of firm 2, it is being subjected to limit pricing with probability h_1.

At the separating equilibrium, expected profits are 39.12 for firm 1 if $c_1 = \underline{c}_1$ and $22.25 + 7.11h_2$ if $c_1 = \bar{c}_1$. For firm 2 they are $2h_1$ for the low value of c_2 and $0.11h_1$ for the high value. Firm 2 cannot do better, for the value of q_{11} signals the actual value of c_1. It enters if $c_1 = \bar{c}_1$ and stays out if $c_1 = \underline{c}_1$. Meanwhile, firm 1 also can do no better. If it has the low marginal cost, raising q_{11} will merely lower first-period profit, whereas lowering q_{11} will cause entry and will reduce second-period profit by far more than can be recouped in period 1. On the other hand, if firm 1 has the high marginal cost, it can do no better than to reap monopoly profits in period 1 and accept entry in period 2. If it should forestall entry by choosing $q_{11} = 7.2$, the period-2 gains will not offset the profit reduction in period 1.

Here, too, firm 1 engages in entry-preventing behavior part of the time: when it has low cost. It does not fool firm 2. Quite the contrary, it signals its costs to firm 2, and firm 2 stays out knowing that entry would be unprofitable. At the same time, the strategy followed by firm 2 makes the cost-revealing strategy of firm 1 optimal for firm 1.

Other separating equilibria exist, and they are like the one shown in equations (8.16) and (8.17), with 7.2 replaced by another output level. A higher level can be used, but if 7.2 is lowered more than negligibly, then it is worthwhile for firm 1, when $c_1 = \bar{c}_1$, to choose this level in the first period in order to deter entry. Such behavior destroys the equilibrium. For example, if firm 2 will enter if $q_{11} < 7.1$ and will stay out otherwise, then firm 1 will be best off always choosing $q_{11} = 7.1$, no matter what the value of c_1. But not only does this destroy the separating equilibrium, these strategies do not even form a pooling equilibrium, because firm 2 can do better by following a strategy similar to its pooling equilibrium strategy in equation (8.15).

Two aspects of the Milgrom and Roberts model deserve comment. First, it may seem unreasonable that the firms learn one another's marginal costs as soon as the entrant comes into the market. Second, limiting the analysis to two periods is substantially less general than analyzing an infinite horizon model. It is very likely that both of these generalizations can be made with no change in the essential nature of the results; however, the analysis will become more complex. If costs do not become immediately known, the firms probably will choose outputs for an expected noncooperative equilibrium. If the horizon is also lengthened, it is possible that the true costs will become known over time as the firms infer one another's costs from observed output choices. With only one possible entrant, the model has a two-period character even if the horizon is infinite, because once the entrant comes into the market, the market switches from a stage-1 situation with an active firm and a possible entrant on the sidelines to a stage-2 situation with two active firms and no entry threat. One difference between two periods and many periods is that the established firm must keep up its entry-preventing behavior indefinitely if the behavior is success-ful in deterring entry, whereas in the two-period model, if entry is deterred in the first half (period 1), then straight monopoly profits are reaped in the second (period 2).

8.2. Capital stocks and scale economies as entry barriers

Independent of one another, Bain (1956) and Sylos-Labini (1962) proposed the idea that scale economies in the firm can cause entry barriers, resulting in positive profits for the firms in the industry. Bain's study is largely empirical, although the underlying theoretical arguments are made clear.

Sylos-Labini's example of static entry

The following example of static entry is in the spirit of Sylos-Labini's presentation and serves to illustrate the idea. Imag-ine there are three possible technologies available to a firm. Each is characterized by a plant size, and each firm consists of one plant. The *small technology* has constant marginal cost of 20, maximum output level of 100, and fixed cost of 100. The *medium technology* has constant marginal cost of 15, maximum output of 500, and fixed cost of 1,000. The figures for the *large technology* are 8 for marginal cost, 2,000 for plant capacity, and 10,000 for fixed cost. These figures are summarized in Table 8.1.

The optimal technology depends, of course, on industry demand for the homogeneous good produced by the firms. Suppose *inverse demand* to be given by $p = 30 - Q/800$, where Q is *total industry output,* and look at a Cournot equilibrium for six large firms. Output of each is at the maximum of 2,000, market price is 15, and profits are 4,000 per firm. Given the firms already in the market, neither small nor medium-size entrants would be viable. The equi-librium price of 15 is below the marginal cost of small firms and just

Table 8.1. *Illustration of entry barriers based on scale economies*

Technology	Marginal cost	Maximum output	Fixed cost
Small	20	100	100
Medium	15	500	1,000
Large	8	2,000	10,000

equal to the marginal cost of medium firms; therefore, either type of firm would have a loss if it were in the market. Meanwhile, a seventh large firm also would not be viable. Calculating the Cournot equilibrium for $n = 7$, each firm produces 2,000, price is 12.5, and profit is $-1,000$ per firm. Thus, there is an equilibrium in which each firm has positive profit of 4,000, and no additional firm of any size can enter profitably. This is clearly due to indivisibilities, for if a large firm could be scaled to any size, keeping marginal cost constant and allowing both maximum output and fixed cost to shrink in the same proportion, the equilibrium market price would have to be 13, which is the minimum average total cost of the large-scale plant $(8 + 10,000/2,000)$. Any time a higher price prevailed, it would be in the interest of an entrant to come in on a small scale, produce to its small capacity, obtain a price in excess of 13, and reap profits of price minus 13 on each unit sold.

Before leaving this example, imagine two other inverse demand functions. First, let $p = 30 - Q/200$. One equilibrium has five medium firms, with each producing 500 units, price at 17.5, and profit at 250 per firm. Although no firm of any of the three sizes can profitably enter, other equilibria are possible. Consider one large and one medium firm. The large firm will produce 1,950 and the medium firm 500; price is 17.75, and profits for the two firms are 9,550 and 387.5, respectively. Yet another equilibrium consists of two large firms, with output at $1,466\frac{2}{3}$, price at $15\frac{1}{2}$, and profit at $3,333\frac{1}{3}$ each. If the inverse demand function is $p = 30 - Q/50$, the equilibrium will consist of four small firms, each producing 100, with price at 22 and profit at 100.

A dynamic model of entry with a rational, maximizing entrant

We turn now to a dynamic model of entry with two economic agents. The first, firm 1, is an established monopolist, and the second is a potential entrant, firm 2. There is a *demand function* $q_{it} = f(p_{1t})$ that the monopolist faces as long as it is alone in the market. Should firm 2 enter, the *two firms' demand functions* are, respectively, $q_{1t} = f_1(p_{1t}, p_{2t}) = f_1(p_t)$ and $q_{2t} = f_2(p_t)$. These demand functions are assumed to satisfy the assumptions given in Chapter 3, Section 3.3. A consistency requirement is needed for $f(p_{1t})$ and $f_1(p_{1t}, p_{2t})$ to ensure that if p_{2t} is so high that firm 2 sells nothing, then the two demand functions specify the same level of demand. That is, if $f_2(p_{1t}, p_{2t}) = 0$, then $f_1(p_{1t}, p_{2t}) = f(p_{1t})$.

The cost functions for the two firms are those specified in Chapter 7, Section 7.2, where the *cost of production* is $C_i(q_{it}, K_{it})$ for firm i, and the capital stock is related to investment by $K_{i,t+1} = \delta K_{it} + I_{it}$. Finally, it is required that for all prices that exceed marginal cost $[p_{it} \geq C_i^1(q_{it}, K_{it})]$, the single-period profit function be concave. That is, $\partial^2 \pi_i / \partial p_{it}^2 = (2 - C_i'' f_i^i) f_i^i + (p_{it} - C_i') f_i^{ii} < 0$, $\partial^2 \pi_i / \partial K_{it}^2 = -C_i'' < 0$, and $(\partial^2 \pi_i / \partial p_{it}^2)(\partial^2 \pi_i / \partial K_{it}^2) - (\partial^2 \pi_i / \partial p_{it} \partial K_{it})^2 \geq 0$.

Of particular interest is the way the firms make decisions and the nature of the resulting equilibrium. It is assumed that both firms know the structure that has been outlined. Firm 1, as the established firm, is assumed to choose K_{11} in period 0. The first period in which it produces and sells is period 1. The entrant can make no decisions prior to period 1. From period 1 onward, it is free to elect to enter the market at any time. If it decides to enter at time t, that decision is made known to firm 1 prior to the selection of p_{1t} and I_{1t}. In period t, $I_{2t} = K_{2,t+1}$ is selected, and period $t + 1$ is the first in which the entrant can produce and sell.

Firm 1 makes no threats. That is, it makes no statements that in the event of entry it will pursue such low prices that the entrant will suffer losses. Rather, it is understood by both that should the entrant come into the market, they will choose from that time forth in a noncooperative equilibrium fashion. The equilibrium strategies are described next after the firms' objective functions are specified.

Assume for the moment that firm 2 decides to enter the market in period t. Then the two *firms' discounted cash flows* are

$$-K_{11} + \sum_{\tau=1}^{t-1} \alpha^\tau \{p_{1\tau}f(p_{1\tau}) - C_1[f(p_{1\tau}), K_{1\tau}] - (K_{1,\tau+1} - \delta K_{1\tau})\}$$

$$+ [\alpha^t \{p_{1t}f(p_{1t}) - C_1[f(p_{1t}), K_{1t}] - (K_{1,t+1} - \delta K_{1t})\}$$

$$+ \sum_{\tau=t+1}^{\infty} \alpha^\tau \{p_{1\tau}f_1(p_\tau) - C_1[f_1(p_\tau), K_{1\tau}] - (K_{1,\tau+1} - \delta K_{1\tau})\}] \quad (8.22)$$

$$\alpha^t K_{2,t+1} + \sum_{\tau=t+1}^{\infty} \alpha^\tau \{p_{2\tau}f_2(p_\tau) - C_2[f_2(p_\tau), K_{2\tau}] - (K_{2,\tau+1} - \delta K_{2t})\}$$

$$(8.23)$$

In equation (8.22), the expression in double brackets is the discounted profit to firm 1 from period t onward. Recall that K_{1t} is already determined when period t begins and that firm 2 chooses only $K_{2,t+1}$ in period t.

The strategies of the two firms are considered in steps. The first step is to determine equilibrium behavior from period t onward, given the decision of firm 2 to enter in period t. After that, it can be determined if there are actually any conditions under which it is in the interest of firm 2 to enter, and, if so, what is the optimal period to do so. Finally, with the decision process of firm 2 fully understood, it will be seen whether or not it is possible for firm 1 to engage in entry-preventing behavior and, if it is possible, whether or not it is optimal.

To anticipate these steps in outline, first note that K_{1t} is already determined when period t is entered, which means that K_{1t} is an initial condition for the duopoly market commencing in that period. Thus, it should not be surprising that the equilibrium discounted profits of both firms from period t onward are functions of K_{1t}. If there is no value of K_{1t} for which firm 2 will obtain positive discounted profits, then firm 2 will never enter. Conversely, if firm 2 will always have positive discounted profits, no matter what the value of K_{1t}, then firm 2 cannot be prevented from coming into the market. The intermediate case is, of course, the most interesting, where some values of K_{1t} correspond to positive profits for firm 2 and others correspond to negative profits. By keeping K_{1t} in the range of values corresponding to negative profits for firm 2, firm 1 can prevent entry. It is assumed that the decision process used by firm 2 to decide on entry is known to firm 1 and that firm 1 takes advantage of this information in making plans. Thus, the decision is by a Stackelberg leader-follower process in which the established firm moves first, setting conditions that are transmitted to the entrant. The entrant is in the follower's role, reacting to the leader's decision. The model and results presented here are from Friedman (1979); however, other models in which entry prevention can occur through the established firm's investment policy are those of Spence (1979) and Dixit (1980).

To return to the two-firm market commencing with the entry of firm 2 in period t, the two firms' *strategies* are, respectively, $(p_{1t}, K_{1,t+1}, p_{1,t+1}, K_{1,t+2}, p_{1,t+2}, \ldots)$ and $(K_{2,t+1}, p_{2,t+1}, K_{2,t+2}, p_{2,t+2}, \ldots)$. Note that the choice of p_{1t} by firm 1 has no strategic import whatever. It is chosen to maximize the period-t profits of firm 1, at which time firm 1 is still the only seller active in the market. From Friedman (1979) it is known that a noncooperative equilibrium exists for this market. The equilibrium is unique if the following additional conditions are satisfied: $f_i^{ii} + |f_i^{12}| \leq 0$ and $0 \geq C_i^{12} > \max[-1, -C_i^{22}/(|f_i^1| + |f_i^2|)]$ for $i = 1, 2$. Note, however, that uniqueness obtains when strategies are restricted to the simple strategies outlined earlier, where the action taken in each period is precisely specified in advance. There are no contingent plans that would, for example; make the price or capital decision of a firm depend on the past history of the market. For the remaining discussion of the model, the additional conditions that ensure uniqueness of equilibrium are retained.

Recall that capital is assumed to have no resale market; therefore, the smallest possible value of $K_{i,t+1}$, obtained when investment in period t is zero, is δK_{it}. Two important facts about the equilibrium behavior of capital stocks are that, in equilibrium, capital stocks will converge to steady-state values that can be denoted (K_1^*, K_2^*), and, for each firm, the higher its capital stock, the lower its marginal cost at any given output level. With that in mind, imagine the sequence of events following the entry of firm 2 when K_{1t} is above the steady-state value K_1^*. First, K_1 will fall at the fastest technically feasible rate to K_1^*. Because K_1 is falling, the marginal cost curve of firm 1 is rising. While it is below the steady-state level, it causes the equilibrium path of prices to be below the steady-state equilibrium prices, exerting a depressing effect on the discounted profits of firm 2. Because there is a unique equilibrium path associated with each initial capital stock of firm 1, the equilibrium discounted profits of the two firms can be written $F_1(K_{1t})$ and $F_2(K_{1t})$. Therefore, given entry at period t and equilibrium behavior following entry, equations (8.22) and (8.23) become

$$-K_{11} + \sum_{\tau=1}^{t-1} \alpha^\tau \{p_{1\tau} f(p_{1\tau}) - C_1[f(p_{1\tau}), K_{1\tau}] - (K_{1,\tau+1} - \delta K_{1\tau})\}$$
$$+ \alpha^t F_1(K_{1t}) \tag{8.24}$$

$$\alpha^t F_2(K_{1t}) \tag{8.25}$$

$F_2(K_{1t})$ is decreasing in K_{1t}. That is, $dF_2/dK_{1t} < 0$; therefore, if there is $\overline{K}_1$ for which $F_2(\overline{K}_1) = 0$, then entry prevention is possible. To carry further the examination of equilibrium requires that the remaining parts of the two agents' strategies be specified. For the entrant, there are two reasonable possibilities. One is to enter the first time that a value of K_1 is observed to be below $\overline{K}_1$. The second is to choose a discounted profit-maximizing response to the preentry plan of firm 1. These two variants are discussed in turn.

Let K_1^{**} denote the capital stock that will be optimal for the monopolist if there is no possibility of entry. If $K_1^{**} \geq \overline{K}_1$, then the monopolist will automatically prevent entry by engaging in profit maximization, ignoring the possibility of entry. Take the case where $K_1^{**} < \overline{K}_1$. Firm 1 must compare its discounted profits if it prevents entry (which will be greatest if $K_{1t} = \overline{K}_1$ for all t) with the best it can do if it allows entry. Concavity of the firm's profit with respect to K_1 ensures that if entry is prevented and $K_1^{**} < \overline{K}_1$, then the optimum entry-preventing capital is $\overline{K}_1$. If entry is to be allowed, firm 1 wishes to maximize $-K_{11} + \alpha F_1(K_{11})$ with respect to K_{11} subject to $0 \leq K_{11} < \overline{K}_1$. If $F_1(K_{11})$ is increasing in K_{11} throughout the allowed interval, then a maximum will not be reached; however, that is not a difficulty. The maximum would have $-\overline{K}_1 + \alpha F_1(\overline{K}_1)$ as its least upper bound. This can be compared with the firm's best entry-preventing profits. If entry-preventing profits are less, then the monopolist can earn arbitrarily close to $-\overline{K}_1 + \alpha F_1(\overline{K}_1)$ by choosing a value of K_{11} that is below, but very close to, $\overline{K}_1$.

Under the second specification for firm 2, firm 1 chooses a capital stock and price sequence $(K_{11}, P_{11}, K_{12}, p_{12}, \ldots)$ that it will follow as long as firm 2 has not decided to enter the market. As soon as firm 2 decides to enter, firm 1 switches to the policy associated with $F_1(K_{1t})$ and $F_2(K_{1t})$. Firm 2 chooses an entry time that maximizes its discounted profits, given the preentry policy of firm 1. This means that firm 2 evaluates $\alpha^t F_2(K_{1t})$ for all t. If $\alpha^t F_2(K_{1t})$ is never positive, firm 2 never enters the market. As before, that would require $K_{1t} \geq \overline{K}_1$ for all t. If a positive value is sometimes attained, then the firm enters at that time for which a maximum is attained. If the maximum occurs at more than one time, the firm enters in the first period in which the maximum occurs. As before, firm 1 simply examines all possible plans it can follow and chooses one that maximizes its discounted profits, if such exists, or, if not, chooses one that is arbitrarily close to the upper bound on its discounted profits. Looking more closely at how the plan of firm 1 is related to its discounted profits, imagine a particular preentry policy. Firm 1 knows whether or not a given preentry policy will induce entry, and when it will induce entry; hence, the discounted profits associated with any policy are readily calculated.

Comments on the dynamic entry model

Note that both specifications of the firms' decision processes have the Stackelberg leader-follower feature. Firm 1 chooses a course of action that firm 2 takes as given and with respect to which firm 2 maximizes. Whether or not both of these specifications are, essentially, noncooperative equilibria depends on precisely how the strategy of firm 1 is stated. Note, however, that under either specification, firm 1 is not guaranteed to be using a profit-maximizing strategy. Its strategy may be within some small ϵ of attaining maximized profits; hence, the equilibria are, at best, ε-*noncooperative equilibria*. This occurs when firm 1 can achieve any level of discounted profit up to, but not including, some amount F_1^*. It can then come within a small ε of achieving F_1^*.

In comparing the two ways of treating firm 2, the first, in which it enters on first observing $K_{1t} \leq \overline{K}_1$, has the advantage that firm 2 is not presumed to predict the preentry policy of firm 1 far into the future. In exchange, firm 2 can enter at a time when profits are less than they would have been if it had delayed entry for a while. The second way of treating the entry of firm 2 requires it to know the preentry policy that firm 1 will follow into the indefinite future, and this allows firm 2 to enter at the best possible moment.

It cannot be emphasized too strongly that the driving force behind entry prevention in this model is the imperfect reversibility of investment. If firm 1 obtains a very large capital stock, it will be stuck with it when firm 2 enters. Were investment perfectly reversible, preentry capital stock would have no bearing on the entry decision. This point is underscored by looking at the work of Flaherty (1980*b*), in which capital does not enter, but a firm pays an adjustment cost if it wishes to alter its production rate. This causes imperfect reversibility of the production rate and makes it possible for the established firm to prevent entry by a high preentry production rate. Were the entrant to come into the market, the monopolist's output level would fall, but it would fall gradually because of the adjustment cost, and while it was falling, the entrant's profit rate would be below the rate that would prevail in the steady state.

There is another fundamentally important feature of the equilibrium with entry prevention, found in the work of Flaherty (1980*b*), Spence (1979), and Dixit (1980), as well as the model from Friedman (1979) presented earlier. There are no empty threats. To see what is meant by an empty threat, imagine a situation in which the monopolist can charge one of two prices, high or low, and the entrant can enter or not enter. The entrant makes his choice and tells the monopolist, and then the monopolist makes his price choice. This is illustrated in Figure 8.1. If the entrant stays out, the profits are 10 for the monopolist and 0 for the entrant, provided the

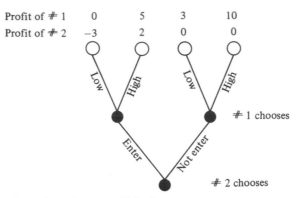

Figure 8.1. A noncredible threat.

monopolist chooses the high price. If the entrant comes in, they are 5 and 2, respectively, if the monopolist chooses a high price, and 0 and −3 if he chooses low. Now note the following two noncooperative equilibria: (1) The entrant chooses to stay out, and the monopolist chooses high if the entrant is out and low if he is in. (2) The entrant chooses to come into the market, and the monopolist chooses high no matter what the entrant does. Check that these are actually both equilibria. In equilibrium 1, if the entrant switches from stay out to enter, its payoff drops from 0 to −3; so it is maximizing, given the monopolist's strategy. If the monopolist chooses low in place of high for the not-enter condition, profit will drop to 3 from 10; if it changes from low to high in the enter condition, profit will not change. It is left as an exercise to the reader to verify that equilibrium 2 is indeed an equilibrium.

Equilibrium 1 has an undesirable feature that can be interpreted as a noncredible threat. Note that for the entrant, staying out is preferable to entering, because if it enters, the monopolist will play low. But consider the situation from the perspective of the monopolist, assuming that the entrant has just announced a commitment to enter. The monopolist is faced with the entrant committed and can, itself, choose high to obtain 5 or low to obtain 0. Faced with actual entry, it is not credible that the monopolist will really choose low. The monopolist may tell the entrant in advance that it will do so, in order to frighten the entrant into staying out, but once the entrant is actually in, only loss and no gain comes of playing low. The second equilibrium is said to be a *perfect noncooperative equilibrium,* because, looking at any intermediate point that might be reached by the agents in the game, the strategies that are being followed are a noncooperative equilibrium for the subgame.[1] This condition is violated in equilibrium 1.

8.3. Sequential entry

Sequential entry is discussed later in only a schematic way, because clear-cut formal results are not available. Nonetheless, certain conclusions appear so plausible that it is worthwhile to suggest them. First, a differentiated products model is specified in which firms can choose the nature of their products. Using this model as a vehicle, there follows a discussion of entry-preventing behavior. The principal suggestion of this section is that the existing firms may engage in entry-preventing behavior to such a great extent that their prices will be driven to levels well below the Cournot equilibrium for a model in which entry cannot occur. In effect, there is competition among firms to induce entrants to settle near one's rivals. This competition narrows the range of choices for each firm in a way that does not occur when there is only one established firm. Imagine a single-quality continuum represented by the real line, along which a firm is assumed to choose a location denoted i. Thus, i, which can be any real number, denotes both the firm and its location. Suppose the firms to be price choosers, and suppose the consumers to have tastes that are uniformly distributed. Letting the set of firms be denoted A, the *inverse demand function* of firm i is assumed to have the following linear form:

$$p_{it} = a - b \sum_{j \in A} \lambda^{|i-j|} q_{jt} \tag{8.26}$$

where $a, b > 0$ and $\lambda \in (0, 1)$. With this formulation there is no need to distinguish between a nonexistent firm and a firm that produces zero. The *cost of production,* identical for each firm, is

$$C_{it} = \frac{cq_{it}^2}{K_{it} - k} \tag{8.27}$$

where the parameter $k > 0$ is the smallest capital stock with which a firm can possibly produce. *Investment* in period t is

$$K_{i,t+1} - \delta K_{it} \tag{8.28}$$

where $\delta \in (0, 1)$, and $1 - \delta$ is the rate of depreciation.

It is plausible that the firms will, in equilibrium, be spaced at equal intervals. Henceforth it is assumed that they are spaced at equal intervals if not noted explicitly otherwise. Letting $\mu^j = \lambda^{|i-j|}$, where i and j are any two adjacent firms, equation (8.26) can be rewritten more simply, and the firms can be indexed in the customary way, with indexes taking on (positive and negative) integer values:

$$p_{it} = a - bq_{it} - b \sum_{j=1}^{\infty} \mu^j(q_{i-j,t} + q_{i+j,t}) \tag{8.29}$$

With α being the common discount parameter, the *firm's objective function* is

$$\sum_{t=1}^{\infty} \alpha^t \left(q_{it} p_{it} - \frac{cq_{it}^2}{K_{it} - k} - \frac{1 - \alpha\delta}{\alpha} K_{it} \right) \tag{8.30}$$

For a model having no threat of entry, it is easily seen that a *noncooperative equilibrium* is characterized by

$$q_{it} = \frac{1 - \mu}{2b} [a - 2(\gamma c)^{\frac{1}{2}}] \tag{8.31}$$

$$p_{it} = \frac{1 - \mu}{2} a + (1 + \mu)(\gamma c)^{\frac{1}{2}} \tag{8.32}$$

where $\gamma = (1 - \alpha\delta)/\alpha$. The steady-state capital stock is

$$K_{it} = k + \frac{1 - \mu}{2b} \left[a \left(\frac{c}{\gamma} \right)^{\frac{1}{2}} - 2c \right] \tag{8.33}$$

and the cash flow per period is

$$\pi_{it}^* = (1 - \mu)^2 \left[\frac{a - 2(\gamma c)^{\frac{1}{2}}}{2(b)^{\frac{1}{2}}} \right]^2 - \gamma k \tag{8.34}$$

The parameter μ indicates the number and closeness of firms. As μ increases and approaches 1, the firms are becoming ever closer, and as can be seen from equations (8.31) through (8.34), output per firm, price, capital, and profit all fall. However, if $k = 0$, equilibrium profit will be positive, no matter how closely the firms are spaced.

Now consider entry into the market. If firms can costlessly change locations, then it is expected that they will always remain evenly spaced. If they select their capital stocks without intending to prevent entry, then entry will continue until equilibrium profits are zero. This occurs when

$$\mu = 1 - \frac{2(b\gamma k)^{\frac{1}{2}}}{a - 2(\gamma c)^{\frac{1}{2}}} \qquad (8.35)$$

Now consider the situation if μ is below the critical level given by equation (8.35) and the firms are sensitive to the possibility of entry. First note that for an individual firm, its concern is that new firms do not locate near it and that neighboring firms do not inch toward it. Therefore, it is acceptable to the firm that an entrant can locate profitably nearby if there are more profitable locations far away. The reason is, of course, that if better locations exist at a distance, then firms will not locate nearby even if doing so would yield positive profits. Thus, the incentive of a single firm is to increase its capital stock enough so that locating in its immediate vicinity is inferior to locating elsewhere and so that it still obtains at least as much profit as if entry did occur nearby.

Of course, all firms have the same incentives; hence, they are likely to continually increase their capital stocks to the point where all their profit levels are very small and no new firm can enter anywhere and make a profit. In a model in which firms can costlessly change location, this equilibrium requires that all firms make zero profits. The situation is opposite to Lancaster's firehouse example, for there are too few firms, each with too much capital. At the same time, each is earning zero profits; therefore, none achieves any gain by attempting to prevent entry. Meanwhile, note the effect on a single firm stemming from the entry-preventing policies of the other firms. They all have very large capital stocks that decrease the profit opportunities of the firm in question. Certainly, by acting to lower the potential profits of a possible entrant, they lower the profit possibilities of existing firms.

8.4. Exit

In this section, exit is considered in only an informal and schematic way. Analogous to the question of whether or not to enter a market and when to enter is the question of when to leave it. And, just as an established firm may be able to prevent entry, such a firm may be able to cause the exit of a rival. A striking difference between entry and exit is that the fundamental asymmetry in the entry situation is absent. Rather than having established firms and potential entrants, in the exit situation there need be only established firms. If the market is symmetric in the sense that all firms are identical, it is difficult to see how one can drive another out without driving itself out at the same time.

Consider a market having two established firms that seek to maximize discounted profits. One firm, say the first, can drive out the second if it has a strategy that will ensure that, from some time t_0 onward, firm 2 will have negative discounted profits. If firm 1 follows this strategy, then in maximizing its discounted profits, firm 2 will exit at some time no later than t_0. Whether or not firm 1 will carry out the strategy will depend, of course, on the diminished profit it will receive over the time until firm 2 exits and the additional profit it can reap after it is alone in the market.

A second way of modeling exit is the ruin approach (Shubik, 1959). For each firm it is necessary to keep track of its net worth (or, alternatively, cash reserve). A firm will seek to stay in the market as long as the rules allow and will seek to maximize profits (or minimize losses), but it must exit if its net worth drops below zero. As in the sketch in the preceding paragraph, one firm will drive another out if it can do so and if doing so will yield to it the highest discounted profit.

Before leaving the topics of entry and exit, it should be noted that everything covered in this chapter can be regarded as preliminaries to the study of markets in which firms enter and leave over time, in which demand and cost conditions change, perhaps in unpredictable ways, and in which new firms possess vigor and flexibility that lessen as they grow and age. Marshall (1890) discusses such a process when he writes of the life cycle of the firm using a biological analogy. More recently, Alchian (1950) and Winter (1964) have considered competitive markets in this way.

8.5. Summary

It cannot be too strongly emphasized that entry and exit are intrinsically dynamic processes; therefore, they must be studied with the aid of dynamic models. To claim to study entry with static models, which is called static entry in this chapter, is not the study of entry at all. It is the determination of the maximum number of firms that can coexist, once established, at equilibrium. The crucial difference between entry and static entry is that when properly examining entry, one takes into account that market conditions undergo changes when a new firm comes in. They do not change instantaneously from an n-firm equilibrium to equilibrium of $n + 1$ firms. The nature and speed of that adjustment process can affect the predisposition of firms to enter, and the preentry behavior of entrenched firms can affect the adjustment process.

Two important themes run through the (dynamic) entry discussion. The first concerns whether or not existing firms can prevent or retard the entry of new firms, and the second concerns the tendency of entry threats to bring about more competitive behavior. Regarding the former, two avenues are found to prevent entry. One is through precommitment to behavior that will affect the postentry prospects of the new firm. For example, where capital investment is irreversible, and where higher capital for the established firm at the time of entry will bring lower postentry profits to the new firm, carrying a very high capital stock can prevent entry by making the early postentry periods sufficiently unprofitable.

The second avenue is information provision; this obtains when the entrant is lacking some information about the structure of the market that it can infer from the preentry behavior of the established firm.

The preceding results, of course, are developed in two-agent models, where one agent is an established firm and the other is a potential entrant. Where entry prevention does occur in these models, it is accompanied by lower preentry prices and higher preentry output than would obtain if there were no entry threat. Profits are not, in general, eliminated, nor is marginal cost pricing caused. The informal discussion of markets having many established firms and many potential entrants suggests a kind of rivalry among established firms that can serve to largely eliminate profits. Each firm wants its own neighborhood to be less profitable to an entrant than some other neighborhood where an entrant might settle. This competition to exclude entry probably causes less product variety and lower prices for existing products than is socially optimal; however, this conjecture awaits careful investigation.

Although the two-agent models (one entrant and one established firm) yield suggestive results, I am skeptical that they can be carried over fully to many-firm, many-entrant situations. This determination remains to be carried out, as does a full investigation of how uncertainty and incomplete information affect the entry process.

9

Oligopoly and noncooperative game theory

The reader familiar with game theory will have noticed that the models discussed in earlier chapters are treated as noncooperative games of strategy, and the reader who is totally unfamiliar with noncooperative game theory will have obtained a lengthy introduction to the subject, together with an application of the topic to oligopoly theory. Game theory has been applied to many areas of economics and used extensively in political science as well. In addition to oligopoly, it has been used in general equilibrium, public goods, voting theory, and committee decision. The role of this chapter is to make the connection explicit between game theory and oligopoly. This is done by providing a brief treatment of noncooperative game theory and then showing explicitly how several of the models of earlier chapters can be viewed as games. Section 9.1 contains a brief general discussion of games and game theory that is intended to set the subject in perspective. Section 9.2 presents a standard model of a noncooperative n-person game, and Section 9.3 connects the model of Section 9.2 directly to some of the oligopoly models of other chapters. Section 9.4 presents an important refinement of the noncooperative equilibrium, called the perfect equilibrium. Section 9.5 has some concluding remarks.

9.1. Overview of game theory

Essential features of many games of strategy include the following: (a) There are two or more decision makers, called *players.* (b) Each player wishes to maximize his own utility, called his *payoff.* (c) Each player is aware that any other player's individual action can affect the payoff he receives. (d) The interests of one player vis-à-vis the others are neither perfectly opposed nor perfectly coincident. Looking at (a), were there only one player, he would face a straightforward maximization problem. Such a problem is sometimes called a *game against nature,* and although technically it can be classified as a game of strategy, it is not very interesting from that point of view. The stipulation in (b) that each player wishes to maximize his own payoff is a statement that each player is a rational and conscious decision maker. Condition (c) states that if the decisions of all players except one are frozen, then as the behavior of that one player is altered, the payoffs to the other players will change, and they realize this. Finally, in (d), as one player's behavior is altered, anything can happen to the payoffs to others. A change that benefits one player can either help or hurt another, and although certain actions can simultaneously help all players, the combination of actions that maximizes the payoff of one player will, in general, not maximize the payoffs to all.

Of course, (a) and (b) are standard features of economic models; however, (c) is not. In some models (most prominently, competitive models), the behavior of one single player (economic agent – consumer or firm) has no effect on any others. Condition (d) is present in many economic models, although, like (c), it is absent in competitive models. As a group taking concerted action, economic agents have some scope for mutually beneficial action, but the best outcome for one individual will not be the best outcome for all. If the agents are viewed as acting individually, rather than as forming cooperative groups (*coalitions*), then a competitive economic model is a model of many intertwined games against nature. Indeed, the dominant tradition of competitive analysis in economics consists in viewing the interactions of economic agents as being an interplay among many mutually determining games against nature. This viewpoint is the genius of the competitive approach, and it has been extremely fruitful. Certain situations in economics do not lend themselves readily to competitive analysis; hence the need for game theory. Oligopoly, where condition (c) obtains, is an outstanding example.

Games are often categorized according to (i) cooperativeness, (ii) number of players, and (iii) payoff structure. By cooperativeness, games are divided into the cooperative and noncooperative. *Cooperative games* are those in which the players have the capacity to make binding agreements. Labor-management negotiations provide an example of a two-person cooperative game if it is understood that management and labor are each single players and it is impossible for either player to violate any contract that they both sign. A *noncooperative game* is one in which the players cannot make binding agreements. It is usual to regard the opportunity for binding agreements as totally present or totally absent, rather than to allow for various degrees of enforceability being available at various costs. Cournot oligopoly is an example of an n-person noncooperative game. Oligopoly in general, in an unregulated industry and where antitrust legislation rules out legally enforceable agreements, is an example of a noncooperative game. Interestingly, a regulated oligopoly can be a cooperative game. This hinges on two things. First, the regulating agency must have the ability to set, and enforce, critical decision variables such as prices. Second, the firms must be in a position to induce the agency to force on them the arrangements of their (the firms') choice.

When games are categorized by the number of players, the main distinction is whether $n = 2$ or $n > 2$. Often two-person games are simpler than their general n-person counterparts, whereas the differences between $n = 3$ and $n > 3$ are slight. The primary distinction concerning payoff structure is constant sum versus general sum. A *constant-sum game* is one in which the players' payoffs add up to a constant such as zero, no matter what strategies are chosen. Of course, to speak meaningfully of a constant-sum game requires that the players' utilities can be compared. This may be acceptable when the players are firms and utility is identified with profit; however, it is not readily acceptable if the players are consumers. It turns out that the crucial feature of a constant-sum game is that all possible outcomes are Pareto optimal. That is, in comparing any two outcomes where the players do not, individually, receive the same payoff, there is at least one player who is strictly better off at the second outcome and one who is strictly better off at the first.

Thus, a useful distinction can be made between games in which all payoffs are Pareto optimal and games in which some payoffs are not Pareto optimal. A payoff vector is Pareto optimal if it is attainable by the players and if any other attainable payoff vector must cause a lower payoff to at least one player. Among games in which all payoff vectors are Pareto optimal, the distinction between games of two players and more than two players is particularly interesting. Imagine a two-person, cooperative, constant-sum game. Cooperation may be allowed by the rules, but there is no contract that the players can sign that does more for each of them than what they can achieve without contract. Contract is beneficial when there is mutual gain to be obtained by its use. Compare this to a three-person constant-sum game, such as the majority game in which three people are to split 100 dollars. Any contract signed by two or more players is binding, and in the absence of a contract, the money is divided equally. Although the game is constant-sum, two players can form a coalition and make a contract that gives zero to the third player. Two players, by cooperating, stand to gain the $33\frac{1}{3}$ dollars that would go by default to the remaining player.

The games most characteristic of economic life are n-person variable-sum games. Two-person constant-sum games, though much studied by mathematicians working in game theory, have little or no applicability to economics. Even general two-person games are narrow for most game theoretic economic situations. As between cooperative and noncooperative games, one probably could make a very long list of applications of either, and, as noted in Section 9.3, in some games that are nominally noncooperative, the distinction between cooperative and noncooperative can blur.

9.2. A model of a noncooperative game

There are several standard ways to represent a game: the extensive form, the characteristic function form, and the strategic (or normal) form. The extensive form is used primarily for introductory exposition, the characteristic function form is well adapted for some cooperative games, and the strategic form is the primary vehicle for noncooperative games. See Luce and Raiffa (1957) for exposition of the extensive and characteristic function forms.

A formal description of a game

A *game in strategic form* is described by three sets: the set of players (N), the set of strategies (S), and the payoffs (P). The *set of players, $N = \{1, 2, \ldots, n\}$,* is, of course, the set of rational decision makers whose behavior is being studied. Each player, $i \in N$, has a *strategy set S_i* from which he must choose some particular element (*strategy*) s_i. The nature and meaning of strategy need further elaboration after the payoffs are described. A *strategy combination* is a selection of one strategy for each player and is denoted $s = (s_1, \ldots, s_n)$; s is a member of the (Cartesian) product set $S = S_1 \times, \ldots, \times S_n$, and therefore it is assumed that the set of strategies available to a player is independent of the strategy choices made by the remaining players.[1] Each player i has a scalar-valued *payoff function, $P_i(s)$*, whose value depends on the strategies of all players. The vector of payoffs is $P(s) = [P_1(s), \ldots, P_n(s)]$. That the players play the game means that each chooses a strategy, with all players making their selections simultaneously. It remains to determine the strategies the players are expected to choose, and then, in Section 9.3, to translate the insights of this section to several illustrative oligopoly models.

The meaning of strategy

Loosely speaking, the *strategy of a player* is his total battle plan for the whole game, which must be distinguished from a move. A *move* is an action taken at a particular moment, whereas a strategy is a player's overall plan indicating the particular moves that are to be taken at each conceivable point in the game at which the player must make a move. An illustration from a parlor game like chess may illuminate further the concept of strategy. Player one, who will make the first move in the game, has a choice of ten pieces that he can move, two possible moves per piece, and therefore a total of twenty moves from which to choose. The initial part of his strategy names the particular one of those twenty moves that he chooses. Player two has a parallel choice of twenty opening moves; however, player one cannot know in advance which move player two will select. Thus, player one's second move is contingent on the initial move of his opponent, and player one must specify precisely which move he will take at his second turn for each possible initial move of his opponent. Continuing in this way, player one knows, for each move he may make, the various configurations that the board can have; and for each move and each possible configuration at each move, he knows what move he will make. The strategy of player one is the complete listing of moves for each conceivable situation he may face in the course of the game. Although it is clearly beyond the capacity of the human mind to consider explicitly all possible chess strategies, and although most individual strategies are, likewise, too long and detailed to hold in the mind at one time, it is usually assumed in game theoretic models that players do know their entire strategy spaces and that each player explicitly chooses one strategy from among those available to him. This abstraction is fruitful, as are many analogous assumptions in economics that presume tremendous memories and calculating abilities on the part of economic agents.

A strategy, then, is a complete specification for a player of what to do in each possible contingency that may arise. Games are generally analyzed as if each player assesses the game before it begins and chooses a strategy at the start. Thus, all judgments are made before the start of play, and, in a sense, a player is never surprised. At least no player ever changes his mind midstream about the appropriate move for some contingency.

The Nash equilibrium

The equilibrium concept virtually always applied in noncooperative games is the Nash (1951) noncooperative equilibrium: s^* is a *Nash equilibrium* (or a *noncooperative equilibrium*) if $s^* \in S$ and

$$P_i(s^*) \geq P_i(s_1^*, \ldots, s_{i-1}^*, s_i, s_{i+1}^*, \ldots, s_n^*) \tag{9.1}$$

for any $s_i \in S_i$ and for $i = 1, \ldots, n$. That is, the strategy combination s^* is a Nash equilibrium if each s_i^* is in the appropriate strategy set (i.e., is available to the player to choose) and if it is impossible that any single player can obtain a higher payoff through the use of a different strategy, given the strategy choices of the other $n - 1$ players.

That the Nash equilibrium is a straightforward generalization of the Cournot equilibrium can be seen by interpreting the Cournot oligopoly model of Chapter 2 as a game. The firms are the players. For each player, the strategy set is the interval $[0, Q_i]$ of output levels from which firm i must choose its output level, and the profit function $\pi_i(q)$ is the payoff function of the ith firm. The firm's output level is, of course, its strategy. Using the two-firm example specified in equations (2.1) through (2.6) in Chapter 2, the strategy sets are naturally derived from the demand function, $p = 100 - 0.1(q_1 + q_2)$. For $q_1 + q_2 > 1,000$, the expression $100 - 0.1(q_1 + q_2)$ is negative; however, the firms are not actually forced to sell at a negative price, and so p is taken to be zero for such output levels. No single firm will ever produce above $Q_i = 1,000$, which leads to a natural definition of S_1 as $[0, 1,000]$ and S_2 as $[0, 1,000]$. Note that the demand and payoff functions must be defined for $q_1 + q_2$ as great as 2,000, because each firm is allowed to go as high as 1,000. The payoff function for player 1 is

$$P_1(q) = 84q_1 - 0.1q_1^2 - 0.1q_1q_2 - 6,000$$
$$\text{for } 0 \le q_1 + q_2 \le 1,000 \quad (9.2)$$

$$P_1(q) = -16q_1 - 6,000 \quad \text{for } q_1 + q_2 > 1,000 \quad (9.3)$$

For player 2, it is

$$P_2(q) = 90q_2 - 0.1q_2^2 - 0.1q_1q_2 - 9,000$$
$$\text{for } 0 \le q_1 + q_2 \le 1,000 \quad (9.4)$$

$$P_2(q) = -10q_2 - 9,000 \quad \text{for } q_1 + q_2 > 1,000 \quad (9.5)$$

The Cournot equilibrium, $q_1^c = 260$ and $q_2^c = 320$, is defined in precisely the same way as the Nash noncooperative equilibrium: $q_1^c = 260$ maximizes the payoff to firm 1, given the strategy

($q_2^c = 320$) of firm 2. Similarly for firm 2. One respect in which the Cournot oligopoly model is a very simple game is that it consists of only one move for each firm; hence, that move, the choice of an output level, is identical with a firm's strategy.

Although the underlying concept of equilibrium is essentially the same, the Nash model is much more general than that of Cournot. This becomes apparent if a typical noncooperative game model is examined somewhat more closely and if the notion of strategy, outlined earlier, is borne in mind. The assumptions given next describe a noncooperative game model that is not the most general such model; however, it is quite general, it is easily explained, and it provides a useful illustration. The model satisfies the following conditions: (a) The number of players, n, is finite. (b) Each strategy set, S_i, is a compact and convex subset of R^m, the m-dimensional Euclidean space.[2] (c) Each payoff function, $P_i(s)$, is continuous in s. (d) Each payoff function, $P_i(s)$, is quasi-concave in s_i. To be *quasi-concave in s_i* means that for any fixed values of the s'_j ($j \neq i$) and any given profit level z, the set of s_i values for which $P_i(s_i, \bar{s}'_i) \geq z$ is convex [where $\bar{s}'_i = (s'_1, \ldots , s'_{i-1}, s'_{i+1}, \ldots , s'_n)$]. A game satisfying conditions (a) through (d) possesses a noncooperative equilibrium, although the equilibrium need not be unique. Condition (b) can, under many circumstances, be replaced by a condition allowing the dimensionality of S_i to be infinite. The great scope for S_i allows the model to represent a game of many moves. For example, imagine a Cournot oligopoly with the proviso that the firms are to operate for m periods. Then an individual strategy, $s_i = (s_{i1}, \ldots , s_{im})$, could be a sequence of output choices. That is, the s_{it} would be the output levels of firm i in each period t, with t running from 1 to m.

The Nash equilibrium can be justified by the appealing consistency condition that it embodies: If s^* is a Nash equilibrium strategy combination, no player has an incentive to reconsider his strategy choice if he believes that the other players ($j \neq i$) will choose s_j^*, and he sees no reason to suppose that any other individual player will have an incentive to alter his choice. Another way to say the same thing is to note that if a Nash equilibrium strategy combination is played and a player asks himself if, in retrospect, he could have done better by selecting a different strategy, the answer is no for each player.

As with any equilibrium in economics, it is natural to ask whether or not the economic agents can actually be expected to choose equilibrium behavior. That is, how do the players find their way to equilibrium? If the equilibrium were unique, it could be argued that all players would be able to calculate it, that its consistency property would be attractive, and that any alternative would be ruled out because its lack of the consistency property would render it unacceptable.

9.3. Applications of game theory to oligopoly

Each of the following subsections shows one model from an earlier chapter discussed as a noncooperative game. The purpose of doing this is to provide concrete examples of noncooperative games that appeared earlier in this volume and to relate those examples in a precise way to the abstract formulation of noncooperative games that is given here. No effort is made to be exhaustive by covering all the models from earlier chapters. The ones chosen feature ease of presentation and variety, and they allow illustration of pertinent points relating to the application of game theory to economics. The models to follow are Chamberlinian single-period oligopoly (Chapter 3), Stackelberg leader-follower (Chapter 5), n-firm dynamic reaction function oligopoly (Chapter 5), and n-firm multiperiod advertising (Chapter 6).

The differentiated products price model

In this, as in all examples, each firm is a player, and in this model (see Chapter 3, Section 3.3) there are n firms. Recall that each firm chooses only its own price, p_i for the ith firm, and its price falls into the interval $[0, p_i^+]$. Thus, $S_i = [0, p_i^+]$, and $s_i = p_i$. The payoff function is single-period profits; hence, $P_i(s) = \pi_i(p)$. It is easily seen that the Cournot equilibrium, p^c, is the Nash noncooperative equilibrium by comparing the two definitions.

As a numerical example, consider the illustration in equations

(5.3) through (5.5) in Chapter 5. The two demand and cost functions are

$$q_1 = \max\{0, \ 100 - 5p_1 + 4p_2\} \quad \text{and}$$
$$q_2 = \max\{0, \ 80 - 3p_2 + 2p_1\} \tag{9.6}$$

$$C_1 = 10q_1 + q_1^2, \qquad C_2 = 7q_2 + q_2^2 \tag{9.7}$$

The strategy space for firm 1 is [0, 88.57], and for firm 2 [0, 85.71]. These are found by solving the simultaneous equations

$$100 - 5p_1 + 4p_2 = 0, \qquad 80 - 3p_2 + 2p_1 = 0 \tag{9.8}$$

The payoff function for the first firm is

$$P_1(p) = p_1 q_1 - 10q_1 - q_1^2 \tag{9.9}$$

However, the boundary conditions cause the specifications of q_1 to be tedious. If $100 - 5p_1 + 4p_2 \le 0$, then $q_1 = 0$. This reflects the condition that demand cannot be negative. If $80 - 3p_2 + 2p_1 \le 0$, then $q_1 = 100 - 5p_1 + 4(80 + 2p_1)/3 = 206\frac{2}{3} - 2\frac{1}{3}p_1$; p_2 is treated as if it takes the value satisfying $80 - 3p_2 + 2p_1 = 0$, which reflects the condition that once q_2 is zero, further increases in p_2 cannot affect the demand of firm 1. For q_1 and q_2 both positive, the two payoff functions are

$$P_1(p) = -11{,}000 + 1{,}150p_1 - 840p_2 - 30p_1^2$$
$$+ 44p_1 p_2 - 16p_2^2 \tag{9.10}$$

$$P_2(p) = -6{,}960 + 581p_2 - 334p_1 - 12p_2^2$$
$$+ 14p_1 p_2 - 4p_1^2 \tag{9.11}$$

Again, as with the preceding quantity example, the Cournot and Nash equilibria coincide: $p_1^c = 64.519$, and $p_2^c = 61.845$. Neither player can obtain larger profit by choosing another strategy (price), given the strategy (price) of the other player.

The Stackelberg leader-follower model

If the Stackelberg leader-follower model is to make sense as a single-period model, it must be part of the rules of the game that the leader (player 1, say) choose its price before the follower (player 2) and that the price choice of the leader be communicated to the follower before the latter makes a price commitment. In this model, $n = 2$, of course. For player 1, the strategy set is $[0, p_1^+]$; however, the strategy set of the follower is much larger. The follower chooses a price after seeing the price commitment of firm 1; thus, it chooses a function $h(p_1)$ that associates a value of p_2 from the interval $[0, p_2^+]$ with any possible p_1 in the interval $[0, p_1^+]$. Let H denote the set of all such functions. Then $H = S_2$, and $[0, p_1^+] = S_1$. The two payoff functions are $P_1(s) = \pi_1[p_1, h(p_1)]$ and $P_2(s) = \pi_2[p_1, h(p_1)]$.

The numerical example from the previous section can be used again. Writing the payoff functions that obtain when both output levels are positive,

$$P_1[p_1, h(p_1)] = -11{,}000 + 1{,}150p_1 - 840h(p_1)$$
$$- 30p_1^2 + 44p_1h(p_1) - 16[h(p_1)]^2 \quad (9.12)$$

$$P_2[p_1, h(p_1)] = -6{,}960 + 581h(p_1) - 334p_1$$
$$- 12[h(p_1)]^2 + 14p_1h(p_1) - 4p_1^2 \quad (9.13)$$

Taking first the strategy choice of player 2, $h(p_1)$ must satisfy

$$\frac{\partial P_2}{\partial h(p_1)} = 581 - 24h(p_1) + 14p_1 = 0 \quad (9.14)$$

$$\frac{\partial^2 P_2}{\partial[h(p_1)]^2} = -24 < 0 \quad (9.15)$$

That equation (9.15) is negative assures that the solution to equation (9.14) is a maximum. Solving equation (9.14) for $h(p_1)$ gives an optimal strategy for player 2 of

$$p_2 = h(p_1) = \frac{581 + 14p_1}{24} \quad (9.16)$$

The sequential nature of this game allows the equilibrium to be solved recursively, by solving for the strategy of the last player to move (player 2), then the next to last (player 1). For player 1, the optimal p_1 must satisfy

$$\frac{\partial P_1}{\partial p_1} = 1{,}150 - 840h'(p_1) - 60p_1 + 44h(p_1) + 44p_1h'(p_1)$$
$$- 32h(p_1)h'(p_1) = 0 \quad (9.17)$$

$$\frac{\partial^2 P_1}{\partial p_1^2} = -840h'' - 60 + 88h' + 44p_1 h''$$

$$- 32hh'' - 32(h')^2 < 0 \qquad (9.18)$$

In evaluating equation (9.18), equation (9.16) makes clear that $h'' = 0$ and $h' = \frac{7}{12}$; hence,

$$\frac{\partial^2 P_1}{\partial p_1^2} = -60 + 88 \left(\frac{7}{12}\right) - 32 \left(\frac{7}{12}\right)^2 = -19\frac{5}{9} < 0 \qquad (9.19)$$

Therefore, equation (9.14) does give a maximum, which is $p_1 = 65.11$. Using this in equation (9.16), the actual price choice of player 2 is seen to be $p_2 = 62.19$, and the two payoffs are $P_1 = 740.37$ and $P_2 = 745.93$. It is interesting to note that this game yields both players higher profits than the Cournot game described in the preceding section and that player 2, the follower, gains more by the Stackelberg rules than player 1. The higher profits arise because player 1 can get p_2 above the Cournot level (p_2^c) by selecting p_1 above p_1^c. But p_2 is increased by only $\frac{7}{12}$ for each unit rise in p_1, which is bound to relatively favor player 2.

The Stackelberg leader-follower equilibrium is easily seen to be the Nash noncooperative equilibrium for this game. Although the model is logically tight, and the equilibrium is certainly appropriate to the model, there is a basic economic assumption that can be questioned: Why do the rules require that firm 1 choose its price prior to firm 2? From the standpoint of understanding economic behavior, it is desirable to formulate a model in which some of the timing of decisions is endogenous to the model and then see the conditions under which a leader-follower situation will emerge as an equilibrium outcome.

Smooth reaction functions in multiperiod models

In the traditional reaction function models of Section 5.3, Chapter 5, each firm chooses its price according to a rule, $p_{it} = \phi_i(p_{t-1})$. Assuming that the firms make decisions beginning with period 1, there is a start-up problem. Either some price vector, p_0, is specified from outside or else each firm makes a straight price choice in period 1, then uses ϕ_i from period 2 onward. If the latter viewpoint is taken, then the game can be described thus: There are n players, and the strategy of the ith player is $[p_{i1}, \phi_i(p_{t-1})]$, where p_{i1} is the first-period price choice and, for periods $t \geq 2$, $p_{it} = \phi_i(p_{t-1})$. The function ϕ_i must be chosen from the set V_i, which is the set of all functions that has $\times_{j=1}^n [0, p_j^+]$ as domain and $[0, p_i^+]$ as range. The strategy set $S_i = [0, p_i^+] \times V_i$. The payoff function of the ith player is

$$P_i(s) = \pi_i(p_1) + \sum_{t=2}^{\infty} \alpha_i^{t-1} \pi_i[\phi_1(p_{t-1}), \ldots, \phi_n(p_{t-1})] \quad (9.20)$$

Let $\phi = (\phi_1, \ldots, \phi_n)$, and let p^* be the steady-state price vector associated with ϕ^* $[p^* = \phi^*(p^*)]$. Then the strategies (p_i^*, ϕ_i^*) $(i = 1, \ldots, n)$ are a Nash noncooperative equilibrium. But this equilibrium is very special, because the initial price vector is part of it. It would be more satisfactory if there were some reaction functions $\phi_1', \ldots, \phi_n'$ that, in combination with any first-period price choice, would be a Nash equilibrium. Put another way, if the alternative formulation of the model is used in which the reaction functions of the firms are used from period 1 onward, and there is an initial condition p_0 that is part of the data of the model, one will want to find reaction functions that form a Nash equilibrium relative to any initial condition p_0.

Use the same cost and demand functions as used in the preceding two sections, and suppose that $\alpha_1 = \alpha_2 = 0.9$ is the common discount parameter. The strategy set for player 1 is the set of all $s_1 = [p_{10}, \phi_1(p)]$, where $0 \leq p_{10} \leq p_1^+ = 88.57$; ϕ_1 is any continuous and continuously differentiable function whose arguments (p_1, p_2) satisfy $0 \leq p_1 \leq 88.57$ and $0 \leq p_2 \leq 85.71$, whose value is between 0 and 88.57, and whose derivatives are positive, with $\phi_1^1 + \phi_1^2 < 1$. Parallel rules hold for the strategy set of player 2. Letting $\pi_1(p_t)$ and $\pi_2(p_t)$ represent the single-period payoffs [i.e., equations (9.10) and (9.11) with time subscripts appended], the payoff functions are

$$P_1(s) = \sum_{t=1}^{\infty} \alpha_1^{t-1} \pi_1[\phi(p_{t-1})] \quad (9.21)$$

$$P_2(s) = \sum_{t=1}^{\infty} \alpha_2^{t-1} \pi_2[\phi(p_{t-1})] \tag{9.22}$$

At the steady-state prices, p^*, the reaction functions ϕ_1^* and ϕ_2^* must satisfy

$$p_1^* = \phi_1^*(p^*) \tag{9.23}$$

$$p_2^* = \phi_2^*(p^*) \tag{9.24}$$

$$\pi_1^1(p^*) + 0.9\pi_1^2(p^*)\phi_2^{*1}(p^*) \sum_{t=0}^{\infty} [0.9\phi_2^{*2}(p^*)]^t = 0 \tag{9.25}$$

$$\pi_2^2(p^*) + 0.9\pi_2^1(p^*)\phi_1^{*2}(p^*) \sum_{t=0}^{\infty} [0.9\phi_1^{*1}(p^*)]^t = 0 \tag{9.26}$$

Equations (9.25) and (9.26) are the infinite horizon counterparts of equation (5.19) and can be written as

$$1,150 - 60p_1^* + 44p_2^*$$
$$+ \frac{0.9\phi_2^{*1}}{1 - 0.9\phi_2^{*2}} (-840 + 44p_1^* - 32p_2^*) = 0 \tag{9.27}$$

$$581 - 24p_2^* + 14p_1^*$$
$$+ \frac{0.9\phi_1^{*2}}{1 - 0.9\phi_1^{*1}} (-334 + 14p_2^* - 8p_1^*) = 0 \tag{9.28}$$

There are many (p^*, ϕ^*) that can satisfy equations (9.23) through (9.26). Suppose ϕ_1^* and ϕ_2^* to be

$$p_{1t} = 9.855 + 0.515p_{1,t-1} + 0.35p_{2,t-1} \tag{9.29}$$

$$p_{2t} = 5.76 + 0.4p_{1,t-1} + 0.492p_{2,t-1} \tag{9.30}$$

Then $p^* = (66, 63.3)$. The strategy sets in this game are not compact, because the reaction functions, ϕ_i, are not drawn from compact sets. Also, it is not true, in general, that the discounted payoff of a player is a concave, or quasi-concave, function of its strategy. The import of these facts is that standard techniques and results in game theory cannot be used to assure existence of an equilibrium. For the specific numerical example, there is an equilibrium, as exhibited earlier. Also, using the techniques of Friedman (1977, Chapter 5), equilibrium is established for a large class of games; however, to repeat a point made earlier, noncooperative equilibrium is assured for strategies (p_i, ϕ_i), where p_i is the initial price. Only an approximation to noncooperative equilibrium is assured when strategies are reaction functions, ϕ_i, alone.

A multiperiod model with advertising

In the advertising model presented in Section 6.4 of Chapter 6, the firms' strategies are described as being sequences of output and goodwill levels. In the notation of that section, $(q_{i1}, S_{i1}, q_{i2}, S_{i2}, \ldots)$ is a strategy for firm i. Each q_{it} must fall into the interval $[0, q_i^0]$, where q_i^0 is defined by the condition $C_i(q_i^0) = M/(1 - \alpha_i)$. That is, the firm will never choose an output level so high that the cost of production in a single period will be higher than the largest possible discounted revenue it can achieve. S_{it} is bounded above by a similar sort of cost condition and below by the condition that advertising expenditure cannot fall below zero. The upper bound is denoted S_i^0. Let the lower bound be denoted $v_i(S_{i,t-1})$. Then the strategy set for the ith player is the set of sequences of output and goodwill that fall within the required bounds:

$$\{(q_{i1}, S_{i1}, q_{i2}, S_{i2}, \ldots) | q_{it} \in [0, q_i^0] \quad \text{and}$$
$$S_{it} \in [v_i(S_{i,t-1}), S_i^0] \quad \text{for } t = 1, 2, \ldots \text{ and}$$
$$\text{for } S_{i0} = 0\} \quad (9.31)$$

The payoff functions are $\sum_{t=1}^{\infty} \alpha_i^{t-1} \pi_i(q_t, S_t, S_{i,t-1})$, and the equilibrium is a Nash noncooperative equilibrium.

The model has a soft spot that should be pointed out, relating to the strategy sets. At any time $t \geq 2$, the firms have some accumulated knowledge concerning past moves. Specifically, the history of the game at time t can be denoted $z_t = (q_1, S_1, \ldots, q_{t-1}, S_{t-1})$; z_t is defined for $t = 2$ and onward, and it is reasonable to suppose that any firm might choose a strategy under which its move in period t will depend on the history as of that time. Thus, a strategy for firm i might be in the form

$$\sigma_i = [q_{i1}, S_{i1}, g_{i2}(z_2), g_{i3}(z_3), \ldots, g_{it}(z_t), \ldots] \quad (9.32)$$

Equation (9.31) defines the possible histories of the whole game; therefore, each g_{it} must choose a pair (q_{it}, S_{it}) that satisfies equation (9.31) and do so for any history that, likewise, satisfies equation (9.31).

The reason these appealingly more general strategies have not been used is that they form a class of strategies that cannot be dealt with satisfactorily. Proving the existence of equilibrium, a primary task, has proved impossible. Such strategies as those defined in equation (9.32) are sometimes called *closed-loop strategies* or *feedback strategies,* and the simpler strategies defined in equation (9.31) are called *open-loop* or *nonfeedback strategies.* In the particular model being discussed, the (open-loop) equilibrium properties of the Nash equilibrium do not depend on the strategies being restricted to the set of open-loop strategies. That is, even in a model where closed-loop strategies are allowed, the open-loop equilibrium is still a Nash equilibrium. This will not be true for all possible models. For example, if there is a random mechanism in the model, say a random component to each firm's demand, and the random element for each period is made known to the firms prior to their moves for that period, a Nash equilibrium for a model confined to open-loop strategies will not typically be a Nash equilibrium if the model is changed to allow closed-loop strategies. This is because the closed-loop strategy allows players to take advantage, at each period, of new information that comes to them and that could not have been foreseen. Thus, the specific moves can be adjusted, time by time, to the random events. With an open-loop strategy, all moves are precisely determined at the outset of the game.

9.4. Perfect equilibrium points

In essence, Selten's invention (1975), the *perfect equilibrium,* is a noncooperative equilibrium that preserves the noncooperative equilibrium property from any conceivable decision point in the game. To return to the example of chess, imagine a strategy for each player that specifies the move he will take at any time as a function of the configuration of the board. Call these strategies s_1^0 and s_2^0. To say (s_1^0, s_2^0) is a noncooperative equilibrium means, of course, that if the board is arranged in the customary starting fashion, neither player can choose a different strategy and increase his payoff.

Now imagine that the chessboard is rearranged in a totally arbitrary way, with, perhaps, some pieces being removed. Starting from this arbitrary point, the players can use their strategies s_1^0 and s_2^0. The fact that (s_1^0, s_2^0) is a noncooperative equilibrium for a game begun from the usual starting point does not imply that (s_1^0, s_2^0) is a noncooperative equilibrium for a game started from such an arbitrary configuration. If (s_1^0, s_2^0) is a perfect equilibrium, then it will be a noncooperative equilibrium for any game that can be imagined by choosing an arbitrary starting point.

More generally, s^* is a perfect equilibrium point if, starting from any conceivable decision point in the game, s^* is a noncooperative equilibrium for a game starting at that point. This condition holds even for decision points that will never actually be reached when following s^* from the normal starting point of the game.

An important feature of perfect equilibrium points is that they do not allow threats unless the threats are credible. Ordinary noncooperative equilibrium points need not rule out empty threats, as an example from Chapter 8 shows. In Figure 8.1, the following strategies form an equilibrium that is not perfect: For s_1', firm 1 chooses a low price if firm 2 enters the market and a high price if it does not enter. For s_2', firm 2 does not enter. Neither can alter its strategy and increase its payoff. But consider the situation if firm 2 does enter: s_1' calls for a low price, but it is not believable that firm 1 will choose a low price if firm 2 actually enters. This low price must be seen as a (noncredible) threat intended to deter entry.

Suppose that (s_1^*, s_2^*) is a pair of strategies that form a perfect equilibrium, where s_1^* is that firm 1 chooses a high price whether or not firm 2 enters, and s_2^* is that firm 2 enters. Now firm 1 has a strategy that is best after the decision of firm 2, no matter which decision firm 2 selects.

The fault with (s_1', s_2') is not that it contains a threat. The fault is that the threat is not credible, because if firm 1 is put in a position where the threat action is called for, it is not in firm 1's interest to carry it out. Credible threats are consistent with perfect equilibrium.

The notion of perfect equilibrium and its relation to credible and noncredible threats can be illustrated with a modified version of the game used in the preceding section. Suppose the two players' payoff functions are

$$\sum_{t=1}^{\infty} 0.9^{t-1}\pi_i(p_t) \qquad (i = 1, 2) \tag{9.33}$$

with $\pi_i(p_t)$ given by equations (9.10) and (9.11). The strategy set of player 1, S_1, is the set of all $s_i = [p_{11}, g_{12}(p_1), g_{13}(p_1, p_2), g_{14}(p_1, p_2, p_3), \ldots]$, where $0 \le p_{11} \le p_1^+$ and, for any $t \ge 2$, $0 \le g_{1t}(p_1, \ldots, p_{t-1}) \le p_1^+$. Thus, the first move is some specific price, and each subsequent move is allowed to be an arbitrary function of the known price history of the market, restricted only by the condition that each price fall into the interval $[0, p_1^+]$. In other words, the functions g_{it} need not be differentiable or even continuous. The strategy set of player 2 is similarly defined.

Note, first, that the very simple strategies $s_1^c = (p_1^c, p_1^c, \ldots)$ and $s_2^c = (p_2^c, p_2^c, p_2^c, \ldots)$, which call for choosing single-period Cournot equilibrium prices in each period, form a perfect noncooperative equilibrium. As of the start of the game, neither player can choose a different strategy and obtain a higher payoff (i.e., s^c is noncooperative equilibrium), and from any time t onward, s^c is a noncooperative equilibrium irrespective of the past history of the game to that point (i.e., s^c is a perfect equilibrium).

Now consider the strategies described in Section 5.4 of Chapter 5 as $T1$-$T2$ strategies. As an example, s_1^* is defined thus: $p_{11} = 68.897$, and, for $t \ge 2$, $p_{1t} = 68.897$ if $p_{2\tau} = 66.529$ for $\tau = 1, \ldots, t-1$. Otherwise, $p_{1t} = 64.519$. Then, s_2^* is defined thus: $p_{21} = 66.529$, and, for each $t \ge 2$, $p_{2t} = 66.529$ if $p_{1\tau} = 68.897$ for $\tau = 1, \ldots, t-1$. Otherwise, $p_{2t} = 61.845$. These strategies will give payoffs of $8,061.4$ to player 1 and $7,523.2$ to player 2. Neither player can deviate unilaterally from his strategy and increase his payoff. Thus, s^* is a noncooperative equilibrium. Now consider whether or not it is also perfect. Suppose it is period t and the observed price history is

$(p_1, \ldots, p_{t-1})$. If $p_\tau = (68.897, 66.529)$ for $\tau = 1, \ldots, t-1$, then the situation at time t is identical with the situation at $t = 1$. Player 1 will choose $p_{1t} = 68.897$, and player 2 will choose $p_{2t} = 66.529$, and they cannot improve on using s_1^* and s_2^*. If at least one price differs at least once from $p_{1\tau} = 68.897$ or $p_{2\tau} = 66.529$ for $\tau = 1, \ldots, t-1$, then they will choose $p_{1\tau} = 64.519$ and $p_{2t} = 61.845$ for $\tau = t, t+1, \ldots$. This, of course, is a noncooperative equilibrium for the subgame starting from time t. Thus, s^* is a noncooperative equilibrium from any time t onward, irrespective of the history of the game up to time t.

Now consider a proposition made by player 1 to player 2. Player 1 suggests they choose $p_1 = 75.452$ and $p_2 = 76.033$ in each period, stating that if player 2 will not agree, then player 1 will choose $p_1 = 0$ in each period. This strategy for player 1, call it s_1', is like s_1^* with 75.452 in place of 68.897 and 0 in place of 64.519. If player 2 agrees, this will give payoffs of 10,366.9 (1,036.69 per period) to player 1 and 1,859 to player 2. Suppose the strategy of player 2, s_2', to be that he chooses 76.033 in each period unless he sees that player 1 has deviated from 75.452, in which case he switches to 24.208. Player 1 points out that his threat to choose $p_1 = 0$, if carried out, will leave player 2 able to obtain 725.2 (i.e., 72.52 per period) at the maximum.

It is true that s' is a noncooperative equilibrium. Neither player can change his strategy and increase his payoff, but the equilibrium is not perfect. Suppose a price history for which one of the players has deviated from the high prices proposed by player 1. The players then choose (0, 24.208). Player 2's choice of 24.208 is payoff-maximizing for $p_1 = 0$, but $p_1 = 0$ is not payoff-maximizing for $p_2 = 24.208$. Indeed, there is no value of p_2 for which $p_1 = 0$ is best for player 1. Thus, s' is not a perfect equilibrium.

To make the same point in a slightly different way, suppose player 2 does not go along with s_2', and player 1 chooses $p_1 = 0$ according to strategy s_1'. Such a choice is not forced on player 1 (no binding agreements), and given the fait accompli of player 2, it is not in the interest of player 1 to select $p_1 = 0$. Should player 2 choose 61.845 in each period, player 1 can do better than $p_1 = 0$.

The best choice for player 1 is 64.519, and the fact that the choice of $p_1 = 0$ cannot be in the interest of player 1 under any circumstances makes an empty gesture of the threat to choose it.

9.5. Concluding comments

Many of the numerical examples used in this chapter are based on the same two-firm differentiated products market model specified in equations (5.3) through (5.5). Many different games with appropriately different economic interpretations, payoff functions, and strategy sets are made from the same basic materials. It is important to remember that these represent several truly different economic markets. Too much confusion is generated in discussing economic issues and "truths" by being incomplete and/or unclear in specifying a model, with the consequent result that several discussants will have different models in mind, though each believes that they are all discussing his. Merely to specify differentiated products or to say that the approach is game theoretic leaves a great deal that must still be stated. As the examples show, the Nash noncooperative equilibrium takes many different forms, depending on the details of the model, and it coincides with the Cournot equilibrium only in special circumstances.

The preceding sections are no substitute for a thorough treatment of noncooperative game theory, but they may convey some of the flavor and power of it. Of course, there are books one can consult for further information. A book by Vorob'ev (1977) has a very clearly written text, at a modest mathematical level, that covers the basics. The work of Luce and Raiffa (1957) remains an excellently written and enlightening source in which many models, approaches, and basic ideas of the subject can be found. Books by Friedman (1977) and Harsanyi (1977) are technically more difficult than the other two books, but Friedman (1977) has several chapters on multiperiod games (supergames), which are of considerable interest in economics, and Harsanyi has a superb exposition of that part of cooperative game theory dealing with the Nash cooperative models, the Shapley value, and Harsanyi's generalization of them.

NOTES

Chapter 2. The Cournot model of oligopoly

1 In denoting the derivatives of a function, primes are used in the usual way for functions of a single variable: $f' = df/dx$, and $f'' = d^2f/dx^2$. For functions of several variables, such as $f(x,y,z)$, superscripts are used: f^i denotes the first partial derivative with respect to the ith argument. For example, $f^2 = \partial f/\partial y$; f^{ij} denotes the second partial derivative with respect to the ith and jth arguments.

2 The notation used here for vector inequalities is as follows: $x \geq y$ means $x_i \geq y_i$ for all i; $x > y$ means $x \geq y$ and, for at least one component, $x_i > y_i$; $x \gg y$ means $x_i > y_i$ for all i. Note that these vector comparisons are meaningful only if x and y have the same number of components. Furthermore, these inequalities are partial orderings, which means that not all pairs of vectors can be compared.

3 Strictly speaking, the usual condition is that the profit of the ith firm is a quasi-concave function of its own decision variable. An exception to this requirement can be found in the work of Nishimura and Friedman (1981).

4 There is one known instance of an analytical solution to a two-person strategic decision problem. Published in 1713 and attributed to James Waldegrave, it contains the saddle-point solution to a two-person gambling game called Le Her; it appears in the work of Montmort (1713) and has been reproduced in English translation by Baumol and Goldfeld (1968). It is highly unlikely that Cournot was aware of this work, which anticipates the minimax theorem of John von Neumann (von Neumann and Morgenstern, 1944).

5 Cournot's discussion was framed slightly differently. He discussed stability only for the two-firm model and assumed that the firms alternated in making decisions. Firm 1 would choose q_{11}, then firm 2 would choose $q_{22} = w_2(q_{11})$, then firm 1 would choose $q_{13} = w_1(q_{22})$, then firm 2 would choose $q_{24} = w_2(q_{13})$, etc. Cyert and DeGroot (1970) have a two-firm dynamic model with alternate decisions. There is a large body of literature elaborating the static stability analysis sketched in the foregoing text that appeared mostly in the *Review of Economic Studies;* however, much of it is summarized by Okuguchi (1976), and many references are given there.

227

6 Although this point is not germane to treating oligopoly theory, it is interesting that Cournot influenced other economists in the nineteenth century. Walras (1874) acknowledges two people above all who influenced his thinking, his father and his father's friend Cournot. Likewise, Alfred Marshall apparently read Cournot at a formative stage of his development, probably in the late 1860s. See Marshall's early works (1975) and the preface to the first edition of his *Principles* (1890). Finally, on the occasion of the English translation of Cournot, Fisher (1897) wrote a very laudatory review article.

Chapter 4. Product choice and location

1 Stipulating that all consumers reach the same utility level implies that income be distributed appropriately. This condition is not central to the example and is used only to make calculations easier. And having a numerical utility index attain the same value for all consumers does not imply anything about interpersonal utility comparison.

2 Hotelling (1929) suggested that his model is suitable for explaining political candidates' choices of positions on campaign issues. This has been elaborated by Downs (1957) and developed further by many others. See Riker and Ordeshook (1973).

Chapter 5. Reaction functions

1 Actually, Bowley wrote $D_{p_1}(p_2)$ in place of $\phi_1'(p_1)$. His discussion is so brief that much of his meaning must be inferred; however, the interpretation given here seems to be the only reasonable one.

2 In private communication, Edward Green has given me his impression that many scholars believe that the equilibrium described here will necessarily be accompanied by some amount of price cutting (deviation from p^*) by one or more firms. Under the conditions used here and elsewhere (Friedman, 1977, Chapter 8), as well as in the work of Radner (1980), price cutting is impossible as a part of equilibrium behavior. One of two circumstances must hold: (a) The strategies $T1, \ldots, Tn$ form a noncooperative equilibrium, in which case the firms always actually choose p^*, because it is in no one's interest to choose differently. (b) $T1, \ldots, Tn$ do not form a noncooperative equilibrium, in which case the firms will never choose p^* in the first place. They will, perhaps, choose p^c in every period. Green (1980) has shown elegantly that neither fewness nor largeness of firms is essential to the $T_1, \ldots, Tn$ equilibrium by proving that an infinite number of infinitesimal firms (literally, a nonatomic measure space of firms) can support such an equilibrium. It is only necessary that price cutting by one firm can be detected by the others.

It is quite possible that price cutting would be difficult to detect if demand were subject to random shocks. Then firms might be able to get away with some price cutting without causing a move from p^* to p^c. Of course, the strategies Ti would have to be suitably reformulated for the stochastic environment. On this topic, see Green and Porter (1981) and Porter (1981).

Chapter 6. Oligopoly and advertising

1 My claims about the milk industry or other industries may not be true; however, if the reader accepts them as hypothetical examples, then they can be used to illustrate various aspects of advertising.

2 For a serious study of advertising in the cigarette industry, see Telser (1962). One point that emerges from Telser's work is that the advertising pattern in cigarettes has changed from time to time in ways too complex to be detailed here. For example, when smokers first became seriously concerned about the link between smoking and lung cancer, sales of unfiltered cigarettes dropped, and many filtered brands were introduced. The introduction of new brands was accompanied by large increases in advertising budgets until they were well established.

3 The definition of the message unit is, admittedly, rather vague here. I hope that the intuitive notion is clear, for I agree with Schmalensee (1972) that it is often important to make a clear conceptual distinction between the advertising message and advertising expenditure. In the models described throughout the remainder of this chapter, advertising messages do not play an explicit role; hence, the conceptual distinction is not crucial for them.

4 Strictly speaking, equation (6.4) defines a *discounted cash flow,* because goodwill, being a long-lived asset, has a tangible value. Thus, the true profit for period t is cash flow plus the increase in the value of goodwill. Because the market for the sale of the firm itself is not considered here, and because the owners' satisfaction from the firm is assumed to derive from the cash flow it provides for personal consumption, the terms *discounted cash flow* and *discounted profit* (as well as *cash flow* and *profit*) are used interchangeably in models having long-lived assets such as goodwill and physical capital.

5 This pie is $\Sigma_{i=1}^{n} h_{it}$. Hence, nothing specific is said of the effect of h_{it} on demand.

6 Any initial conditions for which $S_{i0} \geq 0$ $(i = 1, \ldots, n)$ can be easily handled.

Chapter 7. Oligopoly with capital

1 See note 4 in Chapter 6.

2 It is well known that the sum of concave functions is concave (Berge, 1963), a fact used in many of the models presented in earlier chapters. Although both the total revenue function and the investment function in equation (7.5) are concave, the total cost of production function, $c_i q_i$, is not. It is linear (hence concave) in each variable separately, but decidedly not concave in c_i and q_i jointly. As a result, Flaherty must force either total revenue or $g(c_{it}, c_{i,t+1})$ to be sufficiently strongly concave that the objective function is concave. She accomplishes this, in fact, by additional restrictions on g (Flaherty, 1980a, p. 1190).

Chapter 8. Entry

1 On perfect equilibrium points, see Selten (1975). What is sketched here is called *subgame perfect,* which is less general than perfect, but is fully adequate for present needs. This concept is discussed further in Chapter 9.

Chapter 9. Oligopoly and noncooperative game theory

1 The Cartesian product of two sets A and B, denoted $A \times B$, consists of elements $(a, b) \in A \times B$ where $a \in A$ and $b \in B$. For example, suppose A is a two-dimensional price-advertising space for firm 1, with elements denoted (p_1, a_1), and B is an analogous space for firm 2. Then an element of $A \times B$ is (p_1, a_1, p_2, a_2).

2 A compact set in an n-dimensional Euclidean space is a set in which the distance between any two points is no more than some finite number (the set is bounded), and the boundary points of the set are members of it (the set is closed). A set is convex if the straight line segment connecting any two points in the set is also in the set.

REFERENCES

Where two dates are given for a reference, the earlier date is the year of publication of the original edition, and the second date refers to the edition that is actually cited. The earlier date is always given in the text to emphasize the historical timing of the contribution.

Alchian, Armen A. 1950. "Uncertainty, Evolution and Economic Theory." *Journal of Political Economy* 58:211–21.

Arrow, Kenneth J., and Frank H. Hahn. 1971. *General Competitive Analysis.* San Francisco: Holden Day.

Bain, Joe S. 1949. "A Note on Pricing in Monopoly and Oligopoly." *American Economic Review* 39:448–64.

——. 1956. *Barriers to New Competition.* Cambridge, Mass.: Harvard University Press.

Baumol, William J., and Stephen M. Goldfeld (editors). 1968. *Precursors in Mathematical Economics: An Anthology.* London School of Economics and Political Science.

Berge, Claude. 1963. *Topological Spaces.* New York: Macmillan.

Bertrand, Joseph. 1883. Book review of *Théorie Mathématique de la Richesse Sociale* and of *Recherches sur les Principes Mathématiques de la Théorie des Richesses. Journal des Savants,* pp. 499–508.

Bliss, Christopher J. 1975. *Capital Theory and the Distribution of Income.* Amsterdam: North-Holland.

Bourguignon, Françoise, and Suresh P. Sethi. 1981. "Dynamic Optimal Pricing and (Possibly) Advertising in the Face of Various Kinds of Potential Entrants." *Journal of Economic Dynamics and Control* 3:119–40.

Bowley, Arthur L. 1924. *The Mathematical Groundwork of Economics.* Oxford University Press.

Braithwaite, Dorothea. 1928. "The Economic Effects of Advertising." *Economic Journal* 38:16–37.

Brems, Hans. 1951. *Product Equilibrium under Monopolistic Competition.* Cambridge, Mass.: Harvard University Press.

Bresnahan, Timothy F. 1982. "Duopoly Models with Consistent Conjectures." *American Economic Review* 71:934–45.

Buchanan, Norman S. 1942. "Advertising Expenditures: A Suggested Treatment." *Journal of Political Economy* 50:537–57.

Chamberlin, Edward H. (1933) 1956. *The Theory of Monopolistic Competition,* 7th edition. Cambridge, Mass.: Harvard University Press.

Cournot, Augustin A. (1838) 1927. *Researches into the Mathematical Principles of the Theory of Wealth,* translated by Nathaniel T. Bacon (with an essay on Cournot and mathematical economics and a bibliography of mathematical economics by Irving Fisher). New York: Macmillan.

Cyert, Richard M., and Morris DeGroot, 1970. "Multiperiod Decision Models with Alternating Choice as a Solution to the Duopoly Problem." *Quarterly Journal of Economics* 84:410–29.

D'Aspremont, C., J. Jaskold Gabszewicz, and J. F. Thisse. 1979. "On Hotelling's 'Stability in Competition'." *Econometrica* 47:1145–50.

Dixit, Avinash K. 1980. "The Role of Investment in Entry Deterrence." *Economic Journal* 90:95–106.

Dorfman, Robert, and Peter O. Steiner, 1954. "Optimal Advertising and Optimal Quality." *American Economic Review* 44:826–36.

Downs, Anthony, 1957. *An Economic Theory of Democracy.* New York: Harper & Row.

Economides, Nicholas S. 1981. "Oligopoly in Markets for Products Differentiated by their Characteristics." Unpublished doctoral dissertation, University of California, Berkeley.

Edgeworth, Francis Y. (1897) 1925. "The Pure Theory of Monopoly." Papers relating to political economy, Royal Economic Society, London, 111–42.

Fellner, William J. 1949. *Competition among the Few.* New York: Knopf.

Fisher, Irving 1897. "Cournot and mathematical economics." *Quarterly Journal of Economics* 12:119–38.

Flaherty, M. Thérèse. 1980*a.* "Industry Structure and Cost-Reducing Investment." *Econometrica* 48:1187–209.

1980*b.* "Dynamic Limit Pricing, Barriers to Entry, and Rational Firms." *Journal of Economic Theory* 23:160–82.

Friedman, James W. 1968. "Reaction Functions and the Theory of Duopoly." *Review of Economic Studies* 35:257–72.

1977. *Oligopoly and the Theory of Games.* Amsterdam: North-Holland.

1979. "On Entry Preventing Behavior and Limit Price Models of Entry." In: *Applied Game Theory,* edited by S. J. Brams, A. Schotter, and G. Schwödiauer, pp. 236–53. Würzburg: Physica-Verlag.

1980. "Advertising and Oligopolistic Equilibrium." Unpublished manuscript.

Friedman, Milton. 1953. *The Methodology of Positive Economics, Essays in Positive Economics,* pp. 3–43. University of Chicago Press.

Frisch, Ragnar. 1933. *Monopole–Polypole – La Notion de Force dans L'Economie, Festschrift til Harald Westergaard.* Supplement to *Nationalekonomisk Tidsskrift.*

Gale, David, and Hukukane Nikaido. 1965. "The Jacobian Matrix and the Global Univalence of Mappings." *Mathematische Annalen* 159:81–93.

Green, Edward J. 1980. "Noncooperative Price Taking in Large Dynamic Markets." *Journal of Economic Theory* 22:155–82.

Green, Edward J., and Robert H. Porter. 1981. "Noncooperative Collusion under Imperfect Price Information." Social Science Working Paper 367, Division of the Humanities and Social Sciences, California Institute of Technology, Pasadena.

Harsanyi, John C. 1977. *Rational Behavior and Bargaining Equilibrium in Games and Social Situations*. Cambridge University Press.

Hildenbrand, Werner, and Alan P. Kirman. 1976. *Introduction to General Equilibrium Analysis*. Amsterdam: North-Holland.

Hotelling, Harold. 1929. "Stability in Competition." *Economic Journal* 39:41–57.

Kaldor, Nicholas. 1935. "Market Imperfection and Excess Capacity." *Economica* 2:33 50.

Kamien, Morton I., and Nancy L. Schwartz. 1971. "Limit Pricing and Uncertain Entry." *Econometrica* 39:441–54.

——— 1981. "Conjectural Variations." Discussion Paper 466 S, Center for Mathematical Studies in Economics and Management Science, Northwestern University.

Kirman, Alan, and Matthew Sobel, 1974. "Dynamic Oligopoly with Inventories." *Econometrica* 42:279–87.

Koopmans, Tjalling C. 1957. *The Construction of Economic Knowledge, Three Essays on the State of Economic Science*, pp. 127–66. New York: McGraw-Hill.

Lancaster, Kelvin. 1966. "A New Approach to Consumer Theory." *Journal of Political Economy* 74:132–57.

——— 1971. *Consumer Demand: A New Approach*. New York: Columbia University Press.

——— 1979. *Variety, Equity and Efficiency*. New York: Columbia University Press.

Leland, Hayne. 1977. "Quality Choice and Competition." *American Economic Review* 67:127–37.

Lerner, Abba, and H. W. Singer, 1937. "Some Notes on Duopoly and Spatial Competition," *Journal of Political Economy* 45:145–86.

Luce, R. Duncan, and Howard Raiffa. 1957. *Games and Decisions* New York: Wiley.

Marschak, Thomas, and Reinhard Selten. 1977. "Oligopolistic Economies as Games of Limited Information." *Zeitschrift für die Gesamte Staatswissenschaft* 133:385–410.

——— 1978. "Restabilizing Responses, Inertia Supergames, and Oligopolistic Equilibria." *Quarterly Journal of Economics* 92:71–93.

Marshall, Alfred. (1890) 1961. *Principles of Economics*, 9th (variorum) edition, with annotations by C. W. Guillebaud. London: Macmillan.

——— (1919) 1923. *Industry and Trade*, 4th edition. London: Macmillan.

——— 1975. *The Early Writings of Alfred Marshall, 1867–1890*, edited by J. K. Whitaker. London: Macmillan.

Milgrom, Paul, and John Roberts. 1982. "Limit Pricing and Entry under Incomplete Information: An Equilibrium Analysis." *Econometrica* 50:443–59.

Miller, Charles L. 1982. "A Reaction Function Equilibrium for a Simple Dynamic

Duopoly Model with Random Demand." Department of Political Economy, Johns Hopkins University.

Montmort, Pierre Remond de. 1713. *Essay d'Analyse sur les Jeux de Hasard,* 2nd edition. Paris: Jacque Quillau.

Nash, John F., Jr. 1951. "Noncooperative Games." *Annals of Mathematics* 45: 286–95.

Nerlove, Marc, and Kenneth Arrow. 1962. "Optimal Advertising Policy under Dynamic Conditions." *Economica* (N. S.) 29:129–42.

Nikaido, Hukukane. 1975. *Monopolistic Competition and Effective Demand.* Princeton University Press.

Nishimura, Kazuo, and James Friedman. 1981. "Existence of Nash Equilibrium in *n* Person Games without Quasiconcavity." *International Economic Review* 22:637–48.

Okuguchi, Koji. 1976. *Expectations and Stability in Oligopoly Models.* Berlin: Springer.

Porter, Robert H. 1981. "Optimal Cartel Trigger Price Strategies." Discussion Paper No. 81–143, Center for Economic Research, University of Minnesota, Minneapolis.

Prescott, Edward C. 1973. "Market Structure and Monopoly Profits: A Dynamic Theory." *Journey of Economic Theory* 6:546–57.

Radner, Roy. 1980, "Collusive Behavior in Noncooperative Epsilon-Equilibria of Oligopolies with Long but Finite Lives." *Journal of Economic Theory* 22: 136–54.

Riker, William H., and Peter C. Ordeshook, 1973. *An Introduction to Positive Political Theory.* Englewood Cliffs, N.J.: Prentice-Hall.

Roberts, John, and Hugo Sonnenschein. 1977. "On the Foundations of the Theory of Monopolistic Competition." *Econometrica* 45:101–13.

Ruffin, Roy J. 1971. "Cournot Oligopoly and Competitive Behavior." *Review of Economic Studies* 38:493–502.

Salant, David J. 1980. "Quality Location Choice and Imperfect Competition." Unpublished doctoral dissertation, University of Rochester.

Salop, Steven C. 1979. "Monopolistic Competition with Outside Goods." *Bell Journal of Economics* 10:141–56.

Schmalensee, Richard. 1972. *The Economics of Advertising.* Amsterdam: North-Holland.

Scitovsky, Tibor. 1976. *The Joyless Economy.* Oxford University Press.

Selten, Reinhard. 1975. "Reexamination of the Perfectness Concept for Equilibrium Points in Extensive Games." *International Journal of Game Theory* 4:25–55.

Shapiro, Leonard. 1980. "Decentralized Dynamics in Duopoly with Pareto Optimal Outcomes." *Bell Journal of Economics* 11:730–44.

Shubik, Martin. 1959. *Strategy and Market Structure.* New York: Wiley.

1980. *Market Structure and Behavior* (with Richard Levitan). Cambridge, Mass.: Harvard University Press.

Smith, Adam. (1776) 1976. *An Inquiry Into the Nature and Causes of the Wealth of Nations,* edited by R. H. Campbell, A. S. Skinner, and W. M. Todd. Oxford: Clarendon Press.

1795. *History of Astronomy, Essays on Philosophical Subjects,* edited by Joseph Black and James Hutton. Edinburgh.

Smithies, Arthur, and L. J. Savage. 1940. "A Dynamic Problem in Duopoly." *Econometrica* 8:130–43.

Spence, A. Michael. 1979. "Investment Strategy and Growth in a New Market," *Bell Journal of Economics* 10:1–19.

Stackelberg, Heinrich von. 1934. *Marktform und Gleichgewicht.* Vienna: Julius Springer.

Sylos-Labini, Paolo. 1962. *Oligopoly and Technical Progress.* Cambridge, Mass · Harvard University Press.

Szidarovsky, F., and S. Yakowitz. 1977. "A New Proof of the Existence and Uniqueness of the Cournot Equilibrium." *International Economic Review* 18:787–9.

Telser, Lester G. 1962. "Advertising and Cigarettes." *Journal of Political Economy* 70:471–99.

Triffin, Robert. 1940. *Monopolistic Competition and General Equilibrium Theory.* Cambridge, Mass.: Harvard University Press.

von Neumann, John, and Oskar Morgenstern. (1944) 1953. *The Theory of Games and Economic Behavior,* 3rd edition. Princeton University Press.

Vorob'ev, N. N. 1977. *Game Theory,* translated by S. Kotz. Berlin: Springer.

Walras, Leon. (1874) 1954. *Elements of Pure Economics,* translated by William Jaffé. Homewood, Ill.: Irwin.

Winter, Sidney G. 1964. "Economic 'Natural Selection' and the Theory of the Firm." Yale Economic Essays.

Zeuthen, Frederik. 1930. *Problems of Monopoly and Economic Warfare.* London: Routledge & Kegan Paul.

AUTHOR INDEX

237

SUBJECT INDEX